... years of
... ...int and online media.
...ralian newspaper in the 1980s, he
...d fall of the entrepreneurs. Adam joined
...work in 1991, reporting for *Business Sunday*
...ydney and Melbourne, before leaving to wander Africa
for three years as a freelance journalist for Nine and other
media organisations. Since 1997 he has been an investigative
reporter and he is currently working for News Ltd and the
Triple M network. His research on the Melbourne gangland
murders was carried out as a joint investigation for the
Bulletin magazine and the Nine Network's *Sunday* pro-
gramme, both late and lamented. Adam is also the author
of the true crime books *The Skull* and *King of Thieves: The
Adventures of Arthur Delaney and the Kangaroo Gang.*

BIGSHOTS

THE CHILLING TRUE STORY BEHIND
THE GANGLAND WARS THAT INSPIRED
THE SERIES *UNDERBELLY*

ADAM SHAND

JOHN BLAKE

Published by John Blake Publishing Ltd,
3 Bramber Court, 2 Bramber Road,
London W14 9PB, England

www.johnblakepublishing.co.uk

First published by Penguin Group (Australia), 2007
Revised edition published by Penguin Group (Australia), 2010
This edition published by John Blake Publishing, 2011

ISBN: 978 1 84358 347 9

British Library Cataloguing-in-Publication Data:

A catalogue record for this book is available from the British Library.

Design by www.envydesign.co.uk

Printed in Great Britain by CPI Bookmarque, Croydon CRO 4TD

1 3 5 7 9 10 8 6 4 2

Papers used by John Blake Publishing are natural, recyclable products
made from wood grown in sustainable forests. The manufacturing
processes conform to the environmental regulations of the
country of origin.

*For my parents and my children,
who taught me that understanding is
more valuable than judgement*

CONTENTS

Those intending to embark on a career in the underworld would do well to sit down and watch an old James Cagney movie, *The Roaring Twenties*. Make the time, because the one thing you have now is time, and later you won't. Call it a training film, or maybe even a prophecy, but it may give you a foretaste of what is to come in this life. The moral is not that crime doesn't pay – it pays well, extraordinarily well if you get it right – but that eventually Death takes its whack.

For the first few reels of *The Roaring Twenties*, it's all going well for Cagney's Eddie Bartlett. He's knocking off his enemies in fine style and driving big, shiny cars. He has friends in high places, who think it's cool to be seen with Eddie. His pockets are full of cash, and the odd policeman too. He's got the lovely Panama on his arm; a squad of pug-faced retainers enforces his will and whim. But the final reel brings the inevitable shoot-out and demise. Alone and gut-shot, Eddie staggers to a church, seeking sanctuary and salvation, but collapses on the steps. Panama catches up to him and cradles Eddie's head on her suitably ample bosom. The credits are about to roll on Eddie when a cop steps from stage right, to ask, 'Who is this guy?'

Panama: 'This is Eddie Bartlett.'

Cop: 'Well, how are you hooked up with him?'

Panama: 'I could never figure it out.'

Cop: 'What was his business?'

Panama: 'He used to be a big shot.'

Carl Anthony Williams was a big shot too. For a brief moment, he was atop the foetid dung heap of the Melbourne underworld. Standing on the corpses of his enemies (and some of his friends), he thought the view was marvellous until he sank into the ooze with the rest of them. His is a tale of glamour, but in the true sense of the word. Glamour is a false and empty concept, a creation of the world of advertising and Hollywood. It's a face made attractive with make-up, a triumph of style over substance. So if by writing his story I have 'glamourised' crime or Carl Williams then I do not apologise. A society that worships glamour and hollow celebrity is fertile ground for people like him.

1 | THE MUNSTER'S LAST STAND

It had rained hard all evening, a summer downpour in the midst of a drought. The bluestone streets of old Melbourne had run like rivers, sending the Christmas shoppers in the city scurrying for cover. A southerly buster had blown in off Port Phillip Bay, sweeping away the dust and grit that settles after a hot week. In December, when north winds scour the city, the heat builds up over a week or so until it feels like it's coming out of footpaths at you. Sleeping becomes difficult and, deprived of rest, you can't think straight at work. On the trams and trains, you can almost hear the unspoken thought among heat-stressed commuters: *something's got to give, something's got to give*.

Once-in-a-hundred-years events were afoot in Melbourne at the close of 2003. As the rain came down in sheets, fully laden trams headed out of the city, their trolley poles sparking blue against the overhead electric wires.

By midnight, the rain had stopped and Belmont Avenue, Kew was slick and glistening under the streetlights. It must have seemed to Graham 'The Munster' Kinniburgh that his old Ford could find its own way down the meandering street as he coasted home. A gentle slope twisted to the left under a pale streetlight and then to the right under another, and soon he would be at number 35. The security cameras he had installed weren't working – he hadn't bothered to fix them. In just ten steps he could get from the car to the heavy security grille and into the house.

Kinniburgh was the Mister Big of crime in Melbourne, and its elder statesman. He had been involved in, or had knowledge of, almost every big heist in the city for decades. He counted among his associates some of the most notorious and violent criminals in the country. The coroner had implicated him in the January 1998 murder of Carlton crime boss Alphonse Gangitano, and he knew about many other killings stretching back to the 1960s. He had serious overseas connections and was as much at home in Las Vegas as Victoria.

Though Kinniburgh was well known to police, Gangitano's murder and the subsequent coronial report had brought him to the attention of the public for the first time. The media had suggested that Kinniburgh helped to position his long-time ally for the hit. His neighbours found all this impossible to reconcile with the friendly senior citizen they saw walking his dog, carrying a plastic bag for its droppings.

Kinniburgh's life story was written in that knockabout face. The heavy lantern jaw, the impassive deep-set eyes that darted away from inquiring gazes – this was a classic 'head', the kind any villain or half-decent copper would recognise instantly.

He hadn't carried a gun in years but tonight he was carrying one tucked into his belt. Just a precaution, he'd told people. He had dined that night in town with friends, a racing writer and some

4

women. Pleasantly full of food and drink, he would slip quietly into bed next to his wife, Sybil, behind the heavy metal shutter that protected them from the morning sun and other less welcome intrusions. He had stopped off on the way to pick up a few groceries. He might even cook breakfast for Sybil.

People were drifting home now from their office Christmas dos. A dinner party for ten was winding up in number 31. The occasional passer-by on foot would trigger the motion sensors at number 35 and the yellow bricks of the driveway would be momentarily bathed in light.

For the two men in the blue Falcon, there was nothing to do but sit and wait for Kinniburgh to return home. They could wait all night and every night until their chance came. Or another team took their place. Melbourne's underworld had come to reclaim its own, and it didn't matter who pulled the trigger.

The Munster must have passed them as he eased into a parking spot outside his house.

Four days earlier, on Monday afternoon, Kinniburgh had been driving down the freeway taking an old friend home.

His friend looked across at Kinniburgh's weathered face (he was nicknamed for a likeness to Herman Munster, the Frankenstein-like star of the 1960s TV comedy *The Munsters*) and wondered just how things had got to this. He had this feeling that he was about to say goodbye to his best friend in the world. And there was nothing he could do about it. He had been an apprentice to the Munster, the safecracking master. Everything he knew about it came from this man. It wasn't just about the money, though there was nothing like seeing a big haul flat-stacked on a table in front of you. There was more to it. It was about beating the system, having the freedom to square up with it. Every day, banks were hitting up their customers with new hidden fees and charges. That was stealing. To liberate some of the banks' money, well, that was a victory for everyone, even if they didn't share in the spoils.

'You know the police won't shed any tears if they knock you, Graham,' he said.

'One in particular. I tell you, son, in 1979 I threw the best punch of my life at him, knocked him on his arse, laid him clean out,' said the Munster with a deep, throaty laugh. The copper had it coming, of course, he continued, trying to keep the discussion off his potential demise. The bloke was renowned for having violated the corpse of a young model in the police mortuary, and had lived with hoons and prostitutes. Still, the hard men of Russell Street wouldn't let such a thing pass. A three-man team turned up at a club two weeks later.

'As soon as one of them came in range I tried another upper cut, but I missed,' he said. 'They squared up with me good and proper. The three of them gave me a terrible flogging, but I copped it sweet.' The Munster had had the last laugh: they threw him in a squad car bruised and battered, and he crapped himself spectacularly in the back seat en route to the watch house. And the officer who had led the beating had to drive home to the suburbs with a message from the Munster in his nostrils.

At sixty-two, Kinniburgh had a contract on his life. He was 'off', as they say in the underworld. Kinniburgh had fallen foul of a new team, led by two of the fastest-rising men of the underworld: Carl Anthony Williams and a man who cannot be named for legal reasons, who we'll call 'The Chief Executive'. This team was powerful enough to run its affairs even from jail. Their money bought the best soldiers, in or out of prison. They boasted that they were so powerful they could bribe judges, fix juries and knock witnesses. And they would take on anybody in town, any time.

In mid-2003, Williams had contracted one of Melbourne's most feared crims to carry out surveillance on the Munster. Let's call him 'The Raptor' for his speed and ruthless killing power. On spring nights, the Raptor would scale the Kinniburghs' security fences to watch his prey through the lounge-room window.

In Melbourne, public killing 'draws the crabs'. Kill a few men and suddenly the constabulary is all over you, booking you for anything and everything, from urinating up a back lane to pinching a bicycle. And the other villains would laugh at you. To avoid all this, there might be a square-up – say, an entree to a job – and pretty soon all would be sweet again. If not, someone might agree to act as a mediator, calling all the men concerned to a certain nightclub. They would show up with all their retainers, full of bullshit and bad manners, but out of respect to the mediator, firearms would be left at home. Lots of grimaces and dramatic posturing would follow, but it would rarely go further, because that was generally in no one's interest.

But this crew didn't care to talk, unless it was about complete and total surrender. They'd made known their utter contempt for the 'standover men and thieves' who ran things in Carlton. And the Munster was a fixture in Carlton, even if he paid homage to no one. Williams' team had been killing people all year – six to date – and the Carlton Crew had yet to return fire.

It wasn't their way to wage open warfare. If the wogs lost a soldier, they would wait a respectable time and then set up the culprit in his driveway or in a restaurant, like they did in those old gangster movies. They would all mill around at the funeral with great decorum, kissing the widows and orphans and professing shock and sorrow at the mysteries of revenge, before getting back to business. But Williams and the soldiers of speed would strike back quickly and strike back hard.

It was said that Carl Williams had three senior men on the Kinniburgh job, a veteran hit man we'll call 'The Savage' and armed robbers Steve Asling and Terry Green. The down payment was said to be two kilos of speed, a pair of handguns and about $20 000 in cash.

The talk of the Munster's contract had reached the ears of his old apprentice. He sat with his friend for hours, trying to get him to take the threat seriously. He was still at him as Kinniburgh drove him home that afternoon. They were crossing enemy territory as they followed the freeway across the suburban tundra of Melbourne's north-west fringe. It was here, in suburbs like Broadmeadows and Sunshine, that the new heroes of the underworld were being created, in the courts and crescents where the police were rarely seen. They were men with no respect for the old codes of behaviour and even less for the reputations of men like the Munster. Only money meant anything, and they had more of that than they could spend.

In reality, there hadn't been a code of honour in Melbourne since

1978, when a team of gunmen led by Raymond Patrick 'Chuck' Bennett had burst into Les Kane's flat and shot him in the bathroom, as his family were held nearby. They bundled the body into the boot of his own car, never to be seen again. Kane had been a force in Melbourne, but the manner of his death sent the message that no one was safe. The ante in the violence had been steadily upped ever since. Now it was only fear that kept people in line, much as it stops children from playing on the road. It occurred to the Munster and his companion that out there in the vast jungle of suburbia there were people who were totally unafraid.

As Kinniburgh pulled up in a quiet street to drop off his passenger, his old friend looked him squarely in the eye. 'You know you have to deal with these people, Graham. You know that, don't you?' he demanded. 'You're going to have do something about this Carl Williams, his father and that wife of his – what's her name? Roberta. Yeah, that one. I've never seen a bloke like this before, never seen a bloke so game. He'll take on all of you. You've got to do something . . .'

They had never heard of Carl Williams before all of this. Williams was a nobody, an errand boy of small-time hoods and suburban drug dealers, or so they believed. All they knew was that the Munster's loyalty to the Moran family had made him a target. Anyone close to the Morans was now a target. Well, so be it. That was the way they had lived their lives. 'If you live through the sweets with a bloke,' the old saying went, 'then you have to be there for the sours too.'

And these were sour days indeed. There was a spontaneity about the killings that year that had disturbed everyone. These were killers looking for an excuse to earn. And the Munster had them given them one. The chain of events began in June 2000, when it was said that one of Carl's shooters, the Savage, had killed Mark Moran, the scion of the family drug empire. Kinniburgh had organised a hit on the shooter in retaliation, but word had reached the Savage before it could be carried out.

Kinniburgh was a threat to Williams but this had become personal for the Savage. He and the Munster had history stretching back to the 1970s: they had been on opposite sides of another feud. It was time to settle old scores. The Savage thought nothing of killing. In 1987, he had put three rounds into the head of a former partner in crime and then shot the man's wife because she was a witness. He had then cut her throat from ear to ear for good measure, all with the couple's three kids cowering in their bedrooms. There were other killings in his past that had yet to come to light. A judge would later say that the Savage had 'a chilling and fearsome resolve' and an 'utter lack of humanity and regard to the sanctity of human life'. He was at his worst when he had a regular supply of speed. He had been clean for about four years in the late nineties but now with lots of powder courtesy of Williams, the blood lust was rising in him like a poisonous sap. He could do anything, or anyone.

But the Munster was convinced that the old firm would still win out. He shrugged and looked away. 'I know, mate . . . But don't worry – it's all under control. Now go on,' he said.

The last week of the Munster's life was a series of meetings and negotiations. He was observed having dinner on the Tuesday in an Italian restaurant, La Villa Romana, on Carlton's Lygon Street with a group of his most trusted friends in the underworld, each one a leader of the old-school crime groups in Melbourne. Murder was apparently on the menu. A lot of the restaurants in Lygon Street have been bugged by police over the years, but this night the surveillance was a little more straightforward – the Carlton CIB was celebrating its Christmas party at the same joint that night. As a group of detectives and their wives stood waiting to be seated, they noticed that the gentlemen in front of them in the queue were very familiar heads indeed. The entire leadership of the Carlton Crew was waiting patiently for a table. Polite nods were exchanged between the two camps.

Though the discussions likely centred on what to do about Carl Williams, there were others there that night possibly with motives of their own. Dominic 'Mick' Gatto was the most powerful man in Carlton these days, but he still paid due respect to the Munster and theoretically had a lot to gain from the Munster's departure. The Munster and Big Mick hadn't always seen eye to eye; in fact, they had only recently begun speaking to each other again after a frosty period. Among other things, Gatto had been questioned over the murder of Melbourne Mafia boss Frank Benvenuto, a man who had, like Kinniburgh, been almost universally liked. Mick's close associate Mario Rocco Condello had never really been comfortable with the Munster's influence over the crew. He believed Calabrians gave the orders in this team, not scruffy Irish heads from Richmond. With a general like Kinniburgh gone, his soldiers would look to men like Gatto and Condello for leadership. New vistas of opportunity would open up.

Kinniburgh's oldest friend, Lewis Moran, was there, a man who had already lost two children, his son Jason and stepson Mark, to the war. Lewis was marked for death himself, but still wouldn't share what he knew with the police. Williams' kill teams were in fact stalking both Moran and Kinniburgh. One of the stalkers was a mate of Lewis's and was passing information back to Williams about when they should strike. At times Lewis would feel like he was already dead. He had lost his dash now, lost the heart to go on with the villainy. Mark and Jason had both been killed, three years apart, after falling out with Carl Williams. It had been a trivial feud over a pill press worth $400 000 – a fraction of what they were making from drugs – but then Jason had shot Carl in the stomach in 1999 and the money became immaterial. It had become a question of principle and Lewis had backed his sons all the way. Now he was on the hit list and Kinniburgh, in trying to settle the dispute, had also put himself in the firing line.

Since Jason and Mark had died Lewis had begun blaming himself for everything that was happening. The thought of the Munster paying for his family's debts was a miserable postscript to the sorry tale of the Morans' demise. But like the Munster, Lewis had been a big shot in his day. At times during their thirty-year friendship, Kinniburgh had apparently carried Moran's handgun for him, a bond between criminals that creates a special kind of intimacy.

But why had the Munster avoided Lewis at the funeral of dock-side worker Harold 'Snowy' Baker a month before the meeting at La Villa Romana? Why had Lewis pushed into the pew next to the Munster, and why had the Munster refused to talk to him?

More curiously, why, on the day before he died, did Kinniburgh have coffee in Lygon Street with a police detective? It was said the detective was a relative of the Munster's. Some of his criminal peers had always been suspicious about Kinniburgh's ability to avoid jail time despite his involvement in so many crimes.

In his youth, Kinniburgh had been renowned for a quick temper and fists to match. But that was when he was shearing, when it paid to advertise your credentials in the sheds and pubs. As he drifted into ever more sophisticated crime, the fighting stopped. He learned to 'nut off', to avert his eyes from police or some knockabout looking for trouble.

A moment's indiscretion in a bar could put an entire criminal enterprise at risk, and possibly cost you your life. He kept secrets even from his closest friends and associates, and certainly from his wife. Tell them nothing and they will never have to lie for you. You can trust no one completely, but ironically, to survive the anarchy of the underworld you have to trust someone, sometime. So you choose your partners in crime very carefully and tell them what they need to know and nothing more. If you run around with a big flashy team, someone's going to lag you eventually – everyone has their unique selling point. If Kinniburgh had a fault it was that he always helped a mate in trouble, even if it meant getting between two blokes in a fight. Things tended to unravel quickly at these moments, he reasoned, so best keep things nice and quiet.

'Graham was into everything. He would be into a shit sandwich without the bread,' the former apprentice told me. 'But he definitely drew the line at violence.' He only ever shot one man, a troublemaker named Steve Sellers who all agreed had it coming. It was 1978 and Kinniburgh's crew had pulled off a mighty heist on a bank in Murwillumbah in northern New South Wales. Sellers believed he should have had a slice and when Kinniburgh refused, he went off tap, threatening to kill him and his family. So the Munster got in first, with a shotgun blast to the chest. But Sellers didn't die and Kinniburgh wasn't going to finish him off. He had made his point, so he rang the ambulance and waited with him.

A safe-cutter is known as a 'tank man' in Melbourne, and Kinniburgh was the best. When you cut safes with him you were working with a perfectionist. Before a big job he would buy a safe of the exact same specifications and his team would practise in a warehouse, simulating the conditions on the day.

'We'd be wanting to go and hang around the pub,' said one comrade from the 1970s, 'but he would have us there till midnight practising, talking the job through in every detail – how the smoke from the torch would flow out of certain safes, how to use hydraulic jacks to lift a safe out of a brick wall.' Anyone who didn't want to put in the hard yards was politely shown the door.

Kinniburgh was the boss of the Magnetic Drill Gang, which was suspected of more than a dozen big-league heists in the 1970s and '80s, including a $5 million haul of gold and jewels in Sydney in 1983.

He was also an associate member of the infamous Kangaroo Gang, a group of Australian shoplifters who tormented retailers in the United Kingdom, France, Belgium and Germany for a generation. Shoplifting wasn't Kinniburgh's go, but he was more than happy to fence the high-class jewellery, furs and assorted accessories that came his way via the gang. Later, some of the Kangaroo Gang veterans re-formed into the Grandfather Mob, which reputedly imported an estimated fifteen tonnes of hashish into Australia in the 1990s. Again Kinniburgh was happy to work with his old mates. Police sources confirmed that the gang was caught bringing the fourth drug shipment, worth around $225 million alone, into Australia via Hervey Bay in Queensland.

It's believed that the deckhands on each run received $1 million for their trouble. Kinniburgh was charged with conspiracy to import, having organised the trawler and outfitted it with communications equipment. But the Crown's case was weak and the jury acquitted him in 1997.

Others did jail time over it but the villains had already made their fortune. Part of the proceeds – $4 million – sat for years in a Dutch bank. In 2003 the family of one of the ringleaders, the late Jack 'The Fibber' Warren, launched legal action aimed at claiming it, but failed, and the Australian government wound up keeping the loot.

Kinniburgh remained active in the underworld even though he was now very wealthy, and in June 1992 he was charged over a $1 million armed robbery in East Melbourne.

By now the Munster's family was progressing in society. In 1994, one of his sons married a girl from a wealthy Melbourne family in St Peter's Eastern Hill and the reception was held in Melbourne's grand old establishment hotel, the Windsor. The *Age* newspaper reported that 'one friend of the bride was startled when introduced to Kinniburgh, not so much by the man himself as by the four who were standing around him. They were all wearing Ray-Bans and it was ten at night. A guest of the bride, a property developer, was dancing with a woman from the groom's side. A friend of the groom, released from prison days earlier after completing his sentence for biting a man's ear from his head, suggested to the property developer that he would be shot if he did not become a wallflower. The developer immediately lost interest in the music and retired to the bar.'

Kinniburgh's daughter married the son of a former Victorian attorney-general, Vernon Wilcox QC, while another of his sons became the teaching professional at a prestigious Melbourne golf club. His wife, Sybil, had opened a bead shop down at the Victoria Market and was dabbling in Buddhism and other eastern religions.

Kinniburgh divided his time between Melbourne's elite and its criminal fraternity. Former Crown Casino chief Lloyd Williams (no relation to Carl) said he regarded Kinniburgh as 'the perfect gentleman' when he occasionally encountered him in the casino or at the races. One of Australia's leading jockeys was a close friend, and Kinniburgh is said to have extended him an interest-free loan of $80 000 to help pay off a tax bill. His barrister, Robert Richter QC, says Kinniburgh was a regular in cafes around the legal district, where he was often seen in conversation with leading solicitors and barristers. 'Even if he wasn't involved, you would still see Graham there. He just liked to know what was going on, to keep up with the latest cases,' says Richter.

The Munster's appetite for food and drink was legendary. He was reputed to be the silent partner in the city's most prestigious Chinese restaurant, having bailed out its owner, who had backed too many slow horses. Kinniburgh told friends, 'I've spent half a million dollars on fried rice.'

After the murder of Alphonse Gangitano in 1998, the coroner concluded that Kinniburgh and one of his young followers, Jason Moran, had been at Gangitano's house the night he was found shot dead in his underpants, and were probably implicated. To be implicated in a murder shattered the Munster's low-key existence. His wealth and his friends among Melbourne's social elite counted for nothing now. High-street friends now found it uncomfortable to be seen with him in public, and he retreated into his old networks. The greatest humiliation came when the Victoria Racing Club warned him off all racetracks as an undesirable person.

Kinniburgh wasn't from this leafy middle-class suburb, but he could have forgiven himself for feeling right at home here. He had grown up in the working-class slums of Richmond, four or five kilometres away down by the river. Now he owned one of the best houses in the street and the neighbours greeted him warmly if they encountered him walking his little fluffy white dog.

He didn't even bother to lap the street checking for potential threats that night as he drove down Belmont Avenue and parked.

The shooter walked straight up to him as he got out of his car and opened fire. A good professional shooter knows the best time to hit your target is when he's getting out of a car. The motor's off, precluding escape, and the target is fumbling with seatbelts and door handles and, in this case, a bag of groceries.

Were it not for that bag of groceries, perhaps Kinniburgh might have got his gun out faster and dealt with the threat. As it was, he got a single shot off, which whizzed past his attacker and lodged in the timber of the carport across the road. Kinniburgh fell where he stood, his groceries scattered on the road by his side, the scene a grisly reminder that there is no such thing as semi-retirement in the underworld.

The police quickly plotted the getaway route the killers took. Within seconds, the gunman was driving north along Belmont Avenue towards Parkhill Road, before doubling back to cross the main Cotham Road. Less than five minutes later, residents in the mansions of Doona Avenue, one kilometre from Kinniburgh's house, saw the blue Falcon ablaze in a driveway down a service lane.

The next stage of the plan called for a 500-metre walk along a leafy alleyway linking Doona Avenue, Barenya Court and the main road where a second escape car was waiting. They would have been driving away just as the first police cars began nearing the Munster's place.

The next day Carl Williams was nursing a hangover but, as usual, was available for comment.

He told *The Sunday Age* he was not involved. 'I don't know him. I've heard of him but I don't know him. All I've ever heard about him is good.'

Carl's wife, Roberta, said: 'It was his lawyer's birthday and he was out with him. He got Chinese and came home drunk as a skunk. They can't blame him for this one.'

The morning after Kinniburgh's murder, Billy 'The Texan' Longley called me at seven o'clock, waking me with the news. 'They've got Mister Big,' he said gravely, without announcing himself. Even in his late seventies Billy Longley appreciated the drama of a good gangland hit. In his day, it was said he had been involved in or had knowledge of fifteen such acts of 'homicidal merriment', as he termed it. They finally got him for one he swore he didn't do: the shooting of rival union official Pat Shannon in a South Melbourne hotel in 1973. They threw him in H Division in Pentridge for thirteen years and it all but broke him. Now he was living quietly in a modest home in Ascot Vale, going to water aerobics classes four days a week.

'This is the biggest happening in the underworld since Jackie Twist got the Frog back in '58. This is going to unleash merry hell, son. And they said it was over . . .' He let rip with a deep, rumbling laugh that contained not a trace of mirth.

Standover king Freddy 'The Frog' Harrison was gunned down on South Wharf back in February 1958. That day, in front of dozens of Harrison's dockside workmates, the gunman strolled up with a twelve-gauge shotgun and, with the words 'This is yours, Fred', blew half his head away. No one saw a thing, not even a man alongside who was splattered with Harrison's brains.

Back then this was how killing was done in Melbourne. It was orderly. A villain's home was his castle, and the newly created widow and orphans would get a telephone call to inform them of their loss, not a blood-spattered corpse on the front porch.

The killing of Graham Kinniburgh, the twenty-first murder in five years, would set off a deadly chain of events, said Billy. There was nothing more certain.

'A vendetta lasts a generation, and that's twenty-five years. Some things only blood will settle,' he said, pausing for dramatic effect.

Then he whispered conspiratorially, 'But I can't talk on the phone. Come and see me, but don't knock on the door. Ring me when you get close and I'll come out and see you. You never know who's listening at a time like this.'

A little murder has always been a part of doing business in the southern capital, but even by Melbourne standards the new spate of killing was right out of hand. It was threatening the fragile status quo that had existed in Melbourne's underworld since the last round of bloodletting in the early 1980s. It had brought a public spotlight onto a class of citizens that normally live entirely in the dark. And nocturnal creatures don't do well when they are hauled into the light of day.

The public interest in the killings was beginning to heighten. Now it was more than just the crime buffs who were gobbling up each morsel of new information. There was talk of crime commissions and extra budgets for the special police taskforce called Purana that had been set up to investigate the murders six months earlier. There was a feeling among the right-minded citizens of Melbourne that the criminal class was running riot, that it had lost its fear of the law and police, and it needed to be put back in its box.

The police, who usually watched the wise guys kill each other with faint amusement, were now taking a special interest in finding the shooters. For decades they had pretty much left the villains to regulate their own affairs. When it fell to violence the underworld was a self-cleaning oven. The hotter it got the less there was for the police to do. 'We catch and kill our own' had been the ethos that governed affairs in Melbourne, but now all this wanton killing was making the police look bad. An unwritten covenant was being broken.

In time, the gangland war would provide an incredible insight into how things were actually run in Melbourne – who held the power and how it was exercised. The conflict would develop into a class struggle between the old and new factions of the underworld. It would reveal that there was a clear nexus between corrupt police and the drug business.

Everyone was getting into the spirit of this gangland saga, it seemed. Melbourne had a new soundtrack that summer, straight from the movies. In Billy's day, men like Freddy Harrison and his cronies were regular cinemagoers. It was how they kept in touch with the gangster fashion coming out of the US. They might pull off a successful heist and then take themselves off to the latest gangster flick starring George Raft or Jimmy Cagney. They would sit there eating ice-creams in their trench coats and fedora hats, consuming the language and mannerisms of the Hollywood men of honour they idolised.

The current crop of bosses, particularly the Carlton variety, had grown up on Marlon Brando's Don Corleone in *The Godfather*, and like that film and the businesses they were running, they were trapped in the 1970s. They always had that slightly passé dress sense – the lumpy black suit over a body shirt or a tight-fitting skivvy. Many of them were older guys. They had put on a little weight now and their slicked-down hair was thinning, but when they ventured into the city's nightclubs, even the toughest bouncers would run over and line up to kiss them on both cheeks.

Now Al Pacino's Tony Montana from the 1983 film *Scarface* was the role model for a new generation of knockabouts. In *Scarface*, the ruthless Cuban immigrant Montana fights his way to the top of the Miami drug business. Along the way he defeats and kills his former mentor, the most senior criminal in Miami, as well as the corrupt police officer who protects him. He makes deals with no one, becoming increasingly paranoid until, in the climactic scene, he plunges his face into a mountain of cocaine. As his enemies pour into his palatial mansion, Montana grabs his favourite assault rifle/grenade launcher and with the words 'Say hello to my little friend' begins to destroy as many as he can, not to mention a good deal of plastering and masonry. Finally he succumbs to a hail of bullets – but it's not in vain, because he pulls off a dramatic death scene, plunging from an upper level into his fishpond.

Of course, the Montanas of Melbourne were dealing methamphetamine, not cocaine, and consequently the Porsches of the movie were in real life second-hand Mazda RX-7s or Subaru WRXs. The new boys could recite great slabs of dialogue from the movie, putting on the accent and swagger of Tony Montana. Not surprisingly, none I ever met was keen to play the death scene. They all wanted to live their own version of gangster life while conveniently leaving out the last reel.

What was going on was so unusual, so exciting, that people were drawn into the drama. Everyone laid their own version of reality over the facts. I had already begun to question my objectivity in this story – was I being pulled into the myth? I had been awoken in a city hotel by a call from a legendary gunnie to say gangland history had been made. In the background I had heard the sound of sirens across the city as Billy gravely said there was much more to come. Hanging up, I had turned to my companion, a troublesome Italian diva on the run from her boyfriend in Sydney, and heard myself saying the immortal words: 'I gotta go. There's been a murder.' 'You're dangerous,' she'd said. How many times in your life do you get to have a conversation like that?

The times were changing. You could feel it at the Munster's funeral. At Kew's Church of the Sacred Heart, I was amazed to see a long-forgotten childhood friend of mine emerge from the church as a pallbearer, sharing the burden of Kinniburgh's coffin with some of the most notorious criminals around. I had lost track of this man over the years and when I saw him I had to find out how he was linked to the Munster. As soon as he set the coffin down I broke ranks, walking through the crowd of mourners to accost him. 'What are you doing here?' I asked.

'I should be asking you the same question,' he said, obviously as surprised to see me as I was to see him. When I told him I was a reporter covering the gangland murders, he stopped short, fixing me with a murderous glare. 'The media got Graham killed – all this talk of him being the big gangster and murderer and stan-dover man. That's what got him killed, that's what made him a target of these animals,' he said, choking back his tears. 'He was my best friend in the world and I can tell you that's what got him killed – the idea that he was a threat to someone trying to take over what they thought was his bloody empire.'

He went to leave but realised he had more to say and turned back to me. 'Listen, if you are going to write about this, tell the truth, please. Tell people who Graham really was. He wasn't a gangster, he didn't terrorise people, he didn't stand over people. He was an old-style crook, and there's a huge difference.'

The day before the funeral I had visited the church, for no

particular reason other than to soak up some atmosphere. Security people were combing the grounds in readiness for the most tense send-off the underworld had seen in years. An unmistakeably criminal 'head' was sitting in an old car outside watching everyone come and go.

I sat in one of the back pews, thinking about how far Kinniburgh had come only to be dragged back into the grime, first with the murder of Alphonse and now once again in the manner of his own demise. I gazed around at the stained-glass windows of the old church, which had been built in the 1920s with money donated by John Wren, another, even more glorious robber baron. My eye fell on one pane in particular, and I wondered if tomorrow any of the mourners would see it and recognise the significance of its message: 'By the grace of God I am what I am'.

Certainly, for the villains who filled the church the next day, it was now too late to be anything else. The men of the old school had nailed their colours to the mast simply by turning up at the funeral.

2 | CARL AND ROBERTA

The suspect agreed to meet but he needed the right location – a secure place where he could pass unnoticed. All the heat surrounding his alleged involvement in murder, mayhem and drug dealing had made him a marked man. Melbourne had been voted as the world's most liveable capital, but for a man like this getting killed was easy here.

After several telephone calls, we settled on a rendezvous point with just the right ambience for this scion of the Victorian underworld. Carl Williams and his wife, Roberta, were standing waiting, as arranged, by the condiments counter at the McDonald's restaurant.

In cop-speak, Williams was regarded as 'a man of the greatest interest' in the investigation into Melbourne's underworld war. With his father, George Williams, Carl was facing charges relating to a $20 million manufacturing operation for amphetamines. It was said that only police surveillance was keeping him alive now. In the meantime, Carl had been despatching his enemies one by one.

This had all been going on without me. Melbourne's newest and least experienced crime reporter was at home in a state of ever-deepening anxiety. Four months before, in a moment of foolhardiness, I had promised my bosses that I would single-handedly crack this underworld story. Having never written a crime story in my life I would write the definitive cover story on the war for *The Bulletin* magazine while simultaneously producing a two-part television version for the Nine Network's *Sunday* program. I had wangled myself a job on *The Bulletin* and *Sunday* on the basis of this promise. Initially I was only to be the producer of the story, but then the executive producer of *Sunday* was moved on and the reporter John Lyons, with whom I was to work on the yarn, was promoted to boss. I had talked myself into a job; now my credibility was hanging by a thread.

On Friday 17 January I was lying motionless in a cheap wading pool in my backyard, just my face exposed to the relentless summer heat. After three months of research I had to face the awful fact that I had gathered nothing more than a caffeine habit, a pile of dog-eared newspaper cuttings, and the telephone numbers of some men who didn't want to speak to me and a few more whom I was too scared to call. I had promised my editors at *Sunday* and *The Bulletin* that we would have the story by the end of January. But the days were slipping past and I could feel a small knot of tension tightening in my forehead as desperation gradually gave way to panic. So I'd retired to the wading pool, wallowing like a stricken white whale.

I had never even considered that gangsters might take holidays just like the rest of us, hadn't considered that all their haunts would be empty for at least another week or two. I had imagined villainy to be a twelve-months-of-the-year thing. I had no idea what was going on and no idea how to find out. But I wasn't telling my bosses that – quite the contrary. I plunged my head deeper into the wading pool, wondering if it was possible to drown oneself in six inches of water. Perhaps a mouthful of grass clippings scraped from the bottom would do the trick.

For weeks that summer I had donned my best dark suit and sunglasses and fronted up at cafes and bars hoping to meet anyone who could help me. And each day I returned to my tiny office at Channel Nine to stare at the family tree of Melbourne's under-world that I had drawn on the whiteboard three months earlier, and at a phone that never rang. No one wanted to speak.

As I lay in the wading pool I could hear the distant sounds of suburban trains moving from station to station, crossing the invis-ible gridlines of another city – the underworld – that I had never visited though I had lived on top of it for nearly a decade. And then, from the depths of my misery, I heard my mobile phone ring. I didn't get there before it diverted to message, so, dripping wet, I dialled to pick it up. Over a hubbub of children playing, adult laughter, car noise and chatter I heard a stranger's voice greet me with absolute familiarity. 'Hello, Adam. This is Carl Williams, buddy . . .'

It was like being struck by a bolt from the blue. Never had such a friendly voice sent such a tremor of fear through me. The voice went on: 'I got your letter from my barrister Nicola [Nicola Gobbo, one of his lawyers] and I thought, if you wanted to, we could catch up over the weekend. Give us a ring if you want to do that, will ya? Cheers.'

'Omigod,' I thought, 'he's not going to leave a number!' But then he continued. I heard him ask someone, 'What's this number,

Bert?' I imagined who Bert might be – some huge tattooed hulk of a man who would be able to snap me in half like a twig. I had underestimated the danger: 'Bert' was in fact Roberta Mercieca, or Mrs Carl Williams as she had become in 2000. As I would later learn, Roberta packed a far heavier punch than her husband. Carl was a veritable man of peace by comparison, and he was supposed to be Melbourne's most ruthless crime boss.

I had written Carl one of my customary begging letters, a mixture of flattery and bravado in which I had suggested that the police, in the absence of any hard evidence linking him to the murders, were running a public relations campaign against him, leaking sensitive snippets of information to reporters who were on side, to discredit him. They were softening him up, poisoning him in the minds of potential jurors. 'I believe the media coverage of you has cemented an image in the public's mind that will impact on your upcoming legal proceedings and may also have a bearing on whether you are charged with further offences,' I had written. 'With such publicity coups to influence potential jurors, the DPP has a better-than-even chance of securing a conviction. And the odds are shortening every day as police feed more disinformation to sympathetic media. All they can charge you with is making some ill-advised comments on the telephone after you'd had a dozen beers. If that's a crime, then I will be giving myself up tomorrow, along with every other drunk in Melbourne.

'I believe this situation to be in no one's interest as it degrades the quality of justice for all Victorians. It also sets the scene for a major attack on civil liberties by lazy politicians and ambitious police. And meanwhile we have the spectacle of police officers entrapping citizens in drug busts and then being unable to testify because of their own crimes. This is further evidence of a system going mad.

'To your credit, you have been able to spot the set-ups, and perhaps that is the starting point for our discussion. You too have the ability to influence public opinion, in fact this may yet be crucial to your fortunes.'

It was completely illogical, of course, because by the time I was finished there would hardly be a person in Australia who hadn't heard of Carl and Roberta. Looking back now, I don't think Carl needed me to explain PR – there was no one in the underworld more adept at that black art than he. There was nothing preventing him from using the same public relations machine to further his defence. He liked my letter and agreed to meet.

I knew there was no mileage whatsoever for him in doing an interview with me, and he knew it too. Still, he had always liked meeting people. Over the years he had made friends with all kinds of strange heads, from child killers to rapists to homicidal maniacs. A reporter would be an interesting addition. This gang war had taken him into new territory in his life and he was curious to go further – even to find out about my world.

When I met Carl, far from the gangster of press repute he was dressed as if for a day in Bay 13 at the Melbourne Cricket Ground: faded long denim shorts, a white sports top and lairy high-top runners. At thirty-three, he still had a fleshy, baby face and a ready smile, and big brown eyes that fixed you in a disarmingly innocent sort of way. This was off-putting – to my mind career criminals had to look the part. They had to have the sallow complexion, the sunken cheeks and hollowed-out eyes that were the hallmarks of someone who did their best work at night. They needed that furtive, hunted expression that comes from spending too much time in prison. Not Carl. If you had put him in polyester pants and a baseball cap he could have passed for a trainee burger-flipper at McDonald's.

Roberta, clutching a big handbag, would have looked every inch the suburban mum and housewife were it not for the glittering diamonds on her fingers. Obviously the maternal sleepwear business she had set up was a very lucrative operation indeed.

'Are you Adam?' asked Carl nervously. We shook hands and exchanged pleasantries for a few moments (nice weather we're having, who's looking after the kids, etc.), then an awkward silence descended. Various questions flashed through my mind. *Do we stay here in McDonald's? Will they want Diet Coke with their meals? Will they even risk dining in? If there are people lining up to kill Carl Williams, do they work on Sundays?*

Before I had left the house, I wrote a note to my sister saying I was going off to meet Melbourne's newest serial killer and here was his telephone number. She was supposed to call Carl if I didn't come home; God knows what she was supposed to say. But his deadly reputation just didn't tally with the chubby, amiable young man with the blond-tipped hair standing before me. He could have been Shane Warne in a particularly heavy off-season. Any apprehension I might have felt disappeared as Carl looked at me awkwardly, shifting his gaze from me to his new basketball shoes. It was he who was nervous. As adept as he was in matters of the underworld, he was still learning the art of dealing with the press. For all the trouble the media were causing him, he still had respect for individual journalists. He gave the impression that he wanted to trust me, but more importantly, he wanted to be liked.

For a man on the underworld's death row, Williams seemed remarkably relaxed despite his initial shyness. He was beaming good health. His face was deeply tanned but for a pale patch on his nose where the zinc cream had protected him from the summer sun on his holidays. I laughed inwardly at the irony: Williams might fall to assassins that year, but he would not succumb to a melanoma. I complimented him on his tan and he smiled broadly, flashing a set of perfect white teeth. Carl always looked after himself, taking pride in following his personal-hygiene regime.

Looking into his calm, unlined face, it occurred to me that I was more worried about events than he was. He was living daily with the threat of execution and I was the one wearing the mask of tension. But, of course, he didn't have to go to work each day and explain why he hadn't cracked the story. He *knew* the whole story, and over time would tell me some of it, even if he left out certain bits that didn't exactly help his cause. By the end, I would know far more than I wanted to.

This was no straightforward tale, least of all in the telling. Over the next year, in dozens of conversations and meetings, Carl would let me look into his world and the forces that had shaped it. Here was a man suspected of conspiring to murder his rivals, welcoming a journalist inside that conspiracy.

Before my images of gangland glamour completely faded, I hustled Roberta and Carl across the road to one of Melbourne's many dark and private cafes. It was still early and the staff were reluctant to open up for us. The Williamses made as if to leave. *What sort of gangsters are these, who are respectful of strangers and take no for an answer?* I thought. They could strike fear into the hearts of their rivals, but they wouldn't demand a table at a restaurant. With a superior attitude and a few choice words in a private-school tone, I soon had the staff running up and down organising a table and taking orders. To a waiter, Melbourne's most notorious underworld couple were just another mister and missus from the suburbs.

On the Gold Coast, good crims will always take you off the strip to the beach to do business, beyond the electronic eyes and ears of the police. In Melbourne, it's all done in cafes and restaurants, the theory being that if things go awry in public, you're less likely to be knocked by your rival. After four months of cafe-crawling, trying to meet the leading lights of the Melbourne underworld, I began to see why they murdered each other. If the boredom of idle plotting in cafes all day didn't send you stir-crazy, the caffeine surely would.

An uneasy calm had descended upon Melbourne after the Munster's death.

For the first few days since the hit, the city was on full-scale murder alert. Every leafy suburb was battening down for the next hit. The media were saying it was only a matter of time before an innocent bystander was shot and killed. The hysteria levels rose and rose in the week before Christmas until suddenly, in the time-honoured Australian tradition, everyone went on holidays.

Carl Williams and his extended family took up residence in three luxury suites at a Surfers Paradise resort for a week's break from the madness and mayhem. Williams was awaiting trial on drugs charges so it had taken a variation of his bail conditions for him to get out of Victoria, but with a phalanx of the best criminal lawyers on side, it appeared he could do almost anything.

Carl and his number-one hit man Andrew 'Benji' Veniamin had earlier spent a few days by themselves in Cairns in delicious anonymity. The rest of the clan met them in Surfers Paradise. Carl's mother and father, Barb and George, had been separated for a few years. Remarkably, George had taken up with Barb's sister Kathleen, while Barb was now living in a house that George and Carl had built for her in Primrose Street, Essendon, but there was no bitterness between them and they presided over the family holiday. Roberta and her elder sister, Michelle, were there, along with a family friend, Deana Falcone. Deana had once been engaged to Carl's late brother, Shane, who had died of a heroin overdose in 1997.

Another man of considerable interest to Victoria Police, the Chief Executive, was also sunning himself in Surfers that week, but not in the Outrigger Resort with the Williams family. The Chief Executive was staying in a suite at the Palazzo Versace, where the best rooms went for $3000 a night. The higher-class digs befitted the Chief Executive's elevated gangland status. It had been a pleasant and quiet week for him – until the arrival of the Williams clan had signalled the resumption of the media frenzy. On 15 January the *Herald Sun*'s front page screamed of Carl's 'BEACH BAIL'. After following the family around for three days, the reporter concluded that the 'unemployed property developer' was 'flaunting his freedom on a court-approved holiday of sun, surf and luxury'. Senior Victorian police were reportedly 'appalled that Mr Williams, who is also facing charges of threatening to kill an officer, is enjoying the high life'.

'For a bloke who doesn't have an official occupation, he's up there sipping on drinks out of pineapples by the pool while we're here sipping on warm cans of Coke in squad cars,' an unnamed detective told the newspaper. The cops needed to be on their guard, for Williams could order hits from his deckchair as easy as picking up the telephone.

Carl could be forgiven for thinking he still had history on his side. In a century of contract killing in Melbourne, only a handful of hit men had ever been brought to justice, and there was no reason to believe this time would be any different. As far as the public was concerned, the villains could go on killing each other to the last man. This was a social good, a cleansing of the underworld. As Purana toiled away, it must have seemed to the holidaying hit men and their bosses that life had taken an expectedly pleasant twist. No one – not even the families of the victims – had the courage to lag them to the police for the murders. Quite the contrary: there were men lining up for a piece of the action. They must have felt they were living without parameters, beyond the law. They had all the guns, drugs and money and it seemed there was not a damn thing the police could do about it. A phalanx of the best lawyers in Australia could keep them out of jail for years to come – ample time to deal with troublesome witnesses or to bribe judges.

Back home, there was only the tedium of court appearances on various drugs charges to look forward to, but that was just a passing irritation to this crew. Once the public got a whiff of the corruption inside Victoria Police's former drug squad, they reasoned, their crimes might pale into insignificance. The right-thinking citizens of Melbourne would be baying for a royal commission, and there were no prizes for guessing who would be the star witnesses. With barristers, solicitors, accountants and even unofficial public relations consultants on hand, there was a strategy in place for almost every contingency. Rarely, if ever, had a group of Australian crims had cause to feel quite so untouchable as this crew did that summer. And even if his close friend the Raptor wasn't there to cook up his trademark pasta dishes for him, Carl Williams must have felt on top of the world. There was always room service.

Even the politicians were ducking for cover. I had called Premier Steve Bracks's press secretary and she had reacted to my interview request with a mixture of contempt and incredulity. 'Why would he want to talk about *that*?' she'd asked with exaggerated emphasis. I pressed on with the request anyway but was rebuffed with a well-rehearsed spiel about how the Bracks Government had restored police numbers that had been decimated in the time of the previous conservative government. She quoted a raft of statistics showing how most of the categories of crime had fallen dramatically under this government. Police had won back the streets, she said. There was no story.

'So why do these guys believe it's okay to go around shooting each other in the streets?' I asked.

'We'll get back to you,' she said curtly, but they never did. There was no reply to my letters and emails to the premier and the police minister. Going into the long summer break, this was a non-issue for the Government. It was not even on the Opposition's radar, particularly as the previous Liberal government had done nothing to deal with the underworld in its time in power – unless you counted the axing of a thousand police jobs. It would be nearly eight months before Premier Bracks deigned to give me an interview. By then it would be hard to avoid: the murders would become the main issue he was being asked to comment on.

Perhaps it was pure coincidence that Carl had chosen to meet at the Maccas just a block away from the grand neo-classical colonnades of state parliament. He was by no means highly intelligent, but even he could see that this dirty business would end up on the steps of that august building. He had been a useful tool for the corrupt and powerful elite that ran the drug business in Melbourne.

Until the puppet had cut his strings and begun murdering everyone, Williams had been nothing more than a bumptious upstart from the suburbs. Now he was calling himself The Premier, the man who called the shots in Victoria.

He'd spent just a couple of years in prison in his twenties, in an undistinguished stretch as a model prisoner. But inside he had learnt fast; he knew how to make friends and allies and how to corrupt the system. While on remand for drugs charges in 2002, Carl had used a corrupt employee of the prison catering company to smuggle contraband into Port Phillip prison. Drugs, guns, mobile phones – whatever you wanted to order, Carl could do it at a price. At Christmas, he had even brought lobsters in for the boys. He wasn't jail-house tough, so to survive in this jungle he had to make himself useful to men who were. It came naturally to him. He had been doing it since childhood.

To this point, Carl's luck had held. By the time I met him he had made $10–15 million from manufacturing and distributing

amphetamines, cocaine and ecstasy. He had begun as a small-time
dealer, but by the late 1990s he had had graduated to a partnership with the Chief Executive and soon they were moving speed by
the pound. He and his father, George, had hit on a way to make
cheap ecstasy, or at least a substitute that satisfied the undiscerning.
Ketamine is a powerful battlefield anaesthetic, used widely up until
the Vietnam War for stabilising wounded troops. It was effective
but had a range of side effects, from hallucinations to convulsions,
that caused most western forces to discontinue its use. By combin-
ing ketamine with speed, Carl was able to produce a fairly exotic
pill on the cheap, even if they were unpredictable in the early days.

George's mate Dennis Reardon agreed to be guinea pig in the
testing phase. Reardon had once been Carl's under-nine football
coach. He had grown so close to Carl that he had a tattoo on his
left calf that read 'The Fat Gang Tribe', signifying their shared love
of food and drink. A co-worker on the ketamine project remembered the first batch. 'Dennis took it and within five minutes he was
in a paralysed state and could only mumble. I thought I had killed
him . . . He was still out of it and dazed for about five hours after,'
he said. So they lessened the dose, hitting on a mix of 28 grams of
speed and 110 grams of ketamine, with 142 grams of glucose to
hold the pills together. The mix of 280 grams yielded about 1000
pills, which Carl and George sold for $15 a pop. Later the mix was
altered and they got 10 per cent more out of each batch, which
is when Carl and George began flogging their pills for as low as
$8–10 each, undercutting the Chief Executive and the Moran clan.
Buying in bulk, the end user could get pills at $20 each, but the
average price was closer to $35. Later in the evening, when they

might be in danger of coming down, nightclubbers would pay up to $50 a pill.

Suddenly Carl's pills, stamped FUBU or UFO, were everywhere. He was doing a batch a week out of his old man's garage. Carl and George were getting rich. They started moving coke and pills from Melbourne to the Gold Coast and Perth. Carl was buying property and planning his own developments. His underworld associates were starting to look at him differently. No longer was he the amiable fat bloke churning out the odd batch of eccies in his garage: he had become a threat in a market that was getting too crowded.

And now his willingness to engage with the media was unsettling to a clique that had always done business quietly and in the dark.

Just how the media had got hold of the travel details that summer was a mystery to Carl. Some of the party suspected that Roberta had tipped off the *Herald Sun*, such was her love–hate relationship with the press. It didn't matter to the Chief Executive – the Williams clan had drawn the media's fire away from him. It suited him that the press had not yet made a connection between him and Carl Williams, even if the police back in Melbourne had. The Chief Executive was the shadowy, malevolent figure just out of reach of everyone. He liked to regard himself as a cut above the riffraff he did business with, as if he was some kind of villain from a James Bond movie surrounded by his henchmen.

The fact that the Chief Executive had humble beginnings, before graduating as a confidence trickster, never lessened his sense of self-importance. Unlike his peers he now had a foot in polite society, having made millions from investments in the property boom that was then reaching its zenith.

The Chief Executive owned several businesses and, until the late 1990s when the Victoria Racing Club banned him from owning horses, a string of thoroughbreds. The VRC ban was a mere irritation; he was still allowed trackside to mingle with jockeys, owners and trainers. In the underworld he was known as the premier race-fixer in Melbourne. In the 1990s he had been the leader of a group of big-spending punters at city race meetings. Police suspected members of the Chief Executive's crew of being involved in daylight robberies of trackside bookmakers.

For much of the 1990s, many of this crew, with Carl Williams, had an interest in a money-making machine tucked away in a nondescript house in inner Melbourne. The speed lab reportedly produced tens of millions worth of product before it blew up, consuming the property. Police found the lab and later caught up with the speed cook, Paul Edward Howden, in the hospital with serious burns to 30 per cent of his body. But Howden stayed staunch; even when he was sentenced to four years' jail, he never lagged his bosses. On the surface it had appeared to be a grievous loss: others, like the Moran clan, had their speed manufactured at the lab on a contract basis, storing the precursors on the premises. The Morans were told that four 25-kilo tubs of pseudoephedrine, worth $300 000, had gone up in the blaze. In reality Williams and his cronies had already stolen the tubs, helping themselves to a multimillion-dollar windfall. If, as the saying goes, there is no honour among thieves, then life among the barons of speed was completely toxic. The lab fire hadn't slowed the Williams faction down at all. A number of

dealers worked for them; one remembers moving 40 000 pills produced from the 'destroyed' pseudoephedrine in a single six-week
period. The Chief Executive, Williams and their pals were getting
fatter and greedier by the day. The Chief Executive stood behind
Williams all the way but generally remained aloof from the grubby
business of murder. Of course, he did benefit from the elimination
of rivals in the drug trade but he knew that no good would come
from all this killing in the end. Williams could carry on with his
vendetta, while the Chief Executive kept raking in the cash.

Meanwhile most were bluffed by the Chief Executive's fearsome
reputation, though it was largely undeserved. It was said that he
travelled in a convoy of shiny black saloons and was attended by
a squad of heavies wherever he went. He moved bundles of cash
around on pallet trucks in an inner city warehouse. He was ruthless, but the perfect gentleman to his friends.

It didn't hurt his profile for such talk to get around. In the underworld people don't mind being known as the culprit in a high-profile
crime, just as long as there is no actual evidence linking them to it.
Gossip gets around quickly, gathering strength as it goes. The idea
that a man is outside normality, that he will deal with his enemies
in the most ruthless manner possible, is a boon for one who is
building and protecting an empire. If a villain has these so-called
'claws and teeth', his enemies will think twice about tangling with
him. They might even switch sides in order to enhance their own
reputation – particularly in the drugs business, where taking over a
franchise can be as easy as shooting a bloke and sitting in his chair.

Until I met Carl, I had viewed the gangland slaughter simply as
a matter of business, a turf war over the $5 billion amphetamine

trade, a problem of supply and demand. It was true that in the background there was a struggle for control of that market.

The 1999 jailing of Australia's biggest speed manufacturer, John Samuel William Higgs, had thrown the market open to newcomers. It had taken police eight years to arrest and convict Higgs. The operation, code-named Phalanx, culminated in 135 arrests, the discovery of fifteen laboratories and the seizure of eight tonnes of precursor chemicals.

Unlike most narcotics, methamphetamine or speed is a highly dilutable commodity. In 2004 a kilo bag of speed, cut with glucose powder to a concentration of just 2.5 per cent, was worth $1 million on the street. And it was relatively easy to make. An underground chemist in the US nicknamed Uncle Fester had taken his revenge on society by publishing on the Internet a step-by-step guide to the production of amphetamines, from small-scale backyard operations to major commercial enterprises. The guide became an instant classic, the bible of a new generation of drug barons. Why go to the time and trouble of organising to import heroin and coke from overseas when there was a fortune to be made using stuff that came out of your own bathroom cabinet? All you needed were the chemicals, a caravan somewhere remote and a couple of blokes with guns to keep an eye on things. You could make a truly staggering amount of money if you got these simple things right.

Uncle Fester has since published a whole suite of books aimed at helping budding drug barons. His list of titles now includes two editions of *Secrets of Methamphetamine Manufacture: Including Recipes for MDA, Ecstasy, and Other Psychedelic Amphetamines*; *Practical LSD Manufacture* and *Advanced LSD Manufacture*; and

The Construction and Operation of Clandestine Psychedelic Drug Laboratories. Recognising the inevitable after-sale issues in the drug industry, Uncle Fester has turned out other helpful tomes such as *Vest Busters: How to Make Your Own Body-Armor-Piercing Bullets*, and *Silent Death*, a DIY guide to chemical warfare. The Aum cult in Japan apparently used the latter manual to produce the sarin gas that killed twelve people and injured 600 in attacks on the Tokyo subway in March 1995.

Since 1998 there had been murders over drug deals gone wrong in Melbourne, but, as I would learn, it wasn't money alone that got you killed. Drug deals were always going wrong in the underworld. Despite Uncle Fester's best advice, a single mistake in a speed cook-up could turn a huge earner into a toxic disaster. Months of scheming and planning to get hold of the all-important pseudoephedrine could come to naught in one careless moment, and cooks could end up as fine pink mist in the terrific explosions that sometimes resulted. Even if you were successful, you still faced the threat of toecutters who would try to rob you. But killing was generally bad for business. There had to be some form of egregious insult, a blow to a man's honour or integrity, before he would reach for the ultimate solution.

That Sunday morning as we dined on ham, cheese and tomato sandwiches and coffee, Carl and Roberta began a long, tortuous dialogue that would take me deep into the ganglands, much deeper, in reality, than I wanted to go. Nearly four years later, the drama would still be dominating my life.

Roberta wanted to talk public relations. As Carl sat quietly by, she told me they wanted to strike back against the police for setting up Carl and trying to blacken his good name. But the campaign didn't end with Carl – Andrew Veniamin had been cast as his bodyguard. The newspaper had said the 'well-muscled' Benji, as he was known, had even remained by Carl's side when he went into the surf. In fact, he'd stayed by Carl because he, Benji, couldn't swim. 'I was looking after *him*,' said Carl impassively. They had stayed between the flags and paddled around in the shallows, Benji kickboxing at the heads of waves as they passed. It seemed that, for all his fearsome reputation, Benji was a strictly terrestrial operator.

Much later, Benji's sister, Helen, told me of their childhood days at the local pool in Sunshine. In my mind's eye I could see the eleven-year-old girl struggling to keep her two little brothers' heads above the water in the local swimming pool and their father calling out from the bleachers, 'Helen, you've got to let them go, otherwise they'll never learn to swim.' One boy swims away but the other – Andrew – holds on ever so tightly to his sister, the thought of the blue depths of the pool sending violent shudders through him.

To call Andrew Veniamin a bodyguard was to undersell grossly his growing status in the underworld, and this morning Carl and Roberta communicated Benji's dissatisfaction with his media portrayal. Of course, just what his role in their life was they did not share with me. 'He's a friend, and a good friend at that,' said Roberta, beaming at the thought of her husband's mercurial offsider.

The truth be told, Benji was one of the most popular men in the underworld. But as everyone in that world knows, a good friend is everyone's enemy. The people you trust the most are the ones who pose you the greatest risk – every gangster dies at the hand of a friend. And Benji had already accounted for a number of people: some friends, some enemies, but all dogs in the end.

Today, the common enemy was the police. With the help of certain media, they were hatching a plan to kill Carl and Andrew, said Roberta. 'Then they can blame all this killing on them and no one will ever know the truth,' she said, smiling and laughing sardonically. There was something unnerving in the smile. Like Carl's, her teeth were perfect, but in her case there were just too many of them, and this gave her a predatory, carnivorous look. She later told me she had spent more than $20 000 on the work, and I imagined the prosthodontist as one of those old circus performers who would fearlessly stick their heads into the mouth of a lion. Roberta was an attractive woman and took great care with her thick brown hair. She had travelled the world and knew how to dress, but in her eyes I could read the ingrained disappointment of her life, see the anger that lay behind them. She was strong and wiry and I could see the sinews in her arms twitching and her fists clenching instinctively as she spoke. She said they were 'just a normal, average suburban family'. She scared me much more than Carl. He had a reputation but she had a physical menace. There was a magnetism about her. 'I can get anyone to do anything for me,' she told me later.

The Special Operations Group had already had a go at provoking Carl, she said, urging him to recount the story of his latest arrest. While he was gathering his thoughts, she quickly jumped in to say that on 17 November Carl had been driving along the beachfront at Port Melbourne when, with no warning, police cars had forced him off the road. The SOGs and officers from Purana Taskforce had surrounded the vehicle and, with automatic weapons drawn, begun to shout commands at Carl. 'Those dogs started screaming, "Put on the handbrake and get out of the car!" But Carl knew enough about Victoria Police to know it was a set-up.'

To someone like me, brought up to trust the police and comply almost instinctively with their commands, this seemed a little odd. But Carl had grown up in the 1980s during a war between the crims and police, a time when suspects had been killed for waving beach umbrellas, and warning shots had been delivered through the chest.

Carl said he had refused to get out of the car, fearing it might be a set-up: 'You go for the handbrake, and they shoot you and say you were going for a handgun.' A stand-off had ensued until Carl crawled out of his four-wheel drive onto the nature strip. He claimed that during his arrest a police officer had whispered softly in his ear: 'We know who you are and what you've been up to, and we're coming for you. You won't know when, but we're coming. Remember that, smartarse.'

Carl had been arrested on charges that he had threatened to kill a Purana Taskforce officer, Detective Sergeant Stuart Bateson, and his girlfriend. A passing photographer from *The Age* newspaper snapped the moment when police slammed Carl's face into the grit of the Port Melbourne nature strip as they handcuffed him. 'The whole thing was a set-up,' Roberta repeated. On telephone intercepts, Carl had been overheard telling the Raptor, who had telephoned from Barwon Prison, that he was going to 'knock fucking Bateson's missus for nothing and chop her up'. On another call, he had told Roberta that if Bateson came to their home looking for him, 'you know what to do: get the gun from under the mattress and shoot him in the head'. Roberta said Carl had been drunk that night, too drunk to know what he was saying. 'He makes jokes like that when he's drunk,' she said, smiling at Carl, who beamed back as if the whole thing was just a naughty practical joke.

Carl said that to add insult to injury, his comments over the telephone to the Raptor had been misheard. 'They're off their heads. You can hear it clearly on the tape. I didn't say I wanted to 'knock' Bateson's girl. I know it's not a nice thing to say,' said Carl, looking sheepish, 'but what I really said was that I wanted to fuck her.' Roberta nodded in agreement, seemingly unfazed by her husband's confession that he wanted to sleep with the girlfriend of a policeman who was dedicated to putting them both behind bars. Her husband's roving eye was not a problem, apparently.

Then there was the media circus as Carl had left the County Court after being released on bail on the threat-to-kill charges. He had been enjoying the attention of the media while cradling his infant daughter, Dhakota, in his arms. He'd thanked his legal team for their excellent work and said now he just wanted to go home and have a drink and a meal. But his smile had vanished when Judy Moran, the mother of slain gangsters Mark and Jason Moran, approached him from behind and jabbed him with a finger, saying in a low growl, 'Why don't you admit you murdered both my children?'

'Is this another set-up?' Williams had cried as he hurried away from Moran, cutting short his media opportunity. 'It's probably why I'm here – another set-up from your family.'

At the mention of Judy Moran, Roberta's demeanour changed dramatically. She forgot that she was playing the sweet suburban wife and bared her teeth and snarled, 'That fucking cow.' Regaining her composure, she explained that the Moran and Williams families went back some time. Some of the children had attended the same grammar school. At one time Carl and the Moran boys had been friends, though it was wrong to say, as some people did, that they had been business associates.

Carl pointed out that he had not fired the first shots in the war. In October 1999 someone had shot him in the stomach from point blank range at a reserve in outer suburban Gladstone Park. Carl flatly denied that he knew who had shot him, and he even disputed the police version of where the incident had taken place. And of course he knew nothing about the talk that the bullet had been in settlement for an unpaid debt of more than $400 000, plus a series of egregious insults. It was widely reported that just before the shooting someone was heard to cry, 'No, Jason, no!', but in the confusion Carl couldn't be sure who had pulled the trigger. 'Nah, I couldn't tell you, mate,' he said, looking unblinkingly into my eyes. 'Of course, the police told me there were surveillance tapes of Mark and Jason discussing shooting me, but nah, I wouldn't know anything about that.'

Roberta and Carl didn't know anything about any of it – even if they seemed to know all the names. 'We've got nothing to do with all this,' said Roberta, with exaggerated sincerity. 'I saw Carl cry when Nik [Radev] was killed. He was our friend.' Radev, 'The Russian', a notorious drug supplier killed in the busy year of 2003, had even come to their daughter's first birthday party. 'To be accused of killing someone you like – well, it's just too much,' said Roberta. Perhaps it was just a slip of the tongue on her part, but I had to agree that it certainly seemed capricious to do it to your friends. The media and bent cops had dreamed up the whole thing, she said.

The last straw for the family came on their Gold Coast holiday, fumed Roberta. The photographer from the *Herald Sun* had followed them all around Surfers Paradise, snapping some particularly unflattering shots of Carl in the surf. In the pictures he looked like any Victorian on holiday up north, his nose smeared with zinc and a generous wodge of brickie's cleavage peeping out of his board shorts. Roberta was like a celebrity complaining about the paparazzi. 'The photographer, the way he took them pictures, he made Carl look fat,' she trilled. Carl looked up from his sandwich, the hurt evident in his big brown eyes.

3 | BEYOND THE PALE

The morning I met Carl and Roberta Williams in January 2004, the cafe was full of ghosts from the past year. By this time, Carl's power was already on the wane, though in his vanity he would never have acknowledged it.

In June 2003, he had overstepped the mark in having his most bitter enemy Jason Moran killed, along with an associate, Pasquale Barbaro. No one would miss Moran, a drug-dealing thug whose only ambition in life had been to be a gangster, but it was the manner in which he and Barbaro were despatched that galvanised police against Williams.

It was 10.40 a.m. on a Saturday morning and scores of kids and their families were at the Cross Keys Reserve in Melbourne's north-west for the weekly Auskick session. The training was finishing up and Moran was in the driver's seat of a pale blue Mitsubishi van, with Barbaro, a sometime Moran drug courier, alongside him. In the back seat there were five children, including Moran's twins. The group must have blended into the family scene but so too did the white van that dropped the Raptor a short distance away. The Raptor rolled down his balaclava, approached

49

the closed driver's side window of Moran's vehicle and produced a sawn-off shotgun, and blasted the startled gangster before he had time to produce a 9mm pistol from his belt. The gunman then pulled a handgun and fired several more rounds into the car, killing Barbaro.

It was the moment that the tone of this affair changed. To that point, crims killing crims could be excused as secret underworld business, but to kill like this, in front of families enjoying a sub-urban ritual, was beyond the pale. Within days, Victoria Police announced the establishment of the Purana Taskforce, a fifty-man squad which would probe a string of sixteen killings stretching back to 1998. Not all of them were connected, but senior police argued that a multi-disciplinary team of investigators, analysts and forensic accountants had a once-in-a-generation opportunity to crack organised crime in Victoria.

Six months later, the cops sitting in their squad cars with their hot Coke and fast food on the Gold Coast knew exactly what the Chief Executive, Williams and their henchmen had been up to in 2003. However, intelligence collected from the state's most inten-sive campaign of physical and electronic surveillance ever was still way short of evidence, even if they were catching a few breaks. They were starting to join the dots to reveal the picture. As one investigator said, Carl Williams had to be lucky all the time to survive. They just had to be lucky once. The officer in charge of Purana, Superintendent Andrew Allen, had to be patient.

'We had to put together the evidence,' he later told the ABC. 'Information wasn't enough for us to move in and arrest and charge. So we did have to step back and we also had to think about what our strategies were going to be, and we were looking at medium- to long-term strategies.'

But as the bodies piled high, holding his nerve would not be easy.

'For a while there, probably for twelve months, it was just full-on during the day and you knew that, if the phone rang at night, 90 per cent chance there was going to be another murder.'

The first of the parade of hits and memories for 2003 was Nikolai 'The Russian' Radev. Radev, a Bulgarian immigrant, had built a fortune over twenty years in Australia, though his only formal record of employment was eight months in a fish-and-chip shop in the early 1980s. He had stood at the top of a chain of small-time drug manufacturers who cooperated, sharing the same speed cooks. Radev was the acme of evil in the Melbourne underworld. He once made an example of a rival by raping him in front of his wife and son. Another man who tried to mediate the dispute ended up dead with a pillowcase over his head and a hot load of speed in him. He also once kidnapped a university science student and forced him to cook up amphetamines for him. No one messed with the Russian.

Carl was worried that Nik had wanted everything. He was planning to kidnap Carl's best cook, hide him on a remote farm and make him churn out fake ecstasy and speed 24/7. So Carl had got in first.

On 15 April 2003, Radev and his bodyguards were in earnest discussion with Carl and George Williams and other associates at the Middle Brighton Baths Cafe. Radev was complaining that the quality of the speed Carl and George had been supplying was no good and he wanted to meet the cook to sort out the problem. This was nothing new – a lot of whingeing went on in the industry – but Carl and George knew it was just a ruse and played along. They offered to arrange a meeting between Radev and the cook, a crim named George Peters. Terms were agreed and a convoy of cars set out for the rendezvous point in Queen Street, Coburg.

But Radev would never meet Peters. Benji and the Raptor had been watching the meeting from their car. Now they raced ahead to get in position to intercept Radev in Queen Street. As it was, they nearly missed him. Radev was already walking away from his black Mercedes when the knocking squad turned up, but then, fatally, he doubled back to the car to get a cigar. It was a poor decision. A car drew up alongside and Veniamin jumped out and poured seven rounds from a revolver and a pistol into Radev's back.

Radev died on that Coburg street wearing Versace from head to toe and with a $20 000 watch on his wrist – at least he was dressed for the occasion. Business had been very good to him: he was buried in a $35 000 gold-plated coffin.

Next to go were Jason Moran and Pasquale Barbaro at the Cross Keys Reserve. At this point, surveillance on the key players was dramatically stepped up with the formation of the Purana Taskforce, but a full scale blood-letting was now underway.

On 21 July, the small-time dealer Willy 'Freckle' Thompson was gunned down outside a gym in Warrigal Road, Chadstone, in the city's east.

At thirty-nine, Willy was still extremely fit. A short, stocky man, he had recently been turned on to the sport of grappling, a form of submission wrestling. On the night of 21 July 2003, he was in

Chadstone training at the Extreme Jiu-Jitsu and Grappling gym. While Willy was coming to grips with his training partner, police believe someone made a telephone call to his killers. At 9.30 Willy came out of the gym talking to a friend, said his goodbyes and walked to his convertible Honda a short distance away. As he prepared to pull away from the kerb, a stolen Ford sedan pulled up alongside and boxed him in. A gunman calmly got out and took aim at Willy and let fly with a full magazine. Willy was known not to carry a gun, so it was only a question of hitting the target. One round ended up in the wall of a book store a few metres behind Willy's car. Thompson's death confounded investigators. Nik Radev had fire-bombed his car sixteen months earlier over a drug dispute but with Radev now dead, police had no clear suspects. The underworld had its own theories.

Willy Thompson made his 'honest' living selling lollipop-vending machines to nightclubs. He had dreamed of a career in the movies, starring in an underground sci-fi hit *The Nightclubber* as a gun-toting action hero. The director, Dale Reeves, said he was perfect for the part. 'Willy had dead eyes. He had seen a lot and he brought a chilling realism to the role.'

Meanwhile former champion kickboxer Michael Ronald Marshall trundled his hot-dog van around the seedy nightclub strips. He and Willy Thompson were mates. They had been bouncers together, but they shared another far more lucrative business venture: a thriving amphetamine trade. Mick lived in a comfortable two-storey home in South Yarra that was fully paid off in three years. Willy also lived in relative luxury, and at the time of his death held $245000 in a Greek bank account and a $150000 slice of a local business. The two men shared a speed cook, and a very good one at that – Murray Tackle. Their business thrived and there was no trouble from the law. They trusted each other.

The trouble began in early 2003, when Willy went to Sydney to buy chemicals from a group of crooks in the south-west of the harbour capital. He drove there with $400 000 in cash and a mission to buy precursor chemicals from the group, but came home with no chemicals and no money. He claimed he had been rolled, that the Lebanese had ripped him off and sent him home. Apparently Mick didn't believe him and there was some unpleasantness, but not enough to commit murder.

It would later emerge that Carl wanted Willy Thompson dead for his own reasons – you could even call it paranoia.

Thompson had been an associate of Mark Moran's and had been passing information to Carl on his brother Jason's movements. Now Carl believed the information was false and that Willy had tried to position him for Jason. Even though Jason was dead, Carl believed Willy was still a threat. One night the Raptor ran into Carl and Andrew 'Benji' Veniamin at a South Melbourne nightclub. Benji whispered in his ear that he needed help with a job – the murder of Willy Thompson. The Raptor was incredulous. 'You're mad!' he said. 'It's too close to the other murders.' The Raptor declined the opportunity; even by his standards this was getting weird.

Carl continued doing business with Thompson after Benji had taken the contract. During one meeting Carl ordered two 25-kilo drums of pseudo from Thompson. Though it was duly supplied, Carl never paid for it.

He was enjoying one of his holidays on the Gold Coast with the

Raptor when Thompson died. Benji had done the job for $100 000 and then flown up to Queensland to join them.

Carl's team quickly spread the rumour that Mick Marshall had knocked Willy over the drug dispute. The Raptor and Carl met Thompson's business partner, Murray Tackle, at Southgate to reinforce the story. Carl swore that he would seek revenge for Willy, but first Murray needed to make good on a $900 000 debt Willy had owed Carl.

Tackle didn't know that he was on trial: Carl wanted to know what he had told the police about the murder. One loose word would have got Tackle killed that night. As it was, he was losing the plot. He told Carl that he changed his clothes for new ones every night, fearing that they and his shoes were bugged. Later, Tackle handed over a bag containing $150 000.

With the lie about Thompson's killer now seeded, Carl had another loose end to tie up.

On 18 August, the charred remains of Mark Mallia, an ally to the late Nik Radev, turned up in a drain in West Sunshine. He had been tortured and strangled, and his body burned.

Mark Mallia had been a childhood friend of Benji's from Sunshine but that gave him no immunity when he had dared to accuse Carl and Benji of knocking Radev. They met Mallia at a seafood restaurant at Southgate and, after prawn cocktails all round, Carl and Benji denied shooting Nik. They committed themselves to finding the real assassins, 'but if word gets out that you are trying to extract revenge on any of us,' said Benji slowly, leaning over the table and pointing his finger at Mallia, 'I will kill you and your family.' Mallia was in tears now; all he wanted to know was who had killed Nik and why. Carl assured him everything would be sweet and urged him not to worry about Benji, who was still glowering at Mallia. Later they heard a vague rumour that Mallia was shopping for a shooter to kill Carl. It was enough. Carl allegedly paid $50 000 to an associate, Terrence Chimirri, to lure Mallia over to his house in Lalor. There a group of men, including Benji, tied him to a chair in the garage and tortured him with a soldering iron to find out where he stooked his drug money, the names of dealers who owed him money who they could now stand over, and what stuff he had at home he could barter for his life. Mallia was then strangled to death with hands and ropes. They stuffed his body in a wheelie bin, poured petrol over him and set him alight.

Even Carl was amazed that Benji had done it so close to home. 'They're mad for doing what they did,' he said.

Mallia now dealt with, Carl and the Raptor had time for some further education. They took a three-hour jet ski course, passing with flying colours. When they went to VicRoads to get their licences, Chimirri rolled up in the flash hotted-up white Commodore he had bought with the $50 000 Carl gave him for luring Mallia out. They were happy days indeed, but it wasn't to last.

The conventional wisdom that Mick Marshall had killed Willy Thompson meant Marshall – though he had done nothing – had offended the Chief Executive. The Chief Executive considered Thompson a close friend. He had no idea that Carl was behind his mate Thompson's murder and in September he offered Williams $300 000 to knock Marshall in retribution

In September, a meeting was organised with Carl, the Raptor and various accomplices at a Red Rooster shop in Brunswick to discuss the deal. (You might notice that a lot of the main action in this story takes place in fast-food joints. It was odds-on the villains wouldn't live long enough to fall victim to high cholesterol.) To Carl, the businessman, murder was a commercial enterprise now. After killing Thompson he had scooped up $150 000 of the dead man's loot, and now another $300 000 would come his way for killing Marshall.

The Raptor was getting impatient, though: he hadn't been paid for the murder of Jason Moran. Carl had set him up in a fully furnished apartment on Southbank and was drip-feeding him with big promises and small amounts of cash. Now there was a new promise of an apartment being built in Frankston and a manila envelope containing $50 000 turned up. Carl had to keep the Raptor sweet to get Marshall knocked before the Chief Executive discovered he had been cheated. The Raptor was happy enough, and blew the entire $50 000 on the horses and at the casino in the four weeks before the plan came to fruition. The Raptor and another henchman, let's call him 'Goggles', carried out surveillance on Marshall, watching his comings and goings from home and his hot-dog stand. Goggles bought a small inconspicuous car, a silver Holden Vectra, for the job, the Chief Executive supplied the guns and all was in readiness. But days before the hit, Goggles told the Raptor that he had found what he thought was a police tracking device in their vehicle. He suggested they delay and find a new clean car, but the Raptor would have none of it. He was focused on the killing and didn't want Carl and the Chief Executive to think he wasn't up to the job. He was feeling the pressure of the deception of the Chief Executive and wanted the job done now. He didn't even mention it to Carl. The Raptor had never trusted Goggles anyway. He had a poor reputation for honesty, even amongst crooks – maybe he was just speaking shit or looking for an excuse to get out of the job. This incredible oversight more than anything else sealed the eventual fate of Carl Williams. For all their careful planning one moment of stupidity would bring the whole team undone.

For nearly two weeks, police had followed the movements of the Raptor and Goggles and listened to their conversations courtesy of that tracking device, reportedly hidden inside one of the indicators of their vehicle.

In the days leading up to the murder, Purana detectives had known the suspects were up to something, but not what that something was. In one week, police tracked the pair four times in the area near Marshall's home. The detectives were listening as they drove there again on the night of Marshall's death, Saturday 25 October.

Towards sunset they listened to 'a chilling series of conversations where it was obvious that a hit was about to occur and we couldn't do anything about it.'

At 6.25 p.m. Marshall parked his car and hot-dog trailer outside his home and was getting out of his vehicle with his five-year-old son when the Raptor stepped up. As the Raptor raised his revolver and fired the first shot, Marshall was lunging at him. The road was wet and the recoil of the weapon caused the killer to slip and fall backwards. Unsure if the first shot had hit Marshall, the Raptor jumped back up and blazed away, with four or five shots hitting Marshall.

When he got back into his car, the killer noticed he had his victim's blood on his clothes – but it didn't bother him. The job was done and it was payday.

But within hours, the Raptor and Goggles would be intercepted by a team from the Special Operations Group, arrested and charged with murder. Marshall was number twenty in the war. To add insult to injury, the Raptor never saw the balance of his $50 000 for killing Marshall. He never got his apartment in Frankston for killing Jason Moran and Pasquale Barbaro. A few days later Carl called from the Raptor's mother's house, where he left just $1500 in cash. Not much for the taking of three lives. Stupidity would be compounded by cheapness. The entire hit team would later turn on Carl.

Soon after Goggles was taken into custody, officers knew they had the weak link in the chain. The Raptor was a hard man. Jail time, even a life sentence, held no terrors for him. But Goggles was weak and malleable. He was an underworld bottom feeder with an undistinguished criminal record of minor assaults, rapes and home invasions. Once he had even tried to ransom the bones of someone's dead granny. If Goggles was placed among the mainstream prisoners, Carl could have him killed just to make sure he didn't deal with the cops. His best chance of survival was a full confession and a magic-carpet ride to an interstate jail. Carl's closest associates wondered why Goggles had made it into the inner sanctum at all; it seemed to leave a question mark over Carl's judgement.

4 | AN AFTERNOON IN CARLTON

On a hot day in October 2003, a few days after the murder of Mick Marshall, two men were sitting waiting outside a Carlton pizza restaurant. They were already on their second coffee and were getting visibly impatient, scanning the street for approaching cars, making telephone calls and gesticulating to each other. The men, a shaven-headed pug with thick glasses, and a wiry hawk-faced jailbird, were clearly not at La Porcella for its famous wood-fired pizzas.

I suspected we were all waiting for the same man, because I had seen the pair the day before when the man in question had stood me up.

La Porcella was a good place for a quiet meeting, a family restaurant that seemed to host families customarily spelt with a capital F. It was far enough from the main drag of Lygon Street to be discreet and difficult for the police to keep under physical surveillance but the lads always assumed the walls had electronic ears. At different times their cars were bugged too, but there were always little spaces in La Porcella where they could retreat for private conversations. It was a big, airy joint with cheery red-and-white checked vinyl tablecloths. A sculpture of a great bulbous chef stood outside as if to ward away any normal diners. This was Mick Gatto's office, and it had been so for a couple of years now.

Gatto and his crew had abandoned their former haunt, Don Camillo's in North Melbourne, complaining that there was too much surveillance there. It was a shame – Don Camillo's is as close to a New Jersey clip joint as you will find in Melbourne. It's a place where the broadest cross-section of society meets – businessmen, union officials, politicians, champion footballers, kickboxers and the Mafia all mix amiably there. A block or two east is the Queen Victoria Market, the epicentre of Melbourne's Calabrian Mafia for decades. Go west a kilometre and the sombre grey spires of the Star of the Sea church, the scene of most of the important criminal funerals in Melbourne, loom into view. A few doors down, a down-at-heel gun dealer's shop completes the underworld atmosphere.

By comparison, La Porcella was low-key and nondescript and, besides, the owner was Calabrese. And Mick liked the coffee.

He was looking to make peace, sources told me. Gatto's deft negotiating skills had helped ensure some of the biggest building projects in Melbourne were completed on time, on budget. He was unorthodox, but had a way of helping employers and unions see eye to eye. Friends – some police among them – said Gatto's hulking frame concealed a warm, almost sentimental heart. Often characterised as the essential man of honour, Gatto would laugh off the Mafia tag, saying, 'It's my face. I can't help the way I look.'

Despite his imposing bulk and history of violence, he could keep a sense of proportion, even a sense of humour – like the time he had tried to stand over a feisty little Greek businessman who had refused to pay up over a building project. Mick's polite inquiry had been met with a resounding rejection. The Greek told me: 'I said to Mick, "I'm not paying you a cent – so you can go and get fucked!" Now Mick doesn't like being spoken to this way, so he says, "Listen here, you little cunt, who do you think you are? When I get hold of you I'm going to throw you through a fucking window!" "Good," I says, "meet me downstairs at such and such a bar in North Melbourne tomorrow afternoon and you can deal with me then." He turns up there all hot and heavy and I'm just sitting there smiling at him. And he looks around the room and suddenly realises the joke – the bar has no windows, so where's he going to throw me? I says, "Mick, what are you going to do now, buddy?" Even Mick could see the joke.'

In early October I had tried to contact Gatto through his lawyer, George Defteros, seeking an interview for a segment I was putting together on the murders for the Nine Network's *Sunday* program. I had no idea that Mick would become a central player in what unfolded in the next seven years. In reality he was already in the eye of the storm when I made the call to his lawyer that afternoon.

The only reason I rang was because Gatto had made comments to the press before. Usually he spoke only to deny that he had killed someone or other, but right now anyone willing to say anything was welcome on my show.

To my surprise, Gatto called back the next day to decline in person, perhaps curious as to why anyone would want to delve into the topic. He was adamant and aggressive, and said that he wanted nothing to do with it. 'Whaddya you doing?' he asked incredulously. 'Do you wanna be victim number twenty-two or something?' There was no disrespect or threat intended in his words.

Despite a warning that he wanted nothing to do with murder stories, or any stories for that matter, Gatto agreed to meet the next afternoon at La Porcella. He was still smarting from the press coverage of his 2002 appearance at a royal commission investigating claims that organised crime had taken a grip on Victoria's construction industry and was extorting millions from developers in return for peace on building sites. Gatto had told the commission that he felt he had been vilified for his role as mediator and peacemaker. 'I had a bit of trouble in my earlier days, but I'm a businessman these days,' he said proudly. The conventional wisdom – not to mention the transcript of the royal commission – didn't quite bear that out. Sure, he wasn't running protection rackets on Lygon Street, but his work as a consultant continued to have more than a whiff of standover about it.

Still, he agreed to meet me, which in my inexperience meant two things: he wasn't involved in the current spate of murders, and he had nothing to hide.

I waited for an hour outside La Porcella, which was virtually empty but for a few office workers and the table where the pug and the jailbird sat. Finally I rang Gatto, and he was profuse in his apologies. He had tried to call me to cancel the meet, because the huge storm the night before had flooded his house and he was busy dealing with that. Could we meet the following day? Obviously he hadn't notified my two fellow courtiers, either. *He needs a personal assistant*, I thought.

The next day the three of us – the pug, the jailbird and me – were back again at La Porcella, this time sitting inside. After half an hour, Gatto loomed up in the window outside. There was no mistaking that this was the boss of the Carlton Crew. A huge, formidable figure, he walked like he owned the street, tugging ostentatiously at the lapels of his black suit and letting the fabric fall over his imposing frame. Two paces behind was the venerable old crim Ronnie Bongetti, once the king of Melbourne's SP betting. He now acted as Mick's aide-de-camp, a constant companion who, it was rumoured, carried the big man's gun. He was also the sole director of Mick's latest enterprise, a building industry 'consultancy' company called Arbitrations and Mediations Pty Ltd.

Mick would tell his clients that for a price everything was negotiable between gentlemen. Arbitrations and Mediations had saved Melbourne's construction industry millions of dollars, and Mick was now welcome in the boardroom of many of the big builders in town, whether they liked it or not. There were few people in the city who could stand over him.

Gatto was one of Victoria's leading boxers of the 1970s, and at one stage a genuine contender for the Australian heavyweight title. But that was before he caught the eye of senior men in the Honoured Society.

Through the 1980s, Gatto's stature rose. He was forced to publicly deny that he had murdered leading underworld figure Giuseppe Arena, the so-called 'friendly godfather' who had been shot dead in the driveway of his Bayswater home in 1988. A newspaper report suggested that Gatto was the police's main suspect in the killing, prompting him to make one of his sporadic appearances in the media to deny that he was involved or that he was a standover man. He said his father was a good friend of Mr Arena's, and he himself had been an acquaintance of the dead man. 'I passed on my respects [to the Arenas] and told them I knew nothing about it. They were quite shocked to hear that my name had been mentioned.'

On 21 February 2002 Gatto was subpoenaed to appear before the royal commission into the building industry, over his role as a special 'industrial relations' consultant on Melbourne building sites. He had apparently been hired to act as mediator in the negotiation of a variety of industrial agreements at the National Gallery of Victoria building site.

A few days later, *The Age* reported that the royal commission was investigating events surrounding the payment of about $250 000 from a big contractor to a company that solved awkward industrial relations problems. Mick took the stand, giving the public its first prolonged look at the leader of the Carlton Crew. He claimed he was being made a scapegoat by the inquiry and strenuously denied he was a standover man. He vowed to take on Commissioner Terence Cole QC, thundering from the witness box: 'I will fight you all the way, tooth and nail.' Mr Cole suggested that Mr Gatto 'keep calm', and said that anyone who disrupted the commission faced heavy fines and jail for up to three months.

But Mick was in no mood to be calm. 'My mother is hysterical; my children – their girlfriends and partners want to leave them. I hope one day you're in this position . . . I'm not a standover man. I'm not a man of ill repute. Fair enough, I've got a chequered past . . . but I paid for . . . whatever I have done wrong. I don't appreciate this nonsense that you are looking for someone to blame to justify your existence here today, to justify 300 investigators and teams of lawyers. You won't be justifying your existence with me, I promise you.'

In an interview published in *The Age* on 2 March 2002, Gatto said people were jealous because he dressed well and drove a nice car. He 'mixed well' with people throughout Australia. Melbourne's Lord Mayor, John So, sent him a Christmas card last year. 'It's not right that they seem to think I'm king of the underworld . . . All this nonsense is not right for my family or my children,' Gatto said. 'I shy away from the spotlight and don't like to be in the public arena. Unfortunately this time they have roped me into something they thought was a bonanza.'

By the time I met him eighteen months later, Gatto had roped himself into his next controversy. For a brief period, he had managed to keep out of harm's way.

From his expression I could tell that Gatto wasn't happy. He had clipped his brow with the car door as he was getting out of the vehicle and a little egg was forming rapidly, discernible through the other scars and bumps on his face. Ignoring the pug and the jailbird, he came straight over to my table and, rubbing his brow, absently offered one huge, meaty mitt for me to shake. For all its size, his hand was remarkably soft – but the grip was irresistible.

'So, what we are doing here today, buddy?' I couldn't tell him I had no idea whatsoever – that I was just wanting to attach myself to him for as long as possible in order to understand a tiny sliver of what was going on in the underworld – so I went with a rehearsed spiel. I have always believed that two things determine the outcome of cold calls like this one: the quality of your reference, and the sweetness of your flattery. Light on the first commodity, I decided to lay the second on as thick as possible.

'Mr Gatto, you have no reason to speak to me or to do an interview,' I began, trying to quell the flaming butterflies in my stomach. 'But I have a lot to gain from you if, at the very least, you can take the time to listen to what I am doing.' I paused for effect, letting the bullshit settle on him. 'You are a leader in your community, a man of honour whom everyone respects. I thought that you, of all people, should know that I am going to be about for the next few months doing some research into things . . .' He tried to speak, but I was gabbling now, just riding right over the top of him.

At this point I must confess that since childhood I have been a 'nimmer'. For those not familiar with the condition, 'nimming' refers to a compulsive shaking of the legs or tapping of the heel, usually experienced during pressure situations. (My mother has a theory that it has to do with a deficiency of vitamin A.) Mostly I don't even know when I am doing it, but at this moment the skin of my caffe latte was shimmering and vibrating, such was the frenzy of nimming going on under the table. I'm sure readers will excuse my shaking like a leaf. If ever there was a nim-worthy moment, this was it. It was all I could do to stop myself kicking Mick in the shins.

Just keep talking and eventually something sensible might come out, I thought. Aloud, I said, 'Because, Mr Gatto, if someone says to you, "Hey, there's some journo around asking questions", and you don't know what I'm up to, then I guess it might make you look kinda bad. People are going to ask you, "Don't you know what's going in your own backyard?" And that wouldn't be good, would it?'

67

Mick paused for a moment, trying to digest this rather preposterous idea. I smiled and held my hands out to him as if I had nothing to hide. The pregnant pause brought on a spasm of nimming that even Mick must have noticed.

It made absolutely no sense, but there was a compliment in there somewhere and a recognition of his authority. We nodded at each other in agreement, and this seemed to put Mick at ease. He was polite and even charming as we exchanged pleasantries about his waterlogged house, but a dark cloud passed over his face when I introduced the word 'murder'. He put one warm, plate-sized palm on my shoulder and squeezed ever so gently. 'Leave me out of all this murder business, will you, buddy? It's not my fight and there's no way I want to get dragged into this.'

But then he talked about the changes that had taken place in his community, how people didn't pay respect to each other anymore. Boxing had taught him how to stand in front of a man without fear, to respect his capabilities and his strengths, and to recognise his own limitations. Such knowledge guides behaviour, he said. But it was every man for himself in the new generation. The new boys were happy to consort with the police if it meant saving their own skin. 'But not my boys,' he said wistfully, looking quietly into the distance.

Gatto didn't know it back then, but soon many of 'his boys' would be found wanting. In the storm that would soon envelop him, many of his mates would turn into 'flags', as traitors are known in the underworld. These flags would flutter and flap whichever way the wind blew. Worse still, some of them would remain loyal, helping Gatto to create one of the greatest messes the Carlton Crew had ever seen.

For now, though, things weren't so bad, and there was time to entertain an obsequious journo like me. Though Gatto was in fact right in the centre of the conflict, he could issue a stinging denial to me that he had any interest in going to war. Looking back, I can only assume that he wanted his rivals to understand that, and I was a convenient vehicle. 'Buddy, things are going along nice and quiet here now, and we don't want any part of this nonsense,' he said sternly, pointing one sausage finger at me in warning.

Then his mood changed entirely. 'Hey, are you going to have some lunch, buddy?' he said, smiling jauntily.

I replied weakly that I had ordered some pasta earlier (I had thought eating would cover the outward signs of terror) but the food hadn't turned up. Gatto swung around to the nearby counter and three waiters snapped to attention. 'Hey, where's this guy's pasta, huh? Come on, let's have it out here before the journo goes and gives the place a bad review,' he laughed, rising to leave the table for his next appointment, with the pug and the jailbird.

Instantaneously, a plate of pasta was produced. The waiter apologised, whispering, 'I didn't want to disturb you while you were doing business.'

Gatto went off to the other table, leaving me with my pasta. I thought that would be the end of my first encounter with a real live Calabrian don. Though it was far less than an interview, he *had* given me a taste of this strange twilight culture. I gulped down a little of the pasta and went to leave, passing Gatto as he hunkered down with the pug and the jailbird. The pug threw me a suspicious glance, perhaps wondering whether I was a new rival for their patron's interest.

'You're not going, are you, buddy?' exclaimed Gatto in surprise, jumping to his feet.

'Well, sure . . .' I began.

'No – stay, stay. I was coming back over when I finished here. I want you to meet some people, have a coffee, whatever,' he said.

As the cliché goes, this was an offer I couldn't refuse. Anyway, where was I going? Back to my hot, stifling little office to pore over newspaper cuttings? This was a chance to step from my world to Mick's, and I wasn't going to miss it.

He ushered me to the inner sanctum of his headquarters, a large table for ten at the back of the restaurant on a raised platform, fenced off from the rest of the place with a thick wooden balustrade. In the dim, cool gloom of that corner Ronnie Bongetti was sitting alone, sipping on a short black wearing gold-rimmed designer sunglasses. Mick took up what looked like his usual position at the other end of the table, from where he could survey the whole restaurant.

'Ronnie, this is Adam Shand. He's a journo, but he's not here for a story. He just wants to meet up with some of the boys. I told him we've got nothing to do with this gangland murder stuff,' he said to Bongetti, who nodded almost imperceptibly, looking straight through me. 'He's given me a rap [vote of confidence], Ronnie, and I figured it would be okay if he hung around for a little while?' Mick asked respectfully. Bongetti signalled his assent with a wave of his hand and a shrug of his shoulders.

'You're going to have a coffee. Relax,' he told me quietly as another waiter appeared as if summoned telepathically. In the 1970s, Bongetti had ruled the SP and numbers rackets of the city, an occupation that had brought him into contact with just about every cashed-up crim in Melbourne. Bongetti had seen his 'brothers' battle for control of the city's organisation, the Honoured Society – or, in Calabrian dialect, L'Onorata or N'Dranghita. He had lived through the market murders of the 1960s, when rival Italian groups had battled each other to control the wholesale fruit-and-vegetable trade. He had looked on as the notorious Painters and Dockers Union had turned the waterfront into a bloodbath as various factions sought to control the criminal empire the union had established in armed robbery, extortion and drug dealing. He had seen half a dozen dons come and go.

The Calabrians had been killing each other in an endless cycle of murder and payback since 1945, when Giuseppe 'Fat Joe' Versace was gunned down. But so neat and tidy were the affairs of the Honoured Society that for years people doubted its existence. However, in 1963, as the market murders grabbed the headlines, police invited American organised crime investigator John T. Cusack to document the activities of the home-grown Mafia that was operating around the produce markets of West Melbourne.

For Cusack, the assignment was a walk-up start. He found all the same dynamics operating in Melbourne that he had observed in the crime capitals of the US, and concluded that the same basic code governed the culture of the Mafia, were it operating in the mean streets of Al Capone's Chicago or Melbourne. Cusack told Victorian police that there were five ironclad rules that governed the Society:

1 The Society would assist its members no matter what the circumstances.

2 Absolute obedience to the office-bearers of the Society was a given.

3 An attack against a member of the Society was an attack on the Society and must be avenged.

4 No member of the Society would turn to a government agency for justice.

5 Omerta, the code of silence, must always be obeyed on pain of death. No member was ever to reveal any of the Society's secrets. 'They realise in silence there is security, while testimony against a Society member can bring death,' Cusack said.

But it was changing now. The Honoured Society was a pale shadow of the old days, having fallen to bitter infighting in a power struggle in the 1990s.

In the 1970s Liborio Benvenuto had been regarded by the community as a shrewd and wise godfather, so for him to get his succession so badly wrong surprised everyone. But a father cannot be blind to the failings of his children, and Liborio was wise enough to know that his son, Frank, was not worthy of succeeding him. Instead, on his deathbed in May 1988 he anointed his son-in-law, Alfonso Muratore, as the new godfather. The mantle of responsibility weighed heavily on the gregarious young man, however, and he later declined the offer. The next year Alfonso added insult to injury by leaving Liborio's daughter, Angela, for his mistress, an outsider called Karen Mansfield. The ungrateful Muratore was dispatched by shotgun outside his Hampton home in 1992, and a coroner's inquest heard sensational allegations that

Frank Benvenuto had ordered the hit on Muratore for snubbing the Honoured Society and his little sister. Frank was never charged.

Liborio's number-one lieutenant, Giuseppe 'Joe' Arena, had also considered himself leadership material upon his boss's death. That delusion lasted just six weeks, until he was blasted from behind with a shotgun as he and his wife returned home from a wedding in August 1988. With Arena and Muratore out of the way Liborio's rejected son, Frank, was, in charge at last. A youthful Mick Gatto quickly pledged allegiance to the new don, prompting speculation that Mick had knocked Arena.

The Society was fragmenting as new businesses were added and factions began to mix with other, non-Italian crime groups in Melbourne. The lines of respect were hard to maintain as wealth brought new confidence. The last of the old-style dons, Frank Benvenuto, was murdered in his car outside his home in May 2000 as he prepared to take some rubbish to the tip. The killer was undoubtedly a friend. He had just slipped into the passenger seat and shot Benvenuto. That's how it goes in Melbourne – your friends can be your most dangerous enemies. And it was a protégé of Mick Gatto, Andrew 'Benji' Veniamin, who had pulled the trigger.

Ronnie Bongetti had seen enough killing for one lifetime. He had terminal cancer and was talking about Tahiti, how he wanted to go there for the beautiful women and the warm sunshine – anything to get away from the tedium of life in Melbourne.

The boys were settling in for the afternoon, and for the next few hours Gatto held court like a big, jolly monarch. Far from the image of the dark, angry don he had shown at the building royal commission, he exuded good humour and self-deprecation. He was a laughing, animated presence as a stream of assorted European types in sunglasses drifted in and out of the cafe to do business, share a coffee or simply catch up.

The first thing that occurred to me was that few of these men were actually Italian: Croatians, Yugoslavs and Greeks came to call on Mick. Still, there was the usual ceremonial kissing and embracing between these men of disparate backgrounds. When they were told a reporter was in their midst they each extended a polite hand-shake, the diamonds of their chunky pinkie rings lending a hint of civilised menace. No one seemed to mind that I was there, and the conversation flowed freely – even though I was darting to the toilet every half-hour due to over-consumption of coffee. The toilet breaks provided me with convenient moments to jot down notes on it all.

The conversation flipped from the recent heavy storm to the price of an introduction to a former senior ALP figure. 'I called him because I want to set up a factory in China and you've got to have an introduction to get anywhere up there, the bigger the better,' said a dour little man across the table. 'So he calls back and says, "That will be $100 000, Tony," so I says, "Get fucked, mate" and slammed the fuckin' phone down. Fuckin' thief.' He complained that there was no incentive to invest any more in his suburban shoe factory. 'No more protection. And the tax system works against you. I'm going to close the fucking thing down and go on holidays forever. Hey Ronnie, we going to go to Tahiti?'

Mattie Tomas, a heavy-set man in his early thirties who was a former business partner of Jason Moran, talked of his new venture in the construction business, Elite Cranes. A while back he had beaten a murder rap in which he was accused of stomping a man to death in a cafe in Lygon Street. At one time Mattie had been headed for a Premier League soccer career with UK glamour club Liverpool, but a severe knee injury had put paid to that. In his late teens he had become a bouncer at city nightclubs and impressed the bosses of Carlton with his dash and loyalty. By now he was a battle-scarred veteran. He said that after the killings of the past five years, he had simply had enough and wanted nothing more to do with the underworld. Now with a new baby and a new business, he was keen to put his past behind him. Elite Cranes, was winning contracts on building sites all over town. It had imported cranes from overseas and was pitching for large-scale government work. Mattie offered to appear on the Nine Network's *Business Sunday* to declare that everything at Elite Cranes was above board. He wanted a fresh start for his business, even if Mick Gatto remained one of its key backers. (Mick later left the board of Elite Cranes and but retains links with the business till today)

Legendary Yugoslav hard man Tony Tsolovic, now over sixty but still a wiry, powerful figure, complained that helping filmmaker Nick Giannopoulos to bring authenticity to his film *The Wog Boy* had brought him some unwelcome attention from the police. 'I see the film and there's this [character] bloody Tony the standover man and drug dealer. I can't believe it. Now twice police have pulled me up in the city and they tell me, "Hey, aren't you Tony the bloody drug dealer and standover man?" Bloody Giannopoulos,' he said, laughing uproariously. (For the record, the Tony character was actually called 'Tony the insane local drug lord', but I certainly wasn't going to correct Tsolovic. One celebrated night back in the

1970s, a group of five police had chased Tony on foot for something or other and he'd climbed a tree to hide. The police had found him and stood below taunting him until he came down – and then Tony gave them all a good flogging.)

I thought this meeting at La Porcella was about as close as the Carlton Crew came to a board meeting. Virtually all the arms of Gatto's empire were represented that afternoon: there were businessmen, standover men, drug dealers, car dealers, construction industry types and union officials. Gatto pushed a glossy black card with gold embossing across the table to me. It declared that Mick Gatto was a consultant to Arbitrations and Mediations Pty Ltd and it featured a curvaceous blindfolded woman holding up the scales of justice with a large sword held discreetly by her side. Mick even had an office and a fax nearby in Carlton. That made La Porcella the unofficial staff canteen.

If this *was* business for the Carlton Crew, it was conducted at a leisurely pace. Every so often Mick would move away to another table to talk business, or disappear through the kitchen into a storeroom for extra privacy. It was just a normal afternoon in Carlton. As the shadows lengthened, Gatto and the boys and me were the only customers left. The waiters brought the tables in off the street and wiped down the vinyl tablecloths, then settled into a game of cards. Before long they were arguing loudly, with one guy in particular banging the table repeatedly. Gatto rose up and, in a booming voice, restored order to his domain: 'Hey, take it easy, buddy – it's only a game,' he said, adjusting his suit.

It was getting a little edgy in there now – a combination of tension and caffeine. I suddenly realised that I was the only one with my back to the street. *In any case, the story isn't here*, I thought. Why would Gatto invite me, a journalist, in here if he was up to his neck in murder and mayhem? It didn't make any sense. *These are the friendly gangsters*, I thought, a caricature of all the tough-guy Mafia shows I had ever seen on TV. Somewhere out in the suburbs there was the real thing, the brutal, callous heirs of the new underworld. La Porcella seemed like a club for middle-aged gents. Gatto talked about his battle to try to lose weight; another associate complained of having missed a dental appointment for his next instalment of root canal therapy.

When I left, all the men of honour pointed at each other in great amusement. 'Hey, write about him.' 'No! Write about *him*.' 'You wanna see a gangster? Hey, get a load of *that* head.'

The next time I saw most of them was at Graham Kinniburgh's funeral two months later. No one was laughing then.

5 | SKULL

'Time wounds all heels,' said Brian Murphy, rolling the words around his mouth. Then, with a lopsided grin, he said, 'Or is that "time heals all wounds"? Either way, it works.' He discarded the menu the waitress had brought. She always brought him one, though Brian had been ordering the same dish at Don Camillo's for years. He would scan the menu intently, examining all the rich, traditional Italian food the place had to offer, before returning to his daily fare.

'Two pieces of vegemite toast and a weak latte, thanks, love,' he said.

In thirty-three years as a police officer, Murphy had required little more than toast and coffee to sustain him through his day on the beat. The fire in him was enough to keep him going. When most officers had been propping up the bar for hours, Murphy the teetotaller was still out talking with his informants, or at the station getting ready for the next day, or having a quiet chat with somebody over a gun. This was much more than a job to Murphy: it was more like a calling. Sometimes it became an obsession, a madness that led him to the darkest places in his soul.

But that was in the 1970s and '80s, when 'Skull' – so called because of his resemblance to the famous pro wrestler of the 1960s – ruled the streets and pubs of Port Melbourne and St Kilda. These days, at seventy-one, he shaved the remaining hair on his head and, sitting there with his powerful arms crossed against his barrel chest, the shiny bald pate made him look even more like that old-time wrestler. A couple of strokes had dulled his edges in recent years, but even today – the day after my meeting with Mick Gatto at La Porcella – there was something in those watery blue eyes that would have made most men stop before taking him on. There was intellect behind those eyes, and an utterly ruthless focus that I found intimidating. Long ago Murphy had decided there was no mileage in fearing anyone. His faith had told him it was God who called the shots. You departed this life when He was ready. 'Of course, others might give Him a helping hand, but the timing is out of my hands,' he said.

As a copper he'd done an on-the-job master's degree in 'sly-chology', a subtle blend of stick and carrot that had helped him build one of the most enduring informer networks Melbourne had ever seen. He'd met one of his best 'fizzes' after nabbing him in the middle of cutting a safe for the Munster back in the 1970s. The Magnetic Drill Gang had been getting bolder with each heist, even leaving a trademark Z, like Zorro, burned onto the broken safes with an oxy torch. When Murphy caught this bloke, he saw something in the villain's eyes – an intelligence and a reasonable-ness that suggested he would respond to gentle persuasion. These qualities set him apart from the rest of the criminal 'heads' he had been nicked with.

Murphy took him down to the end of a darkened pier, hand-cuffed, and hung him over the edge by his belt, then placed his service pistol firmly against the safecutter's genitals. 'Now, cunty, the next person you will see is your lord and saviour Jesus Christ!' he said quietly into the man's ear, dangling him further over the edge while cocking the pistol. Then he continued in a conciliatory tone: 'Is there anything you would like to unburden yourself with before you embark on this final journey?'

The prisoner remembered there was plenty he had to say, and it was enough to help bring many of the best armed robbers and safecutters in Melbourne to heel. Even after Murphy left the force in 1987, this bloke kept on telling him whatever he knew.

Though he'd been out of the service for nearly twenty years, Murphy's heart was still on the beat. He had turned his skills to mediating disputes, helping to persuade recalcitrant debtors to square their commitments, and in his travels around the fringes of business he would see lots of things and hear much more – most of which he kept to himself. He didn't need enemies. But he knew knowledge was power.

Murphy had been a detective in the Consorting Squad, whose task was to map the criminal underworld, to keep an eye on who was mixing with whom. The Consorting Act made it a crime for known crims to hang out together in public, and Murphy enforced this rather archaic law with gusto. It meant he had to show his face in the villains' streets and their pubs. His keen mind could turn the seemingly banal into criminal intelligence. He wrote it all down on little white cards that were filed away for later use, and I could almost hear the cards turning over in his brain that morning as we discussed the 'heads' I had met the previous day in La Porcella. To his great annoyance he couldn't place Carl Williams, nor even Carl's father, George, in his hall of criminal fame. 'There's never been a team like this one here in Melbourne,' he said, with a kind of admiration.

Murphy appreciated a bit of dash in a man, be he copper or villain. He'd grown up among knockabouts in South Melbourne. His father had been a wharfie and had taken on the police in the great strikes of the late 1920s. One day Murphy's father had been coshed by a policeman during a stand-off and had fallen under the boardwalk at Station Pier, unconscious, and nearly drowned as the tide came in. He carried the legacy of that day, the scars and a hatred of police, till his death. When young Murphy came to his father as a teenager and told him he was going to become a policeman, he surprisingly gave his blessing. 'Just mind you be a good one,' said Murphy senior quietly, and the matter was never raised again.

Brian had become one of the most notorious policemen in Melbourne, even if he did cause untold grief for his superiors. Such were his links with known crims that he became known as the most interviewed officer in Melbourne. One New South Wales policeman said that in the mid-1970s he came to interview Murphy regarding his links with a certain Sydney crim. 'Murphy's boss came in with him into the interview room. He said to him, "Now Brian, you take your normal seat while another one of these nice chaps from Sydney asks you a few questions."'

Certainly Murphy was privy to information well beyond the orbit of your average copper. He had found himself in the middle of the last big stoush in Melbourne between the Kane family and legendary armed robber Ray 'Chuck' Bennett and his followers. Murphy was known to be friendly with Brian Kane, a fearsome Painter and Docker who in the 1970s was regarded as the town's toughest gunnie. Murphy and Kane weren't always that way, though. In the mid-'70s Murphy heard that Kane was planning to kill him. This was unsettling, to say the least, considering that the pair had not yet met. One night in a Lygon Street cafe the two Brians became acquainted quite by accident as they both reached for the same short black coffee. The proprietor had made the mistake of saying, 'Here's your coffee, Brian.'

A stand-off ensued over the steaming cup until the proprietor, keen to avoid a scene, sat them at the same table in order that they might get to know each other better. Kane looked at Murphy balefully and said in a low growl, 'You know, Murphy, I was going to kill you, and I still might . . .' It was nearly midnight now, and the cafe was almost deserted. Nobody in their right mind would have testified against the Kanes at the time, so Brian Kane could have killed Murphy then and there.

'What's stopping you then, Brian?' said Murphy.

'Don't kid yourself, copper. I could have killed you many times already. I've been watching you walking with your wife down by Station Pier. You would have been brown bread if she hadn't been with you, you know. Several times I could have had you.'

'Good for you, Brian. That's extremely civilised of you,' said Murphy quietly as he stared into Kane's dark eyes. He was sure Kane was tooled up (armed) – it was an occupational requirement for a man like him. It was time for a little slychology. 'So, Brian, here we are,' said Murphy. 'I suggest we lay our cards out. What would you say if I ask old Giuseppe here to slide back the table so we can all see what's going on here.'

'Sure, Brian,' said Kane. The table was eased back, and to Kane's surprise there was Murphy's .38 service revolver cocked and pointed straight at his groin.

'That's fantastic,' said Kane with admiration. 'You're all right for a jack. Most of the coppers nowadays are just drunken dogs and thieves. I may have misjudged you, Mr Brian Murphy.' Ignoring the .38, Kane then stood and kissed Murphy on the forehead and laughed uproariously. They went through another fourteen short blacks and finally left the cafe at four o'clock in the morning.

Deep in the night, Kane confided a dark secret. 'You know, as a kid I wanted to be a copper, but my old man beat me up just for mentioning it. He said if I wanted to go and get an education and make something of my life, then I'd have to go and steal the books,' he said with a deep sigh. Four hours earlier he'd had a contract in his breast pocket to kill Murphy, and now he was confessing to him like a guilty sinner. Murphy had the skill of looking into a man's heart and seeing the humanity beneath all the bad manners and bullshit.

He was one of a few ex-policeman in Melbourne who got a Christmas card each year from Mick Gatto. Murphy had seen Gatto tearing around South Melbourne as a teenager, and he warned the youngster where a life of crime would lead him. 'Yeah – to a big house in the suburbs and to a life where I never have to work,' Mick had retorted. 'Well, that's right for now,' Murphy told me, 'but I've seen how these movies end. Yeah, it only ever goes one way – they all finish up dying. Maybe not today or tomorrow, but someone will square up for this sooner or later.'

Running a big team of crims at war was a difficult thing, said Murphy. 'You've got to be like a mother. You've got to be able to look forward knowing what your kids are doing behind you, and have a different set of ears for what's going on in that room and what's going on in the kitchen. It's distracting. Mothers can do it, but I don't think men can and I don't think the villains can. Villains are preoccupied with a trip to the morgue.'

The spate of killing was certainly changing things in the underworld, he said. For a start, the Carlton Crew weren't coming to Don Camillo's any more. Gatto and the boys had tried to set up their own cafe across the road, but that plan was progressing too slowly.

Then there was the price of hit men. The voracious demand for professional shooters had driven the going rate through the roof, Murphy said. It was all a result of the drug business: 'The money's around. Years ago ten or fifteen thousand would get somebody killed. Now it's 100 000. I don't think you could get anybody to do a hit for under a hundred, because the benchmark has been set.'

Yes, drugs had been very good for a number of groups in this little community, he said. For instance, the drug barons had also driven up the price of criminal barristers. A good silk who could delay your day in court was worth paying top dollar for. The delay gave you time to knock the witnesses, even bribe a judge, and/or at least make enough money so you were set for life once you came out. And once the hand-up brief (which details the Crown case against the accused and how the police gathered evidence) came down, you would know how the police had caught you, and your barrister could literally teach you how not to get caught the next time. 'These guys walk in with unlimited amounts of money and just slam it down on the barrister's desk. He eyes off the money and the client says, "How much is it going to cost?" "Oh, at least a hundred thousand – or even two hundred thousand",' said Murphy in his best plummy legal accent, 'and the benchmark is set at $200 000, too.'

Why weren't the Carlton Crew firing back if they were under siege, I asked. 'Maybe they can't see the value of firing back. Maybe they're using a little common sense. Maybe they're saying, "Let's settle down – this is all going too far. Nobody is going to win out of this situation." Nobody will.' If this was a chess game, the Italians were taking a frontal assault and sacrificing pawns and knights to protect the royalty safe on the back row.

He paused, trying to recollect another witty aphorism. 'When you live, you live all over, and when you're dead, you're dead all over – no, that's wrong. When you live, you live in clover, but when you're dead, you're dead all over.'

He hinted that Gatto and the Carlton boys had been dragged into a war not of their own making, a war that had already gone further than they could have imagined. Their opponents had sensed weakness and sought to drive home their advantage: 'Some of the Carlton men might have come up wanting because they didn't want to get involved in the nastiest form of conduct we have seen in a long, long time, and even though they get around like they own the world they say, "Do I want to finish up in a pine box? I might lose a little bit of ego here but I'm not going to put my head up".'

One dark night after Murphy had left the force, the then leader of the Carlton Crew, Alphonse Gangitano, came to see him in the lane behind Murphy's house in Middle Park. He had an offer for the newly unemployed Murphy: 'Come and join us, Brian, and we'll look after you.' The Carlton Crew were doing it easy back then. Life consisted of collecting protection money from the restaurant owners of Lygon Street, many of whom were operating illegal casinos and card clubs out the back. Key police at Carlton CIB were sweet with the boys and life was good.

Murphy looked at the tall, pale figure in the moonlight. Gangitano was immaculately dressed in a tailored suit, wearing sunglasses and smoothing his hair back like a matinee Mafioso. It was tempting, for Murphy loved anything with a hint of danger and dash about it, but this was somebody's else's fantasy world.

Alphonse wasn't interested in money per se – he spent most of it on his lawyers and on sending witnesses overseas so they couldn't testify against him. His road would end with little to show for all the trouble he had caused, just a share in a Carlton house bequeathed him by his mother, and another house he shared with his wife and young family in the suburbs. In January 1998 an unknown assailant, probably Jason Moran, shot him in the face, back and chest. They found him lying in a pool of blood in the laundry of his home, dressed only in his underpants and shirt. *The indignity of it all*, Murphy thought when he heard what happened. He commiserated with the widow Gangitano and gave thanks that he had listened to his better judgement. Though many police believed he had changed teams long ago, Murphy knew in his heart that as a cop he had been a trader, not a traitor.

Another day in late summer, as we drove around Port Melbourne, in a moment of hero worship I ventured the opinion that he was as straight as a die. 'Not as straight as you think,' he replied with a chuckle.

Whatever Murphy had done in his working life had been in service of the law, even if he had broken the law in the process. I asked him how many people he had shot in his career and he said casually, 'Oh, forty or fifty.'

'You're joking,' I said.

'But I never killed anyone,' he added.

And that included one Neil Stanley Collingburn, who had died from injuries sustained in police custody under Murphy's watch. Murphy was acquitted of Collingburn's manslaughter in 1971, but the idea that he had beaten the charge followed him. Five years later he was named in Barry Beach QC's inquiry into the Victorian police force. Beach recommended that Murphy be charged with conspiracy to pervert the course of justice, but it went nowhere. Meanwhile, Murphy just kept on locking up crooks with his normal zeal.

At first I wasn't exactly sure where Murphy stood in the current situation, how deep his connections were in this seedy world. I wondered whether it was possible, as he said, to keep good relations with everyone without having to take sides. If he *was* corrupt, I found no evidence of it during my research. He and his wife, Margaret, lived in a comfortable home in Middle Park a street back from the bay, where they walked on the beach every morning before dawn. Their only capital move of any note had been to buy the house next door, which was closer to the water. Murphy's workshop backed onto the old cobbled laneway, and when the roller door was up, anyone from Alphonse Gangitano to the Commissioner of Police was welcome – except, perhaps, the local heroin addicts who for a time frequented the kids' playground directly opposite. One party of junkies had allegedly been set on fire with lawnmower fuel in the lane a couple of years back. Murphy had been questioned by police and declared his complete innocence.

With his beguiling Irish wit, I couldn't help but like him. I wanted to believe that the pluses had outweighed the minuses of his career. He told me, 'If I was going to be a villain, I would not have needed to put on a uniform first to give me the dash. I would have had the courage to be what I was.'

Over time Murphy introduced me to some of the most important characters and folklore of the underworld. We would drive around in his maroon Ford, hopping from cafe to cafe talking to the most influential purveyors of gossip in Melbourne. There was very little that happened in the city that Murphy couldn't run down in twelve or twenty-four hours.

But even he couldn't help me to follow the threads that bound the dense fabric of this story. All he could do was to point me in the direction of others who might be able to help. It would take me nine months to achieve a working understanding of it all, and still I had many details wrong. Six years later, key parts of the tale would assume mythic proportions. Perhaps no one will ever get to the bottom of it.

I thanked Murphy as he finished his vegemite toast and we prepared to leave Don Camillo's with the mid-morning sun now baking the asphalt outside. 'Now mind, if you tell anybody about what I've told you, you will be walking on stumps,' he warned gravely.

'Yeah, sure, Brian,' I said. 'But only one problem, mate,'

'What's that, mate?'

'I'm a journalist. It's my job to tell people . . .'

'Aah, yes, well, I see the problem. See ya,' he said.

6 | ANOTHER AFTERNOON IN CARLTON

I thought I had uncovered the great board meeting of Melbourne Crime Inc. The mail around town suggested that the Chief Executive was very unhappy with the Carlton Crew after a meeting turned into a nasty confrontation in late 2002. The way I first heard it, it was a scene straight out of *The Sopranos*. Australia's most senior mobsters were sitting around a table at a Carlton cafe to discuss a problem, a very pressing problem. And it ended up in a kicking.

In the first of a dozen versions of the story for *The Bulletin*, I wove a tale as dramatic as it was improbable. I laid out the available facts drawing on the idea that organised crime followed a plan, that you could have a meeting of the minds, with the bosses of the east, south, north and west sitting down to carve up the city between them. The reality is that the only time you get the whole crew together is at funerals and weddings, when it's an article of good business to swear allegiance to people you don't like. There is no hierarchy of power, no attempt at central regulation of the community, and the most important meetings ever held are mediations over debts and insults. And this mediation would be the subject of many further mediations and discussions.

Such was the murky nature of the facts that some of the police believed the late 2002 meeting had taken place in a private residence, while others went for a different Carlton eatery. The dozens of sources I spoke to could scarcely agree on anything, not even the time of day the meeting had taken place. I went for an educated guess, the best one I had at the time.

. . . A retinue of thugs, just itching to sink the slipper into each other, stand by their masters' elbows, firing menacing looks around. Some make exaggerated shows of deference to their friends who are now in the employ of their enemies. The sun is sinking low outside, but there is an overabundance of sunglasses in the room.

The smiling host for the evening is Mick Gatto. As the others file in he's sitting at his regular table with the phlegmatic Ronnie Bongetti, who is half in shadow. Mario Condello, Mick's best mate, is by him scowling and posturing. It's a Friday night in spring, but there's hardly a soul in the place. Big black German saloons are looking for parking spots all up and down the street. The delegates file in one by one.

John Kizon has made the trip from Perth in the company of two regular associates, Troy Mercanti and another biker mate. Kizon is one of the West's most colourful criminal identities, with a record for heroin trafficking, assault and financial offences, but for nearly twelve years life has been nice and quiet for the former star boxer. Not that he's been idle – it's not in his nature. These days he tells everyone he's learned his lesson and become a legitimate business-man, running nightclubs and promoting fight nights in Perth. But still they won't leave him alone: the Western Australian media continue to link him with virtually every major crime taking place in the state. Newspaper reports have indicated that as of 1997, Kizon has not held any bank accounts in Australia under his own name. His income over a six-year period has averaged only $3000, yet police intelligence indicates that he has investments worth over $3 million.

It has all been nice and quiet for Kizon until this year, when word has got around that the Chief Executive has a major problem with Mercanti and his mate, the two men who have come to the meeting with Kizon. There is some money owing, but, more importantly, one of them has called the Chief Executive 'a dog' . . .

For what's regarded as the acme of underworld insults, you hear the word 'dog' tossed around constantly. Old hands say it has now virtually lost its meaning and has turned into a term for just about anyone you don't like. It used to be simple: friends were staunch, enemies were dogs. Dogs were police informers; friends kept silent even under physical pressure. But now the code of silence had ceased to exist, if it ever really existed, and you needed a copper in your pocket to prosper in Melbourne. 'Any knockabout who tells you he doesn't have at least one copper sweet is telling you lies,' Billy Longley told me one night. You had to trade information with the police to buy a blind eye to your activities. You needed a copper to fix the blues of your mates and your kids. And the copper needed something in return: the names, addresses and recent activities of villains he could serve up to his superiors.

But in the underworld, a dog is a dangerous thing to be. You are the lowest form of life – a police informer, a traitor and a treacherous two-timer. No one will do business with you – unless you have lots of money – and anyone associated with you will be looked upon with suspicion. You survive at the whim of police. Informers are like manure, say old cops: very useful, but no one wants to handle them.

How the underworld could have invested such malevolence into the character of the humble canine, man's most loyal companion in the animal kingdom, was a matter of some curiosity to me. It seems the term drew on the historical fact that when early man began organised hunting, it was the dog that soon helped him. Man could ride a horse in pursuit of prey but only the dog led him directly to it. The dog betrayed the rest of the animals.

To make matters worse for the Chief Executive, it was two of his trusted men who had 'somersaulted' him to police, sharing intimate details of his operations. In his mind, the Chief Executive had been the victim of some very poor etiquette, to say the least. He had graciously welcomed people into his circle and they had betrayed him. Now he could see his empire crumbling before his eyes. It had been a long way from humble beginnings, but it would be a short trip down the highway to Barwon or Port Phillip prison, and all for the sake of a little respect.

The treachery had arisen from what could be described as a communication breakdown. It got back to one of the men that the Chief Executive had been overheard in telephone intercepts suggesting that his former associate could rot in prison for all he cared. The associate had received a discounted sentence of two and a half years' jail after agreeing to help police bring the Chief Executive down. When he found out, the Chief Executive apparently responded by putting a contract on the man's life.

On 24 August 2001, things got right out of hand. The cops launched Victoria's biggest-ever drug operation, Operation Kayak, a cooperative effort involving 100 Victorian and Australian Federal Police officers. Charges would be laid for the possession and trafficking of amphetamines, ecstasy, ephedrine, cocaine, hashish and LSD. Among others, Lewis Moran, the northern-suburbs crime patriarch, and his son Jason were arrested.

But the Morans and their allies knew that if the police cared to look they would discover that their own officers were up to their necks in the business.

By traditional standards you would have to say there were more dogs in Melbourne than Show Day at Flemington. A group of fast friends had fallen apart, trusted allies were selling out their mates and, worse still, they were working with the cops.

In 2000, Detective Senior Sergeant Wayne Strawhorn was in the front line of society's war on drugs. A distinguished and much admired officer, he had received a couple of commendations for drug busts in the 1980s.

In 1996, Strawhorn returned from an overseas study tour with an audacious new idea for identifying and breaking up the cartels running party drugs in Victoria. The 'Clandestine Laboratories' program involved police finding villains to sell the chemicals required for the production of methamphetamine: barrels of pseudoephedrine and other precursor chemicals. Once the buyers were loaded up with evidence supplied by the police, a net of surveillance closed around the target until the location of the proposed speed cook-up was established – a seedy farmhouse, a fortified suburban home. For the dog, the prospect of getting killed was very real should his buddies discover his treachery. But it was worth the risk, because he could use the police as a cover for his own dealing, and once he had the chemicals he could conduct his business as he saw fit.

One former drug-squad officer, Lachlan McCullough, recalled listening to one of his charges, 'Mad Charlie' Hegyalji, working the system: 'I remember covering a meeting of his with a bunch of crims, and while we were waiting for him to give some chemicals to the crims in a hotel car park, he did several other deals with other people that I witnessed. I suddenly realised that Charlie was using us for cover. It was a perfect way to avoid getting caught for drug dealing – to be covered by us.'

But the sting worked, and the police destabilised the drug elites almost at will. However, it finally dawned on the commanders that they were now in the drug business too. McCullough said, 'When the plan first came out, it was that successful we went from [busting] three or four labs to twelve to fifteen in twelve months – and these are major labs making speed. The only part where it fell down was the possible lack of checks and balances on the actual physical side of delivering the chemicals, because we were in a situation where we were making a profit.'

In fact, the Victoria Police had enriched all the crims, with one of the most adventurous and reckless pieces of law enforcement in the state's history. By 2002, the drug squad's Clandestine Laboratories program had collapsed, and many of the key officers who had run it were in various stages of prosecution and incarceration. It had failed catastrophically, shaking the foundations of the police service, but this did not detract from the fact that it had also been incredibly successful. It had been, in effect, a gigantic bluff that had spread a message of distrust throughout the underworld

The legacy of the operation was a deeply ingrained mistrust among the crooks. It was now even harder to distinguish friend from foe, as rumours circulated as to who was on the payroll of the drug squad.

As McCullough said, 'It caused a great deal of unrest among the crims, because you had a situation where you are a drug dealer and you go to buy chemicals of pseudoephedrine from crims and all of a sudden you are buying chemicals from police and you are arrested, or you buy chemicals and then take them to a lab and you get followed and we get the lab.'

The police bosses failed to account for the human factor. Drug squad officers on $75 000 a year were suddenly dealing in a business where the villains could make that kind of money in a weekend. Lachlan McCullough looked on as his police comrades began to fall one by one. 'Here I was working with colleagues [who were later] found to have been doing exactly what we fought to protect the public from. They were actually doing it. You know, I worked because I wanted to protect the public. I worked because I loved what I did and I was proud of what I did. Some people treated [police work] as a job.'

In early 2000, Wayne Strawhorn was running Operation Vere, which involved supplying Mark Moran with chemicals for making speed through two unregistered police informers. Strawhorn wasn't allowed to supply Moran pure pseudoephedrine without approval of his commander but in May 2000 he did just that. He ordered a fellow detective to purchase two kilos of the chemical from a pharmaceutical company for $340 and had him deliver it to him at a service station. Strawhorn then sold the chemicals through an intermediary to Mark Moran for $12 000.

Strawhorn was nabbed after another officer caught up in an internal investigation agreed to give evidence.

Mark Moran's relationship with Strawhorn and other drug squad officers had boosted the family's name in the underworld, and Jason let everyone know it with the violence and attitude of the untouchable. Perhaps Strawhorn shared this delusion. Maybe it was greed, maybe it was the sheer pleasure of wielding power – he had become a kingmaker by making chemicals available to those he deemed worthy. In 2006, as Justice David Habersberger of the Victorian Supreme Court sentenced Strawhorn to a minimum of four years jail for corruption, he couldn't fathom the motives that led the once-admired cop to detonate his career.

'As to why you, with this most impressive record of dedication, competence, intelligence and integrity, should have so drastically fallen from grace, by this isolated but very serious instance of offending, remains a mystery,' the judge said.

But Strawhorn was not alone.

On 12 July 2002, the *Herald Sun* reported that more than twenty-five Victorian detectives had been accused of corruption in a secret report delivered to Chief Commissioner Christine Nixon. A report by the police ethical standards department recommended that more than eighty charges be laid, mostly against former members of the drug squad. The report uncovered a criminal culture that was operating inside the squad. Officers were alleged to have been involved in the planting of evidence and cash on suspects, the ripping-off of drugs, the protection of dealers and the theft and resale of chemicals. In one telephone intercept the Chief Executive boasted to an informer that he was so close to the drug squad that Wayne Strawhorn had offered him tickets to a police function.

By now Carl Williams had his own connections into the drug squad. It was said a senior officer, Sergeant Paul Dale, was passing on information about the Morans as Williams worked on his plan for revenge.

The Ceja Taskforce was formed to investigate the activities of the former drug squad, seizing the case notes of officers who were under suspicion of working with the villains. At first, it was suggested that the court trials of players like the Chief Executive could wait until Ceja had dealt with the allegations of corrupt officers, but it quickly became apparent that this exercise could take up to five years to complete. It was inappropriate for men like the Chief Executive to be held on remand for years on end while Ceja ran its course. 'Our society will not, and should not, tolerate what is effectively the indefinite detention awaiting trial of persons such as [the Chief Executive] whilst an investigation such as that currently under way takes place,' said a judge in one of many hearings about the Chief Executive.

The Crown had put forward testimony from police informers that underlined just how dangerous the Chief Executive could be if released on bail. He was alleged to have set aside a seven-figure sum to subvert his trial and inquired about bribing a judge. Informers also said he would try to knock witnesses and buy police officers, and would return to every avenue of villainy as soon as he was released.

Chief prosecutor Bill Morgan-Payler, in opposing bail, said that the Chief Executive's record meant there was an overwhelming danger he would try to 'corrupt, pervert and derail this prosecution'.

Con Heliotis QC, for the Chief Executive, said that his claims of being able to bribe police were just empty boasts. 'There is a degree of puffery in almost any conversation that [the Chief Executive] has,' he said.

The Chief Executive got bail in September 2002 with a $1 million surety. Williams also received bail on drugs charges because of corruption in the former drug squad.

While authorities tried to sort the goodies from the baddies in the police force, the Chief Executive, Carl Williams and others were given 'get out of jail free' cards. And they put them to good use.

Little wonder then in these extraordinary times, there was a new arrogance in the Chief Executive. He was hobnobbing with the best of the Melbourne mob, enjoying the company of the city's most feared thugs. One, a big Lebanese heavy called George, was the handiest man with a blade in town. In jail folklore, he was so good he could throw an apple up in the air and quarter it with a razor-sharp blade before it came down (which must have been handy when it came time to make fruit salad). It was said that this man liked to do his killing close up with a knife so the last thing the hapless victim would experience would be George's breath on his face and the hot stink of his aftershave. In the underworld it's never a bad thing to let such stories flourish.

The Chief Executive's friends knew a different person: a quiet, gentle man given to extravagant deeds of generosity – except when it came to paying his debts at the racetrack. Bookmakers and their bowlers (agents who lay big bets with bookies for low-key clients) knew to steer clear of him on big race days. When he was released on bail the Chief Executive went on a punting spree, laying huge bets with a range of bookies. He started his assault using credit, but when he ran up a $1.8 million debt and refused to pay, the tap was turned off. From there he turned to cash, sending runners to place his bets so they couldn't be traced back to him.

'I just remember how much cash he carried around the betting ring,' said one bookie. 'He had it stuffed between his fingers, huge wads of it, I had never seen anything like it before or since,' he said.

There was talk also that the Chief Executive was fixing races using tame jockeys who were prepared to pull horses for him. A disgruntled trainer had come upon one of the jockeys drinking in the Middle Park Hotel and loudly accused him of applying the handbrake to his horse on behalf of that drug-dealing cur the Chief Executive. In front of several off-duty police, the trainer had pulled out a handgun and let go a couple into the ceiling, sending patrons ducking for cover.

Brian 'Skull' Murphy was a known associate of the trainer, so when the Chief Executive came looking for the trainer he started with Murphy. Murphy was instructed to be at a certain cafe, and at the appointed time. Skull watched four shiny black saloons cruise up. Half a dozen burly men in black suits, some with ponytails, all with dark glasses, clambered out of the cars, looking around the street furtively. Only when they were all in position like an underworld Praetorian Guard did the Chief Executive emerge from his limousine. Before the meeting Murphy couldn't recall whether he had met the Chief Executive before, but when the stocky little figure approached, he recognised him instantly. 'Hello there,' Murphy greeted him playfully, 'I remember shining my shoes on your arse in Carlton when you just were a kid.'

It's unlikely the Chief Executive had been spoken to in this manner for a long time, but he didn't take offence. 'Aww, go on, Mr Murphy,' he said sheepishly, before launching into the business at hand. He wanted to know where to find the trainer who had so publicly insulted him, so he could have a quiet discussion with him. Soon the Praetorian Guard and their little underworld emperor were back in their motorcade and away, leaving Murphy to ponder what trouble lay ahead for the trainer, what price he would pay for his indecorous behaviour in the hotel. So he helpfully rang the man, informing him that the Chief Executive would be paying a visit. Murphy needn't have worried; later he heard that the problem had been sorted and the trainer was now ensconced in the Chief Executive's thoroughbred operation. There was no sense knocking a man who could make you money, after all.

The Chief Executive was a reasonable man who thought of himself as civilised and intelligent. He publicly disavowed violence as bad for business. So when Mick Gatto invited him to a Carlton meeting that afternoon to resolve his dispute with the West Australians, he agreed. John Kizon was a close friend of Gatto and most of the Carlton Crew elders, so Mick was hardly neutral, but Gatto had a reputation as someone you could trust in a mediation.

The Chief Executive believed it was Mick's responsibility to ensure his safety that afternoon, so he turned up alone. Accounts differ, but some time later Mercanti and his associate taught him a lesson he wouldn't forget. He was punched to the ground and kicked repeatedly to the head and body as he squirmed and rolled trying to protect himself. The only thing that saved him from death was that the men were wearing runners, rather than the heavy boots usually employed for such tasks.

And what was Gatto the mediator doing while the Chief Executive was thrashing around on the footpath? Word has it that he was standing back with his arms folded across his chest, doing absolutely nothing to stop the slippering. Perhaps he reasoned that the Chief Executive had it coming, that he was too big for his boots and had ceased to respect the primacy of the Carlton Crew in Melbourne. Mick was still a Calabrian, after all.

In 1930–31 another cocky Mafioso, Salvatore C. Lucania, better known as Lucky Luciano, had sparked a war in the New York underworld by thumbing his nose at the old guard. This battle for primacy has been the plotline for scores of underworld movies since, and it probably fit Melbourne in 2004. The traditional Mafia, La Cosa Nostra, had forbade its members getting involved in narcotics and prostitution and despised anyone involved in those businesses, but Luciano decided to extend the franchise from bootlegging and protection rackets into just those areas. To that point the Mafia had left girls and drugs to the powerful Jewish gangs led by such luminaries as 'Legs' Diamond, 'Dutch' Schultz and Meyer Lansky, the men who had dominated organised crime in the 1920s.

After fighting a war that neither could win, Luciano joined forces with Lansky. Both could see that the future lay in forging links with ethnic gangs to broaden the income base of the Mafia, but this was heresy to the old Sicilian bosses who ran Chicago. So they had to go. Lansky introduced Luciano to Benjamin 'Bugsy' Siegel, who needed little encouragement to organise the contract killing of Joe 'The Boss' Masseria, the head of the most powerful Sicilian gang in New York. The hit was carried out in an Italian restaurant on New York's Coney Island. In a classic plot that set the fashion for decades to come, Luciano invited Masseria for dinner and filled him full of good wine and food. Then he excused himself to go to the bathroom, allowing Siegel and three associates to pump the Boss full of lead. In the bloodshed that followed, sixty crime figures perished. The old guard was swept away in a matter of two years.

The handsome and debonair Luciano was the first of a new breed of criminal in the modern age. At meetings after the liquidation of the old guard, Luciano unveiled his blueprint for a nationwide crime cartel, bringing together the leaders of America's twenty-four Mafia 'families'. Lansky and Luciano, with Siegel running the waste disposal unit, led a new generation of mobsters who trampled on the old, traditional Mafia code of honour. While the mild-mannered Lansky counted the beans, Siegel set up the enforcement arm: a contract-killing business that became known as Murder Inc. By 1932 the National Commission was running like clockwork, operating as a kind of alternative government in the underworld in a grotesque parody of the 'legal' capitalist cartels with which Luciano had more than a passing acquaintance.

In his lifetime, Luciano built the Mafia into the most powerful criminal syndicate in the United States, setting up managerial models that were the basis of law enforcement's understanding of organised crime for decades to come. He didn't get long to enjoy his new power: in 1936 he was arrested on prostitution charges and convicted, receiving a sentence of thirty to fifty years. But Lucky lived up to his name, and in 1946 he was released by New York governor Thomas E. Dewey for services he had performed on behalf of the war effort. It was said that Luciano had helped improve security along the waterfront and may even have assisted in the Allied invasion of Italy by encouraging the Mafia there to join the resistance to fascist dictator Benito Mussolini.

And now here was this bumptious little outsider trying to lord it over the Carlton Crew in Melbourne. All of the Chief Executive's drug money still couldn't buy the heritage that Mick Gatto regarded as his birthright. People had been talking of the Chief Executive and his associates as the new team in town, and some of Gatto's friends and enemies had already thrown in their lot with them. It was said they were paying their soldiers $5000 a week, and that bought a lot of loyalty. Perhaps Gatto reasoned that a beating would put the uppity little man back in his place. The Chief Executive was no Lucky Luciano, and Melbourne was still Mick Gatto's town – make no mistake about that. It had taken a lot of killing to create the fragile peace that existed, and Gatto was not about to give anyone a share of the action.

That evening a man already beyond Mick's command was standing alongside him. Andrew 'Benji' Veniamin would have felt right at home in New York in the 1930s and would have given the psychotic Bugsy Siegel a run for his money. Lewis Moran once said of him, 'He's a natural-born killer, that boy.' Benji was about to declare his independence from the Carlton Crew, which in many people's eyes was the same as declaring war on them.

He looked on as the lads continued to tap-dance on the Chief Executive's head, turning the Chief Executive's face into a swollen wreck. Benji didn't like bullies very much – that is, unless it was him doing the bullying. The typical one-on-one street fight in the movies simply didn't exist for him. In Benji's world, you went at it three or four to one because you went into a fight to win, not to lose. In Sunshine, anyone who fought according to the Marquis of Queensberry rules was a fool who deserved a flogging.

However, to be invited to a meeting and then cop a flogging offended even Benji's sense of fair play. For Mick to let these West Australians have their way with the Chief Executive seemed a trifle unfair.

Gatto ordered Benji to take the injured the Chief Executive to a friendly doctor who wouldn't report the assault to police and certainly wouldn't ask any questions. The Fight Doc was good like that. He had met all the western-suburbs crew through his work as the medical man at kickboxing bouts. A blue-blood squarehead who had attended Monash University with the likes of federal treasurer Peter Costello and Victorian Liberal Party heavy Michael Kroger, he enjoyed the racy atmosphere of the underworld. Just about all the young hoods of the kickboxing scene frequented his sports medicine practice in High Street, Armadale. It was a curious meeting point between the underworld and the real world. Suburban mums with tennis elbow mingled with tattooed assassins in the Fight Doc's waiting room.

The Sunshine boys gave his practice an edge the Fight Doc found irresistible, and he had been patching up these gangsters for years. He liked to say he found more wisdom and humanity in these delinquents from the suburbs than in his own middle-class clientele. He thought he could step back any time into his own High Street life. In reality, every time he doled out a prescription for painkillers or Valium, or signed a medical certificate for social security for one of Benji's underworld brothers, he was being dragged further and further in.

It was dark and the Fight Doc was closing his practice for the day when Benji called. The doc would never deny Benji; on other occasions he had opened up at midnight for him and his mates. That night, while the doc treated the Chief Executive's cuts, bruises and black eyes, Benji found that he liked the quiet and charming patient. As they talked, Benji realised that his new friend had enough money to buy and sell the Carlton Crew a dozen times over, and none of the cash had come from standover. The Chief Executive had formed alliances with other up-and-comers – men like Carl Williams and his father, George. They were taking over.

A month or so earlier, Paul Kallipolitis, the most powerful drug dealer in the west, had been shot dead in his home. Someone who knew PK had knocked him for sure: only two people could get into his house without a battering ram and SOG team, and one of them was Benji. When the police found PK his triple-locked security door was open, the surveillance equipment had been turned off and PK was sitting on the floor with his back against the bed. Two shots to the head had done for him. A multi-million dollar trade in amphetamines, cocaine and marijuana was now up for grabs and all it had taken was to pull a trigger. The competition was thinning.

It took about six weeks for the Chief Executive's face to return to normal after the beating. When he next turned up at court it looked like he'd had a little work done too, maybe some botox. He now had a new friend in Andrew Veniamin, and soon Benji would meet another of the Chief Executive's circle, Carl Williams, and the trio would realise they had more in common than they could have ever imagined. To share an enemy is to find common cause.

7 | CHOPPER

For a short, wonderful time in the mid-1990s, the fabric of the underworld had held fast and the bosses had all made millions together – enough to spend every night of the year chopping out their mates with drugs and women in the biggest suite of the best hotel in town, no boundaries, no witnesses and no regrets. For the price of a few scars and a good team of lawyers, they had the run of the town. They were cool to be seen with, they did coke with starlets and barristers, they had places on the Peninsula. But this was the most unlikely group of heads that ever ran Melbourne, and the age of plenty was about to end. Jealousy and paranoia were descending like a fog, and in the confusion the haves and have-mores would bring the castle down upon their own heads. As Skull Murphy said, there could be no winners from this – but, of course, that never stopped them fighting.

It's easy to say in hindsight that I had a handle on what was going on, that the facts were now fitting together to form a coherent picture. Nothing could have been further from the truth. With a month to my deadline I was faced with a jumble of facts. How I arranged them would depend on my own preconceived ideas of how an underworld war would go. As far as establishing a plot, I might as well have been spending my time in the cinema as hanging around the dives of West Melbourne and Carlton.

In my naive mind, I could see two gangs squaring off against each other, settling their commercial differences in the traditional manner. Nothing personal, of course – it was just business. Drawing on twenty years of finance journalism, I created an underworld that was an extension, even if it was a grotesque parody, of the real world. All the same principles applied – the laws of supply and demand, trust, cooperation and negotiation – but when things went wrong, the enforcement of contracts was rather final. The redundancy package was a killer.

In my scenario, the government had chosen to regulate the consumption of legal drugs such as tobacco and alcohol. It made more money out of alcohol and nicotine addictions than the pushers made out of their own trade. Were it not for the church, the politicians might have taken the family franchise into harder drugs, but that was impossible. So they had ceded control of that market to the 'men of honour'. As long as the business was done quietly, with a minimum of bloodshed, the government was happy that others were responsible for keeping working-class people stoned to the eyeballs. The 'self-regulation' of the underworld saved the taxpayer from funding long, unavailing investigations of crimes that nobody in polite society really cared about. As long as no innocent bystanders were killed, police could argue, in private at least, that this was a social good, a cleansing by fire that would eventually consume itself. And it always did.

My underworld was hierarchical, orderly and utterly focused

on itself. I convinced myself that these characteristics mitigated the danger of anyone from the outside looking in. In 1946, when gangster Bugsy Siegel was building the Pink Flamingo Hotel and Casino in the Nevada desert, building contractor Del Webb, who was working on the project, expressed concern for his own personal safety. Webb had noted the growing number of shady characters hanging around the site and wanted to know the odds of his getting caught in a crossfire. Siegel, who was just nine months away from taking two slugs in the head himself, assured Webb that assassins were professionals; he himself had carried out the execution of twelve people and every one had been strictly business. Webb had nothing to fear, said Bugsy, because 'we only kill each other'.

Rather than wander around aimlessly, I did what every cub crime reporter does when faced with the problem of understanding the underworld: I paid a visit to standover-man-turned-celebrity-author Mark Brandon 'Chopper' Read.

After his release from prison in 1998, Read had turned himself into a fully merchandised underworld industry. He had written a dozen crime novels, there had been a heavily mythologised movie of his life, and he had taken his stories on the stage. There were T-shirts and autographed memorabilia, and even a line of beer called Chopper Heavy – '100 per cent guaranteed to get your ears off'.

Many of his former brothers in crime now dismissed Read as a clown, a self-promoter cashing in on a minor underworld career, stealing the yarns of his generation and making them his own in his books. Even media colleagues of mine expressed doubts about the authenticity of anything Read might have to say. I thought about that the first time I met Chopper. What was authenticity, if this man didn't have it? He had spent twenty-three years in jail, most of them in H Division in Pentridge, the most brutal zoo of all Australian jails. He had been stabbed, slashed, bashed, glassed and bottled. He had allowed someone to slice his ears off with a razor just so he could prove to the prison authorities that, contrary to their edicts, he would make it out of H Division (he went to the prison hospital).

To survive all this required not only the application of an iron will, but a certain amount of luck. At forty-nine Chopper was an old man in underworld terms. He had survived three gang wars and numerous attempts on his life. He had grown up in conflict with the men who were now running Carlton and the north-western suburbs, and had little direct contact with the scions of the new underworld, men such as Jason Moran and Carl Williams. But they knew of his reputation. According to Read, Jason had hated him simply because Jason's former criminal mentor, Alphonse Gangitano, had been humiliated in a feud with Chopper in the early 1990s. In 1991, Gangitano had fled Australia for Italy with his de facto wife and child after word had reached him that Read was planning to kill him using landmines. Earlier, Read had stormed Gangitano's card club in Carlton with sticks of gelignite strapped to his waist, demanding that Alphonse hand over money from a recent robbery. Gangitano was believed to have scampered out a back window to escape the lunatic suicide bomber. Even Mick Gatto was understood to have spent time in South Australia in the period Read was storming around Carlton.

By the time Jason joined Gangitano's team in the mid-1990s, the earless one was safely tucked away in Tasmania's Risdon Prison after shooting a former leader of the Victorian Outlaws bikie club, Sydney Collins, in the stomach. Read had been sentenced to be jailed indefinitely and could only be released at the Governor of Tasmania's pleasure. A local official with the Australian Tax Office, Mary-Ann Hodge, began visiting Chopper in jail and in 1995 they married. In 1998, his appeal against his permanent detention was upheld and he went to live with Mary-Ann on a farm outside the village of Richmond, north of Hobart. Rural life didn't suit him and, despite the birth of his son Charlie (named after drug dealer and standover man 'Mad' Charlie Hegyalji), he left Mary-Ann and returned to Melbourne in 2001. There he was reunited with his first love, Margaret Cassar, whom he had met two decades earlier at the local fish-and-chip shop in the north-western suburb of Thomastown, where they had both grown up.

Now a full-time author, Read had bumped into Jason Moran from time to time and could see that the young hood was a man of destiny. On the back cover of his book *Chopper 10½*, published two years before Jason's murder, an illustration depicts a row of three graves that bear the names 'Charlie Hegyalji', 'Alphonse Gangitano' and 'Jason Moran', with a question mark for the date of death on Jason's. Two weeks before Jason's murder, Read had encountered the swaggering young hood in a Collingwood street. As a joke he had suggested Jason join him and former footballer Mark 'Jacko' Jackson on stage to tell stories of his feud with Carl Williams. Jason had stared blankly at Read, not knowing quite what to make of the bizarre offer. 'No thanks, Chopper,' he'd said, turning away. Clearly, his relations with Carl were no laughing matter.

Carl was also dismissive when I mentioned to him later that I had consulted Chopper. He quickly suggested that Chopper was a nobody these days and that I should speak to members of 'the new generation' to understand life in today's netherworld. However, like most of Read's critics, Carl also wanted to know what it was like to hang out with the man, how the reality matched the legend in the *Chopper* movie. He wanted a description of Read's mannerisms, to know how he had endured the removal of his ears. I feel sure that if I had offered to get Carl an autograph, he would have asked Read for a personal dedication. There was no disputing that Chopper had become the first folk hero of the Melbourne underworld since Squizzy Taylor ruled, back in the 1920s. (Perhaps Carl would be the next, and maybe one day they would make a movie of *his* life, Carl told me later.)

Read survived his criminal insanity to become the storyteller of his bloody community. Booksellers say that his crime books (what the author calls 'faction' – a little fact blended with fiction) are the most shoplifted titles around. His brother criminals steal them, perhaps affronted that they have to pay to read their own stories. The week before I met him, the legendary standover man had been manning a stall at Sexpo, the biggest wankers' jamboree in the southern hemisphere. There among the dildo salesmen and titty models stood Chopper, trying to flog his line of red and white wines. He told me he felt like the biggest tool there, but this was a living in the squarehead world.

The second Mrs Chopper, his childhood sweetheart Margaret, was dead against her husband doing any more media. She had a six-week-old baby, little Roy Read, in the bassinette and didn't want Chopper making new enemies with a few smart words. When he got on a roll he was hard to stop, and besides, if he was going to talk about murder and mayhem it should be in his own book, said Margaret. He could write fast – 90 000 words in eight weeks flat, easier than selling plonk at a dildo show.

It wouldn't be possible to have a meeting, said Chopper, glumly. He wasn't doing any more media. I could hear the feisty Margaret driving home the point in the background, baby Roy crying in her arms. But we could meet at his local pub for a quiet chat, he said, almost whispering down the phone. 'I heard that, Mark!' came Margaret's voice – but she knew enough to let him go when he'd made his mind up.

The next day I turned up at Collingwood's Leinster Arms and found Chopper chatting over a soft drink with another regular. He loved the Leinster Arms because it was one of the few pubs that still looked as it had during his heyday as a crim. Every knock-about pub has its page in the murderous history of Melbourne, he said. One night in the Leinster Arms some local villains had taken fatal exception to a young braggart and put a couple of bullets into him, then lobbed him down into the keg cellar for safekeeping until they worked out what to do. They came back two days later and it turned out the bloke was still alive, so they put a couple more into him and dumped him at the foot of a smokestack as a warning to anyone else who dared oppose them.

I had brought all my business theories to test on Chopper, like he was some kind of emeritus professor of the underworld marking my thesis. He listened politely before dismissing every single point I had made. He said it was too easy to get killed in Melbourne at times like this. Forget all the elaborate theories of the media, he said while making short work of a big, thick steak with his cobalt-blue false teeth. 'It's enough that someone simply doesn't like you. In my view, all that's been happening is that people who have been putting holes in their manners are getting shot. It's as simple as that. When the little bell goes off in your head and you keep ignoring it because of drug use or egos gone mad, and you keep fronting up to the same places to do business with the same people, that's what gets you killed in Melbourne.'

Even during his days of gore back in the 1970s and '80s, Read the criminal terrorist knew when to back off. Or perhaps he'd been lucky enough to return to jail before his enemies could get to him. Freedom for Read had been a few brief interludes of parole in twenty-three years of jail time – a chance to settle scores from the inside on the outside.

We walked back to his little worker's cottage to continue our discussion. Twenty-three years in jail had a bestowed a unique gait: a mixture of swagger and waddle, tiny steps for a big man on a long walk in a cramped exercise yard. Carl Williams walked in much the same way, though I think he was just lazy. In the sunlight I could see that the inmate who had shorn off Read's ears had done a nice, thoughtful job – he had left just enough for Chopper to balance his sunglasses on.

Now, in the ultimate irony, Read looked set to outlive the characters in his books. 'I'd like to spread a picnic rug on the banks of the Yarra and watch as the bodies of my enemies float serenely by,' he said as he stood in the backyard of his Collingwood cottage after we got back from the pub, painting a canvas of two boxers smashing each other to pieces. This was a departure for Read the artist, he said. Until now he had been concentrating on a series of Sidney Nolan-like studies of Ned Kelly, the main difference being that Chopper's Ned had enormous, pendulous breasts. I asked him how he would summarise his art, making the point that he was certainly not Picasso. 'Fuck Picasso!' he said, roaring with laughter.

Melbourne's underworld was a combination of 'Chicago, the East End of London and Chikasaw County, Mississippi,' he said. 'Chikasaw County for the inbreeding – a lot of the crims in Melbourne are basically feral because of inbreeding.' Underworld funerals had begun to look just like underworld weddings, because all the same people showed up – minus the bloke in the coffin, of course. 'If no one knows you in the criminal world then you don't exist, because everyone knows everyone or has heard of the deceased. That's how small it is. Things happen and people get killed. In Melbourne we catch and kill our own. We've been doing it for years, since Squizzy Taylor was a boy.'

But Carl Williams and his crew were newcomers. It was hard to place them in the criminal universe. To Read, they were just one more team calling itself a new generation and leaving its calling card. The violence provided the fear essential to the success of any criminal enterprise, he said. Without the capacity to respond to your enemies with extreme violence, they would know you were just a paper tiger. 'You have to be outside the vortex of normality.'

8 | JASON AND CARL

Jason Patrick Moran's family had lorded it over the north-west fringe of the city for three generations. His grandfather Dessie Moran was the leading SP bookmaker in Flemington and Moonee Ponds after World War II and his grandmother had been the number-one backyard abortionist, carrying out her grisly trade in the garage on a kitchen table supplied by a local police sergeant.

Dessie's son eldest son Lewis grew up at the track, practising the 'leather trade' – lifting wallets from unsuspecting punters. They learnt from the best. Mickie Mutch was the prince of pickpockets, or 'dippers' as they were known. On race day Mutch and his team would be trackside, mingling with the punters in the betting ring, or on the trams and trains home from the track, when they would follow any bloke with a smile on his face and relieve him of his winnings. For years, young police officers at the academy were shown a mug shot of Mutch, with a trademark feather in his hat, as part of their training.

The caper depended on giving the racetrack cop on duty a few quid to square him away. The copper would turn a blind eye to Mutch and his crew, not to mention the two-up games that were regular fixtures at the track. Mutch was never more than a dipper, but he retired in a nice double-storey in Coburg and lived there until his death in the mid-1990s. His system relied on confederates who would distract the punters long enough for him to get his nimble fingers into their pockets.

One of Mutch's most faithful apprentices in the 1960s was Dessie Moran's son Lewis. (Lewis's young friend Graham Kinniburgh tried his hand at the trade too, but found it wasn't to his liking: there was something about robbing a worker of his winnings that offended Kinniburgh, though he would never pass judgement on how another knockabout made a dishonest dollar.) From Mutch, Lewis learned that you needed at least one copper in your pocket if you were going to succeed in the villainy game. Fortunately he had grown up in the same street as a boy destined to become one of the most senior officers in Carlton. His mother had virtually brought the future cop up in her own home, and there were strong ties of allegiance between the two families that served Lewis well in later years. As well as his SP activities, Lewis was a major fence for stolen goods in the Flemington and Moonee Ponds area. He was prepared to dabble in whatever criminal enterprise was going.

Mark Moran's father was the noted standover man Les 'Johnny' Cole. In the early 1980s Cole had left Melbourne to work in Sydney for Frederick 'Paddles' Anderson, then the undisputed boss of crime in the harbourside capital, leaving Mark's mother, Judy, and her new partner, Lewis, to raise the boy. Like many former Melbourne gunnies, Cole liked to keep his hand in down south, and was an occasional player in the dock wars that were still raging. He had come back to Sydney from one such foray the day before he was murdered. An earlier attempt to kill him had failed, but this time there was no mistake. Two gunmen thought to be Christopher Dale 'Rentakill' Flannery and Mick Sayers did the job on Cole as he arrived at his fortified home in Kyle Bay. Cole was said to be the first victim of a gangland feud that claimed the lives of eight of Sydney's finest hoods. The reality may be less glamorous: I was told that someone ordered the hit on Cole essentially because they didn't like the way he treated women. Judy herself had been raised surrounded by knockabouts and racetrack types. Her uncle Boysie Brooks was a leading SP bookmaker and a contemporary of Dessie Moran.

Mark and Jason grew up in what looked like a middle-class household, though Lewis was hardly your conventional father. They always had lots of money, though they were careful not to talk about what their dad did to get it. Though three years apart in age, the brothers were always close. Jason idolised his older brother and in return Mark protected Jason, who from an early age found it difficult to run away from a fight. A classmate from Ascot Vale West Primary School remembers Mark standing over another kid at school because Jason was short twenty cents for lunch: 'The kid's first refusal got him a punch in the guts, the second a kick when he was down. Finally he coughed up the twenty cents. All of this happened in the blink of an eye, like no thought had to go into it. It was learned behaviour. Even back then you could see the debt of protection and brotherhood that existed between Mark and Jason.'

Everything came easy to Mark, especially sport. Australian Rules football was his passion, and Jason, a scrapper who had no talent but who would get dirty and be on the bottom of every pack, struggled to keep up. Mark was graceful, the consummate school-yard player and a bright, good-looking kid who 'could charm the pants off teachers and get away with playground murder,' said the school friend. 'He would steal kids' lunches and always had a way to swipe drinks and screw over the milk-bar guy on Langs Road. He'd use his brother to steal stuff all the time.

'Mark and Jason would often get a ride from me and my mum [the friend grew up in a single-parent home] to their grandma's house. We'd play a ton together on weekends if they were there, and there was always trouble to get into – breaking into the show-grounds or the racecourse, ripping off the milk bar or diddling the fish-and-chip guy.'

Mark had a great sense of humour, and if you were in with him, you were there for life. His old classmate, now living overseas, saw him on a trip home about a year before Mark's death. Mark talked of his journey into trade school and chef work, and lots of other 'good stuff' he had going on. He seemed happy and proud of his two kids and wife, Antonella, but was frustrated with Jason. An absence of ten years had not changed Mark's nervous habits. His old classmate couldn't remember a time when Mark wasn't chewing his nails out of anxiety, and he was still doing it. In the last year of his life he was hospitalised twice for what people in his circle described as 'nervous breakdowns'.

Jason became aggressive early in fifth grade. He started fights and then ran for cover behind Mark – who knocked many a kid's teeth in, and then threatened them with a worse beating should they decide to lag him. In Grade 6, the pair began to hang out with another kid from the Kensington Community School, Jedd

Houghton, who would become one of Melbourne's most fearsome armed robbers, later co-authoring a plan to murder two police constables in Walsh Street, South Yarra in 1988. Houghton died in a hail of bullets in a Bendigo caravan park in November that year as members of the Special Operations Group sought to bring him in for questioning over Walsh Street. 'All I can remember [about Jedd] was that he was trouble waiting to happen,' said the schoolmate.

If Mark and Jason were troubled kids, it was mostly others who felt the brunt of their dysfunction. Lewis used his sons as muscle to enforce his will over lesser beings in the local area. For example, one night Lewis was drinking at his favourite hotel, the Laurel in Ascot Vale, with a mate, Herbert Wrout. Lewis regarded the Laurel as his turf, a place where anybody misbehaving could expect summary justice from him. That night a well-known knockabout and his friend were drinking at the bar and the friend decided it would be a lark to pour himself a beer while the barman's back was turned. Lewis was outraged, and decided this would be a good time to put the knockabout in his place. Taking a poker from the fireplace, he crept up behind the bloke and delivered him a stunning blow to the back of the head. This bloke could go, though, and Lewis hadn't knocked him out even though his head was now streaming blood. The knockabout took a bar stool and gave Lewis a severe flogging and then promptly took himself off to hospital. Lewis wasn't going to take this lying down, and quickly summoned Mark and Jason with orders to hunt down any mate of his attacker and deal with them in the customary manner. Three men were shot in the legs or shoulders that night, but everyone copped it sweet. People knew enough not to lag the Morans.

Jason loved the whole gangster image – it was all he ever wanted to be, from when he was eight years old. By fourteen he had his own pistol, which he would bring to football practice and hand ostentatiously to a second while he trained. At fifteen he fell in love with Trisha Kane, the daughter of notorious Painter and Docker Les Kane (he later married her). In October 1978, at the height of another underworld war, Les Kane had been killed while his second wife and their two young children were held at gunpoint in other rooms of their Wantirna unit. The killers stuffed the body in Kane's own car and drove away, and no trace was ever found of him or the car. Four years later Kane's brother, Brian, was shot dead in the bar of a Brunswick hotel. His death wasn't unexpected after the extraordinary murder of Ray 'Chuck' Bennett two months before, inside the Melbourne Magistrates Court while he was under escort by two unarmed detectives. Bennett and two co-accused had been acquitted of Les Kane's murder and Brian Kane, disguised as a solicitor and sporting a newly grown beard, had slipped in and out of the magistrates' complex via a hole cut in the fence. Remarkably, as news of Carl Williams' feud with the Morans began to filter around the underworld, it appeared there was a direct link with the past. Williams' new father figure, the Savage, was a nephew of Chuck Bennett. It had people whispering that perhaps old scores were being settled on new fields.

Jason enjoyed the respect of some of Melbourne's best armed robbers, who knew he was staunch and would never take a backward step in a blue. He traded on his Painter and Docker heritage with these crims, but the drug trade was far more lucrative than any rort the dockers had ever enjoyed. The Moran brothers became key suppliers of amphetamines and party drugs. Through the 1990s, they had interests in several of the top speed labs in Melbourne as well as hydroponic marijuana operations.

Carl's brother, Shane had been a customer, buying dope from a grow house in Broadmeadows that the Moran brothers used as one of their bases. Shane hadn't liked Jason straight away, said his girlfriend Deana Falcone.

'He was a smartarse, arrogant, and Jason wanted you to know he was someone special and you were just a piece of shit,' she said.

Shane had liked Mark. He was okay – polite and charming when he wanted to be. He was a businessman. Mark knew the importance of getting on with others. But only while his family benefitted from the relationship. Beyond that, he was in fact more ruthless than his brother. What had to be done, would be done, without emotion.

The first blows in the war between the Williams and Moran families had been over a piano, believe it or not. Jason was all hot and bothered looking for his piano that had fallen into the hands of a friend of Carl's who had made himself scarce.

Jason bumped into Carl coming out of a cafe on Union Street, Ascot Vale. Carl was recovering from recent shoulder surgery and his right arm was in a sling. Threatening words were soon exchanged over the piano. Carl claimed to know nothing about it – he wasn't into that kind of music. Unamused and glowering, Jason demanded the piano-napper's telephone number on pain of a kicking. Carl refused, saying he would get the bloke to call Jason. That did not please Jason and he pursued Carl up the street, haranguing him and calling him names but Carl was resolute.

Finally, all Jason could do was take a swing at him. However Carl slipped the punch and somehow landed a surprise blow flush on Moran's nose. He expected a fierce kicking but Jason backed off.

He eventually got his piano back, if not his dignity, having lost a fight with a chubby one-armed bogan.

It could have ended a few months later in a little vacant block in Barrington Crescent, Gladstone Park. The reserve was so non-descript, it didn't rate a children's swing or even a name. The events there on the afternoon of 13 October 1999 would lead to the murders of nineteen people, directly or indirectly. Empires would fall and lots of dirty little secrets would tumble out. But they could have ended it there, and maybe they should have.

Carl was expecting trouble. He had tucked a fully loaded Glock semi-automatic into his bum bag. You could normally bank on Jason's 9mm being down the front of his pants, but today it was a snub-nosed .22 revolver.

They had met at a nearby shopping centre and the Moran brothers had suggested a quieter location, so they had driven in separate cars to Barrington Crescent.

There were matters to discuss.

Carl had a pill press that was the Morans' by right, or so Jason believed. It had belonged to a party girl named Danielle Maguire who, by virtue of having slept with Mark Moran, apparently was now a chattel of the Moran clan. Carl could hand it over or pay Mark and Jason $400 000.

Problem was, Carl only had a bit over $5000 in his bum bag.

The Morans couldn't handle that Carl was making cheaper pills than them, flooding the market with his $8 FUBUs and UFOs as against the Morans' $15 flippers. His miserable cash offer added insult to injury. Carl had actually planned to render the press inoperable and then hand it back to enrage them, but couldn't bring himself to kill his own golden goose.

And there was still more. The Morans' mate Dean Stephens had been having trouble with his then wife Roberta Mercieca. He had been bashing her relentlessly and he was afraid she would run off. Carl and Dean had done business together and they were mates. He asked Carl to take care of her when he wasn't at home. Carl repaid the trust by sleeping with Roberta.

Now Carl needed to be pulled into line. A kicking needed to be administered. Mark probably reasoned the fat gormless bastard would cop it sweet. He'd shit his pants, run home and get the pill press.

The pleasantries were soon over. Mark swung at Carl out of the blue with a small wooden bat he had been concealing. He hit him so sweetly the bat broke on Carl's head but it didn't lay him out. Carl ran at Mark and soon they were wrestling on the ground at Jason's feet. And Carl was getting on top of him. This wasn't in the script.

'Shoot him in the head!' cried Mark. 'Shoot him the head, Jason!'

Carl heard the shot, which meant he wasn't dead. Jason had missed him.

He looked into the barrel of the .22 and it was shaking. Jason's hand was shaking badly. He fired again at the writhing mass. One hundred and twenty kilos of Carl Williams was an easy target, but he missed once more.

'Put one in his fuckin' head, Jason,' hissed Mark, pinning Carl for a moment.

A neighbour heard a voice cry out: 'No, Jason, No!'

And remarkably Jason didn't, or couldn't.

Back home in Broadmeadows, Barbara Williams was putting the finishing touches to Carl's birthday cake. He was turning twenty-nine but still she made him a chocolate cake, just as she had done for both her two sons' birthdays every year since they were babies. But she was only making one cake a year these days since she had buried Shane. Her first son's death from a heroin overdose in 1997 made birthdays seem all the more special, so this time she had put extra effort into getting Carl's cake just as he liked it.

Carl had grown up a lot in the two years since Shane's death. She used to worry that he was too soft – a mummy's boy, even. But after Shane went, she noticed a change in him. For years Shane had protected Carl from the bullies that had targeted him, but in later years, as Shane's drug addiction had taken hold of him, it was Carl looking after his accident-prone older brother. Now there was a new hardness there, as if her boy's eyes had been opened to all the cruel and unfair realities of the world his family lived in. In most uncharacteristic fashion, Carl had taken over the arrangements for Shane's funeral, choosing the hymns, organising the church and paying for the lot, even the expensive casket.

Carl was late for the cutting of his birthday cake.

Barb worried about the new crew Carl was hanging out with these days – they were career criminals. Even she could see that. She didn't want to know where the money came from that Carl gave her for the pokies at the club. She didn't ask how he could afford to build her a new home in Essendon. When Carl and George had begun running a pill press in the garage, she just turned a blind eye. Carl had always respected her. There hadn't been more than three occasions in twenty-nine years when her boy had answered her back. They loved a laugh together or a chat over Carl's favourite homemade dish: baked beans, eggs and chips.

But these new mates scared Barb. She had been sunbaking in the backyard one day when one had come out and started shooting at the back fence. Nothing to worry about, he'd said. Just target practice.

When Carl finally turned up that afternoon, he was pale and drawn.

'Where have you been?' asked Barb, but Carl didn't answer. 'I've got your cake for you.'

He barely looked at the cake and went straight to the bedroom she still kept for him. 'What's wrong with you?' she asked.

'Nothing – just going to have a lie-down, Mum,' said Carl, closing the door. A few minutes passed and Carl called out to his father to come in. 'Not Mum – just you, Dad.'

Carl showed his father a small livid hole in the left side of his lower abdomen.

But for the livid burn around the small wound, they could have dismissed the hole in his guts as nothing to worry about. Now, two hours after the shooting, Carl was going into mild shock. He had already made up his mind that he would cop it sweet – there would be no call to the jacks – but the question remained how to get it treated without involving the law. They all looked at the little hole, which was oozing a surprisingly small amount of blood. Carl ventured the opinion that perhaps they could just do nothing, just leave the slug in him and let the wound heal as if there was nothing to worry about. Barb was dispatched to the local GP with a theoretical question: if a bloke had a .22 slug in his tummy and it wasn't hurting too much, could he simply leave it?

If Jason Moran had used a bigger-calibre weapon, they probably could have. A .45 slug delivered from close range will generally go straight through a man, unless it hits lots of bone and vital organs. If you can stop the bleeding and the internal damage is not too severe, surgery is not always necessary. The lighter, smaller .22 slug tends to ricochet around inside, ripping up soft tissue and organs until it comes to rest deep inside the body. In Carl's case, the slug had hit a layer of fat and muscle and travelled straight downwards, lodging inside his pelvis behind his genitals.

The GP recommended a trip to hospital, and Carl somewhat reluctantly agreed. The surgery was straightforward but for the large, ugly incision they made to get at the bullet inside his pelvis. Carl wanted to keep the bullet for a souvenir to put up behind the bar with his Muhammad Ali gloves and *Scarface* portrait of Tony Montana, but when he awoke from the anaesthetic he was disappointed to find that the police had come and taken it away as evidence. He need not have worried – there would be enough bullets flying around in the next five years for everyone to have their own keepsake.

Carl told his father he had been amazed to see how much Jason had been shaking when he shot him.

'No doubt if Jason had a steady hand and any balls I wouldn't be here today,' he told his father. He saw that Jason didn't have the dash, the heart, to kill him. And there was his big brother, Mark, Jason's idol, looking at him saying, 'Shoot him in the head, Jason, put one in his head,' and he couldn't do it. Jason would have died for his brother, but strangely he couldn't kill for him.

For all their big reputation, the Morans were weak. They had too much to lose now, whereas Carl was just on the rise. Of course, Carl hadn't pulled out his Glock either. The confrontation had ended inconclusively. Carl wasn't a killer but the kind of money he was making could buy him the best. He told his father the Morans would regret that they hadn't killed him.

Life changed rapidly for Carl after Jason shot him. Barb never made another chocolate cake for her son again. After that fateful birthday, she noticed a change in her son. He no longer laughed like he used to, and there was a new wariness about him. He said it came from looking over his shoulder all the time. On November 25 1999, four weeks after the confrontation with the Morans, local police knocked on the door of a two-storey townhouse in Broadmeadows to serve a warrant for a minor fraud matter on another man who was registered to the same address. When they approached, the officers heard a strange whirring sound from upstairs, like someone was operating an industrial washing machine. But what sort of house had the laundry upstairs? When Carl opened the door he was wearing a Mambo T-shirt that was dusted with a rather suspicious white powder. No, he didn't have a clue what was going on – he didn't know anything about a pill press. He claimed he had been sleeping at the time, even though he was fully dressed and wearing shoes.

A policeman involved in the arrest said it was 'a Tattslotto moment': to intend to serve a minor fraud warrant and to make a major drug bust by accident was too good to be true. And maybe it was. Carl gets shot and then four weeks later, out of the blue, he gets busted. Was this another set-up from the Morans? A way of taking a troublesome rival out of the market? It was a good haul: 30 000 ecstasy tablets and nearly seven kilograms of various powders, including methylamphetamine, ketamine and pseudoephedrine, with a potential street value of $20 million – which explained the need for the loaded pistol also found.

The drug-squad detective who took over the investigation from the Broadie police ended up beating Carl to jail. In July 2001, Detective Sergeant Malcolm Rosenes was arrested and charged with trafficking cocaine, hashish and ecstasy, and in October 2003 he was sentenced to a minimum of three and a half years.

Carl always said, 'Jason never liked to see anybody else get ahead.' If the bust *was* a set-up, then retribution would have to be exacted on the Morans.

If the Moran family was criminal royalty, the Williams clan was definitely the commonfolk.

George Williams met his future wife, Barbara Denman, when she was thirteen. Barbara was the seventh of eleven children born to a welder and his wife. The Denmans were a typical struggling Richmond family with no money and too many mouths to feed, and her mother kept food on the table by not paying the rent. It kept the wolf from the door but not the landlord, and Barb's early years were filled with memories of moving house hurriedly at various hours of the day and night.

Meanwhile, George's parents split up when he was twelve and left him and his siblings to their own devices. Eventually he moved in with the Denmans as a boarder. Proximity was the homely young George's ally in his pursuit of Barbara, and pretty soon they were inseparable. He found work in the retail trade, and for years they lived in Collingwood and Richmond on top of shops or in tiny units. While Lewis Moran and his cohorts were running with the leading crims of their age and Judy Moran was honing her ballroom-dancing skills at the better clubs of the city, George Williams was digging ditches in the Richmond sewer for the Melbourne & Metropolitan Board of Works. Later he became a debt collector for a whitegoods retailer, rising to the position of manager. Barb worked at a cigarette factory in Richmond and then later at the TAB.

In 1973, when Carl was three years old, the young Williams family moved to Broadmeadows, on the north-west fringe of the city. The move was to be a decisive factor in his education, though not necessarily in an academic sense. Broadmeadows in the early 1980s was a breeding ground for Victoria's jail system. Youth unemployment was high, and in the council flats and dingy pubs you could buy just about anything you wanted, from hot household appliances to hard drugs. Most families had a child in the boob or headed that way. A lot of Carl's schoolmates would become inmates at some time or other. The far-distant city of Melbourne was like another country, still run by the old families who controlled privilege and opportunity. Crims from Broadie found it hard to get a start in the cliques that dominated Melbourne's underworld back then.

In his teens Shane Williams began to explore the drug scene, running with a street crew who admired his dash and fearless attitude. An imposing figure at 188 cm (6'2') and 125 kilos, he was intelligent and humorous, a hit with the girls. Unlike his shy little brother, Shane was an outgoing, gregarious character. But heroin hooked him hard and for fifteen years never let him go. To feed his habit he became involved in the customary petty crime of the heroin addict: shop stealing and the occasional burglary. 'He used to go into the shops and stand there and think he was invisible to people and just stuff things in his shirt and walk off as if nothing had happened,' said his mother. When his younger brother was old enough, he would tag along on some of Shane's adventures, though he had little enthusiasm for planning his own.

Carl's suspected role as an occasional accomplice for his brother had brought him to the attention of the Broadie police by the age of fifteen. The police saw the big, soft kid as an easy mark: a little roughing up would persuade him to lag his brother. But he was staunch. On one occasion when his mother came to pick him up from Broadie, a tearful Carl complained that the officers had hit him on the head with a telephone book. 'He used to want to grow up and be a policeman, but then he started being treated like that and he thought, "I don't want to do that",' his mother said.

He lasted longer in school than most, leaving midway through Year 11 with mathematics being the only subject he had found to his liking. After school he was employed in a service station for a while and then a supermarket, but working for a living didn't much appeal to him when there was a big wide world of opportunity to explore. He became a bookie's runner, a trade that found him mixing with knockabouts and villains who loved a punt but didn't necessarily want to be identified. Living with his parents meant he could subsist comfortably on unemployment benefits and have ample time to run with his mates, who would crowd into the Williams house to play snooker and cards. He was no violent street thug, though he knew plenty of them. His mother actually worried that Carl was a bit of a wimp, but early on he discovered the value of surrounding himself with those of greater physical abilities. In turn, they appreciated Carl's organisational skills and his ability to get on with everybody.

In his early twenties, Carl acted as a courier for some friends running a speed laboratory. He ended up with six months' jail, but he did it easy: he had lots of friends inside already. It was like a finishing school for aspiring underworld types. For the next six years or so after getting out, Carl kept out of trouble, at least officially. There is little evidence that he spent much time working in legitimate jobs.

By the late 1990s he had formed two key friendships. Dino Dibra was a young, flashy punk from Sunshine, a man who had grown up with the most feared drug tsars of the western suburbs and had a liking for cocaine and violence that would eventually prove his undoing. Rocco Arico had spent his childhood in his parents' pool hall – the infamous Johnny's Green Room, where most of the budding young crims of Melbourne found their way sooner or later. Chopper Read told me he gave Alphonse Gangitano his first sawn-off shotgun at Johnny's one night when the young hood was just seventeen. It was that kind of place. Arico was a minor force around Carlton and Brunswick until 2001, when he put five shots in an offending motorist in a road-rage incident and was sentenced to nine years' jail. When Arico was arrested he was trying to board a flight from Melbourne to Perth with Carl. They were travelling light – they had no luggage for what the pair claimed was a three-week trip.

Having men like Dibra and Arico around allowed Carl to get on with business: the relentless search for the raw materials for the next cook-up. It was first suggested that Carl's great value was that he was an amphetamine cook, able to create an awesome cash flow in a short time. In reality he was an organiser, a general manager of operations and a man who brought people together. He learned to operate a pill press, as his arrest in 1999 had shown, but, according to his mother, Carl couldn't boil an egg, let alone cook up a kilo of speed. He existed on a diet of fast food and his mother's cooking.

In one late-night conversation in early 2004 I asked Carl how he supported himself. If he wasn't a leading underworld figure with a sideline in revenge and murder, just what *was* his profession? 'That's a good question,' he said with a chuckle. Perhaps for the benefit of the police on surveillance duty, he quickly denied that he was a drug-dealing murderer. 'Well, I haven't got a trade. I guess I'm . . . a commissioner. Yeah, a commissioner.'

'So what does a commissioner do?' I asked.

'A few mates wholesale jewellery and stuff with me and I sell it on to buyers for a commission,' he said. Carl (or 'The Commissioner', as I dubbed him after that conversation) was a popular figure. He was polite and respectful, a happy-go-lucky character who loved nothing better than a joke and a good belly laugh. He was social and ready to convene with his pals at any hour of the day or night. After the family had all gone to bed Carl would often decide it was time to go out. 'Hey, I'm hungry . . . Anybody want some Macca's?' he would call out, his voice carrying through the thin walls to everyone in the place. This was the prelude to many a nocturnal adventure, and if you wanted the food you would be disappointed. Hours later he might turn up with some stone-cold burgers, full of apologies.

But that Carl Williams died in Barrington Crescent when Jason Moran wounded him. Eight months later, the fat jolly man that everyone loved had become a darker more paranoid character. Even then, most people, including the Morans, continued to under-estimate him.

It was a normal day for Mark Moran on 15 June 2000. He took the kids, Joshua and Tayla, to school, then went shopping with his mother. Later he met his wife, Antonella, for lunch. Then his working day began. At 7.10 p.m. he went to Gladstone Park shop-ping centre to meet an associate, Darren Hafner, to transact some business. He handed over the ecstasy tabs as promised, but had forgotten to bring the cannabis and said he would bring it the next day. Hafner later told the coroner he had been concerned about Moran, saying he seemed distracted, not quite himself. As always, Mark's fingernails were bitten down to the cuticle. The past few months had taken a toll on him – he had been hospitalised twice for depression and had told friends the strain of coping with the violent excesses of his little brother was hard to take. He arrived back home at 7.45 p.m. but was soon off again, this time to deliver some football tickets to another friend.

This was Moran's life – an endless routine of errands and

meetings. The years of armed robbery and drug manufacture with the Ascot Vale crew had been very good to him. He was a qualified pastry chef and part-time personal trainer, yet he lived in a million-dollar home in a yuppie enclave, with no mortgage and his kids attending private schools. The men he had run with had been among the hardest in Melbourne. Jedd Houghton, Graeme Jensen, Gary Abdallah and Mark Militano had all died at the hands of police in the wars of the 1980s, while Victor Peirce would live another two years before he met his own executioner. Their reputations grew in death and invested Moran with a certain cachet that his propensity for violence could never really support.

If he was worried about Carl Williams, Mark Moran hadn't shared with anyone. It was business as usual, but he must have considered the implications from that day in Barrington Crescent. Jason had may have wielded the gun, but it was Mark who told him to shoot Carl in the head. In that situation, who was Carl's bigger foe?

In January 2000 Jason was jailed for twelve months over an affray charge. He and the late Alphonse Gangitano had run through a sports bar in town randomly bashing patrons. Mark had now lost his most valuable ally.

Perhaps he was taking a few precautions. Though he wasn't noted for carrying a gun, police had found a high-tech handgun equipped with laser sights and a silencer in the boot of a car he had rented from the airport.

By 15 June he had been under police surveillance for a long period, but reportedly just days earlier the 'Dog Squad' (as the surveillance wing of Victoria Police was known) had been called off.

Moran had that month bought two kilos of pure pseudoephedrine from the cops, when Detective Sergeant Wayne Strawhorn had begun doing business on his own account. The last thing Strawhorn would have wanted was his new customer under surveillance. If Moran's enemies got wind of that, it would be the perfect time to strike at Mark.

At 8.30 p.m. he was once again getting into his white Holden ute outside his plush residence in Combermere Street, Aberfeldie. The house was better than most of the other neat middle-class residences in that street and inside, all the creature comforts plus a loving family awaited him. But he was about to pay the cost. He was halfway into the car when an assassin with a sawn-off shotgun and a revolver strode up and blasted him twice in the chest.

I wonder whether Mark had the chance to look his assassin in the eye. Did he think of that afternoon in October 1999 when his brother could have stopped this war with one more bullet? There would be no mercy tonight but for a quick and clinical hit. Moran fell back into the car, mortally wounded. When neighbours came out to investigate, all they could see was a pair of long, slender legs sticking out of the vehicle.

Goggles would later tell police that Carl had pulled the trigger on Mark Moran, but it seems extremely unlikely. At 8.50 p.m. Carl arrived at Dennis Reardon's house in Melton South for dinner, a 40-kilometre drive from Mark Moran's house. Minutes earlier he had been captured on closed-circuit TV in a service station en route to Melton. Senior police eventually conceded that it would have been physically impossible to get to Reardon's house so quickly from Essendon. But they have no doubt that Carl ordered the murder. If someone else could do your dirty work you could indeed be in two places at one time. Mark Moran's murder remains unsolved. One persistent theory is that the Savage had been the shooter and Carl had been somewhere on the scene observing the killing.

The Morans held a council of war after Mark's death and the list of suspects was whittled down to three, including Carl Williams. Of the seven men who attended that meeting at Lewis Moran's house, six were killed. Lewis's drinking buddy Bert Wrout would survive but only though good fortune. Though the signs all pointed to Williams, the Morans still underestimated him.

'We still didn't believe we were in a war,' said Wrout later.

Homicide detectives interviewed Williams the day after the murder, but it never went further. Drug squad detectives, including Mark Moran's illicit supplier of pseudoephedrine, Detective Senior Sergeant Wayne Strawhorn, reportedly withheld crucial evidence from the homicide squad because they believed it would jeopardise their long-running operation into the Morans. Perhaps others believed it would jeopardise their personal business with the Morans. Killing was bad for everyone.

There was plenty of evidence linking Williams to Mark Moran's death, but none of it was in police hands.

The shotgun used to kill Mark was one of a pair bought by Carl's close friend 'The Gunsmith' (who cannot be named for legal reasons) from Dino Dibra. The Gunsmith was a jack of all trades for Carl. He helped set up the pill press at the family's garage in Broadmeadows and had been a major distributor of pills, cocaine and pot for the Chief Executive and his family, and the Williamses.

He was a trained fitter and turner and knew the correct method for cutting down weapons. Of the two shotguns, he kept one for himself and gave the older weapon, a 12-gauge under-and-over, to Carl. It had an inscription on the breech that read: 'Mitch on your 21st birthday. from The Boy's. 23/4/56'. Dibra was so pleased to be involved in the deal he never asked for payment for the shotguns and took to claiming Mark Moran's hit for himself.

Mark was sent off two days later, with a service at St Theresa's Church in Essendon. Jason was granted permission from prison authorities to attend, and sat in the church with his head buried in his hands. In a death notice, Jason laid out a challenge to Mark's killer: 'Words could never, ever express the way I am feeling. This is only the beginning. It will never end. Remember, I will never forget.' Most people knew Jason was not up to whacking Carl. Friends had nicknamed Jason 'Billy the Kid' for his brash big talk, but they knew he didn't have it in him.

That night Carl and Roberta Williams were at home in Rae Street, Brunswick when they heard gunshots out the front. Roberta ran from the back to see what was going on. Carl told her someone had been shooting at their front door. He was calm and relaxed, as if this sort of thing happened every day, but Roberta knew they were entering some very weird territory indeed.

I never knew Jason Moran – he died twelve weeks before I began my research – but he was a presence at many places I visited, a friend or an enemy to many whom I was now meeting. His aura was still everywhere as summer rolled into Melbourne. Whether they had been Jason's friend or foe, the one question everyone was asking was why he had spared Carl Williams in October 1999.

None of this drama would be happening if Jason had pointed his .22-calibre pistol at Carl's head rather than his ample girth. Now Williams was coming back at them hard – much harder than anyone would have expected from the once lovable, cuddly bloke.

It was a question Jason was still asking himself four years after the incident, and he was yet to come up with a satisfactory answer. At a function one night early in 2003 Jason took a walk along the Yarra River with an old friend. Finding a bench under a bridge, they sat and talked for an hour. Moran confided that weeks earlier he had taken a telephone call from Williams. Carl was not inquiring about Jason's health.

The idea of being stalked by Carl greatly irritated Jason, but he couldn't get away from the fact that his actions that caused his brother's death and could very well lead to his own demise. As Jason railed against Williams, his friend looked over at him. Even in the moonlight he could see the scars on Jason's head, the legacy of fights in jail or beatings at the hands of cops. He wore them like badges of honour.

Jason had already passed up many opportunities to square up with Carl for Mark. One night after Mark's murder, Jason had walked into a cafe in Essendon to find Carl quietly having a cup of coffee. According to George Williams, Jason turned on his heel and left the cafe, jumped into his car and drove away. On another occasion, as they were 'performing surveillance', as they called it, Carl and the Raptor spotted Jason in a small hatchback being driven by a girlfriend. They gave chase, Carl asking the Raptor to marshal the available weapons for a hit on Moran right there and then. All the Raptor could find was a tyre lever and a screwdriver, but that didn't deter Carl, the hardware hit man. They pursued Moran around a roundabout three or four times and down some back streets, before the hatch of Moran's vehicle popped open. Jason fired off a salvo of shots at the pair, but from twenty metres missed everything.

The Raptor had to shout at Carl to discontinue the pursuit, so focused on his quarry had he become. 'Fucking bastard,' growled Carl as he swung the car around. 'We'll get him another day.'

Carl's obsession was clouding his judgement. The most outlandish, even silly, plans were discussed and entertained. Like the one where Carl would cram himself into Moran's garbage bin for the night, then spring out in the morning to shoot him as he got in his car. This required intricate planning – if they got it wrong Carl could end up in the council tip. In another, Benji would lure Jason to a park for the execution. The Raptor would dress up as a woman in a wig and frock and be pushing a pram. Carl had also got Roberta to pick a fight with Jason's wife, Trish, as she was dropping her kids at school, hoping this might draw her husband out of hiding.

The longer Jason evaded his executioners, the more anxious Carl became that his quarry was stalking him. He worried that Benji was a double agent. He had heard that Benji had taken money and guns from Jason to kill him. Benji was not delivering on his promises to lure Jason to the kill zone; he was making excuses. Carl had never seen Benji so reticent to kill someone before and it made him deeply suspicious. He told Benji to shoot Jason the next time he saw him, but Benji never seemed to get around to it.

Meanwhile, the Morans were not sitting idly by. In May 2001, Lewis and Jason had contracted two Sydney hit men to kill Carl at the christening of his daughter, Dhakota, which was to be held at a Keilor reception centre. Police learned of the plan and decided to intervene to avert a public bloodbath. Williams was on bail awaiting trial for a $20 million bust so any offences would see him returned to custody, beyond the reach of the Morans' hired killers.

Just days before the christening, police set up a sting operation where an undercover officer would buy $100 000 worth of ecstasy (8000 pills) from a Williams associate, Walter Foletti. Once the drugs were bought, it was only a matter of police following the money back to Williams to spring the trap. Both Roberta and Carl were arrested. Roberta got bail in forty-eight hours, but Carl remained inside for fourteen months. The christening was rescheduled for December 2003. The police sting saved Carl's life, but just delayed the inevitable conflict. While on remand in Port Phillip Prison, Carl met and quickly became best mates with the Raptor. The Chief Executive was in Port Phillip on remand, too, on his drug charges.

'After a period of time, [the Chief Executive] became part of our crew' said the Raptor. 'We used to eat together and occasionally drink alcohol. I was working in the kitchen at the time and used to smuggle food out for [the Chief Executive] as he loved his food.' The Chief Executive had been impressed with the Raptor's ability to get anything from drugs and alcohol to mobile phones and guns into the prison.

By the time the Raptor was transferred to Beechworth prison in Victoria's north, the new team was firmly in place. When all three were back on the streets in late 2002, the killing began in earnest. By saving Carl in the sting operation, police had consigned several others to death.

Sitting there by the Yarra in 2003, Jason cut a sad, bewildered figure. He had tried to run, spending nine months bumming around Europe, but had come home to face the threat. Now he was back in Ascot Vale with the kids and Trisha, still doing business but running around with a 9mm pistol down the front of his trousers. A patient foe, as slow and inexorable as the murky river sliding by in the moonlight, was stalking him.

Jason had put the entire family fortune on the line for the want of better judgement. His brother was in the cemetery and anybody else close to him could follow.

9 | TOMMY

Tommy's letter landed on my desk in early March 2004, as I was trying to piece together the fragments of his world – a patch-work of clues and memories, scattered in notebooks and files all over my office floor. The letter lay there for a week or so, hidden under the rubble of mail and unread newspapers, until it dropped to the carpet – a yellow envelope, the sender's name typed with painstaking ceremony: 'Tommy Ivanovic Esquire, Her Majesty's Prison, Barwon'.

I had just published my 7000-word story in *The Bulletin* detailing the state of play in the war as best I could, given the limits of my knowledge. Six months of research into the underworld and there were still great, yawning gaps in my understanding. A kalei-doscope of names and faces swirled before me. The only certainty was that the dead remained departed. A gallery of rogered rogues stared down from the newspaper graphic pinned to my office wall. It was like the kings and queens of old England I had learned about in school – hard to remember who came after whom, how each had met their demise. In the circumstances, an artful weaving of the facts was the best result a reporter could hope for. Like a bald man combing his thinning locks over his head, it looked good from certain angles but a stiff breeze highlighted its shortcomings.

I was thankful the action had paused long enough that the story would have something of a shelf life. At least three times in the saga, things I had written had been completely superseded by events within hours of publication. Some stuff I had written was educated guesswork, a pastiche of fact and inference, and other things were just plain wrong.

In the story I had touched on the strange case of one Thomas Ivanovic, godfather to Carl Williams' daughter. This connection had escaped the media when Tommy stood trial for a road-rage murder in 2002. It would have escaped me also, but for a chance meeting with one of the many legal gadflies of Melbourne who are always willing to chat about the latest gossip. I ventured the opinion that once an innocent bystander was caught in the crossfire, the level of political interest in the killings would skyrocket, leading to earnest speeches in state parliament and the inevitable royal commission that follows such events. 'Yes, but of course you could say there has already been an innocent bystander,' said the gadfly dryly.

He briefly outlined Tommy's story. Driving home one summer evening, a pair of motorcyclists began to follow him. They got all the way to Tommy's gate and still they were following. Tommy parked his car and went across to them and one of the guys pushed Tommy over. So Tommy pulled his .32-calibre pistol from his pants and shot the guy twice. He died later in hospital.

I looked blankly at the lawyer, unable to see the innocent-bystander angle: the story seemed to me a lesson on the dangers of road rage. He explained, 'Tommy was nervous and paranoid. He thought the guy on the motorbike was another gangster trying to shoot him.'

Reading the available news clippings and snippets of court files later, it seemed to me that Tommy's counsel had not led in evidence the fact that his client was an associate of Carl because it would have erased any trace of sympathy the jury might have had. It didn't matter – the jury didn't buy the self-defence argument anyway. The fact that Tommy had fired the second shot a full four seconds after the first, when the victim was no longer a threat to anyone, hadn't helped his case. He got the full whack for murder – life, but with a fifteen-year bottom line.

In Barwon Prison, Tommy had read the few paragraphs I had written about him in the *Bulletin* article, in which I suggested that it might have been difficult for Carl and Roberta to distance themselves from the growing pile of bodies around them when their associates were as trigger-happy as he'd been. Looking back now, it occurs to me that to summarise the worst day in a man's life in a few flippant paragraphs had been grossly unfair. What happened on that balmy evening in January 2002 had been a tragedy for everyone involved and could never be summed up in a few words. It took Tommy's letter to show me this, though.

Tommy's message was delivered in a language so formal and careful that I knew he must have agonised over it. At the time of his trial the newspapers had reported rather condescendingly that his intellect was, at best, modest. That wasn't going to stop him having his say now. 'May this letter find you in good health and good humour . . . I was deeply motivated and troubled with your article of myself as godparent to their infant daughter as you have put it,

and a devoted godparent I must add.' He went on to upbraid me
for the journalistic shorthand I had used in writing his case (okay,
for the mistakes I had made): there was no minor traffic incident,
and two bikers, not one, had followed him home that day. 'Your
source of intelligible information is obviously incorrect, or it has
no idea of the true facts of my case or my present circumstances.'

He called them 'kites' – letters from prison – and over the next
few months Tommy would enlighten me on the facts of his life and
on a range of other things: not the sensitive issues of who had killed
whom, but what it was like to be him, and his journey from chef
to lifer in prison. He was a man desperate to begin again. Now, a
couple of years into his sentence, many of the old friends who been
visiting him were dropping off. The flow of letters of support was
thinning, too. There were still a few, like Carl, who kept in touch,
but the rest were moving on with their lives. They were forgetting
about Tommy.

Yet even in prison he stayed staunch to his mates. My suggestion
that he elaborate on the doings of his former colleagues was met
with a polite refusal: 'I deeply regret that I am unable to elaborate
furthermore on you[r] cover story and my state of affairs. As you
would agree it would be irresponsible to give specifics for further
legal matters.' In other words, jail might be hell, but to rat on his
mates would ensure a trip from the metaphoric to the literal.

Tommy grew up in Brunswick West at a time when Italian and
Greek immigrant families still dominated the inner city. As a child,
he played in his neighbours' vegetable gardens, smelling the richly

scented European herbs and the cooking aromas wafting from the kitchens. Some of his playmates lived in the palazzos with their mock-classical concrete columns and grand facades that were beginning to spring up between the old weatherboard cottages. Some families were wealthier than others, but it never occurred to Tommy to ask why. His family was unusual for the area: his mother was Macedonian and his father Croatian. Their four children grew up with the Italians and Greeks, and Tommy in particular tried hard to be accepted. Even as a youngster he was no general. He had no ambitions of becoming a leader. Though he fell in with the local toughs, some of whom were destined for the underworld, he was an easygoing kid with no propensity for violence. He was just coming along for the ride. It didn't matter where the journey took him, as long as he had his mates.

By the late 1990s, Tommy had completed his apprenticeship and was working as a chef at the popular Brunswick restaurant, Bolero. It was here that he met Roberta Mercieca, a year or two before Carl Williams came on the scene. 'Little Tommy' got on with every-one. In late, boozy nights at Bolero he'd come out from the kitchen to meet film stars, singers and even senior politicians. Like so many diners at the restaurant, Roberta took a shine to the personable, yet naive young man and soon they were speaking almost every day. Later she introduced Carl to Tommy, and Carl recognised a loy-alty rare in his associates. Tommy also knew a cop from the drug squad, Sergeant Paul Dale, who became a regular contact for Carl. They would meet in a swimming pool close by – because waist-deep in water you couldn't conceal a wire in your Speedos – and Dale would pass on information on the Morans. Tommy was very useful to Carl and the young chef's cupboard filled with expensive business suits. He had a designer label for every day of the week. It was all a joke to him – there were no gangs or criminal empire, just little group of wannabes hanging out. Tommy was an entrepreneur. He wanted to save enough money to start his own restaurant, get the boys involved and make an honest pile.

Carl liked having Tommy around. They shared a love of chess and good home-cooked meals. Life in Carl's court was very good for boys like Tommy (not that he spent all of his time with Carl – he kept his cooking job right up until the time he was charged with murder). Tommy was looking the part with his new suits and a late-model silver convertible Mercedes-Benz. He had begin moving a little product for Carl; he was getting a name for himself. Yet Tommy was still living at home with his parents and the car was a cheap import from Japan that he shared with his brother.

By the winter of 2000, Tommy's world had become a smaller, more dangerous place. The walls were closing in on him. Whether it was personal drug use that was driving his paranoia really doesn't matter. There were enough people around him living high on the chemical wire to more than justify his fears.

The pressure was building in the ganglands. Operation Kayak, the joint taskforce between Victoria Police and the Australian Federal Police, was undermining any cooperation and harmony that had existed between the rival camps. The murder of Mark Moran had raised the temperature. Carl was the red-hot suspect and there was a running war of words between the Moran and Williams camps.

At 3.30 a.m. on 16 May 2000, career criminal Richard Mladenich, a small-time dealer with a big-time mouth, was shot dead in a St Kilda motel room. Mladenich had twenty-four aliases but preferred to call himself King Richard or Richard the Lionheart. He was visiting a drug dealer who had used the room at the seedy Esquire Motel as his base. A Williams associate, Rocco Arico, was named by police as the prime suspect in the murder. There were three people other than Mladenich in the room that morning, but none could finger Rocco.

Later, in jail, Arico boasted that he killed Mladenich on behalf of Carl. The talk was that Mladenich had taken a down payment to kill one of the Morans and had reneged, so Carl had contracted Arico to do the job on him. Carl suspected that Mladenich was a double agent intent on another payday, this time for killing him.

Like many others at this time, Tommy was now deeply interested in the security of his home. The Ivanovics lived in a modest weatherboard home in Brunswick. It was in need of a paint and a general spruce-up, but had been a comfortable home to the migrant family. Tommy's mother, Vera, had made a fragrant garden, every corner planted with garlic, spring onions, tomatoes, carrots, beans or pumpkins. She even harvested the stinging nettles that grew behind the house and turned them into a delicacy for the table. Tommy had gone his own way though he lived under the same roof as his father, who was a stern disciplinarian. They had a loving but distant relationship.

In 2000 Tommy installed a security camera under the eaves outside his bedroom and replaced the old gate on the driveway with a remote-controlled roller door. The fence around the imposing shutter was only protected by a shoulder-high strip of lattice work – hardly an obstacle for a determined assassin – but presumably when Tommy parked the Merc behind the roller door it made him feel secure..

In September 2001, Tommy decided he needed a break from all the tension – 'unfortunate times that I would not wish on my nastiest foe', he wrote. There had been a raid on his parents' house and police, including his mate Paul Dale, had found a small quantity of ecstasy. This was a family shame and his father came down heavy on him, so when he got bail Tommy took a trip to New York to visit a brother living in Manhattan. On the morning of 11 September, he had just returned from the gym to his lodgings on Eighth Avenue when the first airliner hit the World Trade Center. He ran out onto the street and was nearly knocked over by people streaming away from Ground Zero. Rather than join the tide of humanity fleeing the disaster zone, Tommy pressed on towards it with an almost insatiable curiosity. 'Then all of a sudden I hear another plane has hit. I can't put it into words the feeling that I was going through. All that I could see was ambulances, police and fire vehicles roar past me,' he wrote.

Tommy had a habit of finding himself in the middle of history's milestones. In December 1999 he had travelled to Croatia with his father to visit relatives, hoping to find some answers to his dilemmas in his roots and heritage. They had landed in the capital, Zagreb, just in time for the announcement that Croatia's veteran president, Franjo Tudjman, had died from complications arising from intestinal surgery. The young man found himself in a city in mourning. It overshadowed his time with his father and, after four weeks of putting up with the national sadness, Tommy came home early. If he wasn't feeling cursed already, his brush with international terrorism in 2001 convinced him that he had been whacked with the trouble stick well and truly. Possibly Melbourne was a safer place for him after all. But Tommy was being pursued by his own demons, and perhaps there was nowhere he could feel truly comfortable.

When 38-year-old trainee motorcyclist Ivan Conabere decided to follow Tommy home, he unwittingly gave form to Tommy's fears. Road rage, always a questionable activity, would now become downright deadly. In Tommy's trial, prosecutor Mark Regan told the court that immediately after the shooting, a witness heard Tommy say to Conabere's companion, 'Well, what was I supposed to do?' Mr Regan said Tommy had tried to explain his actions: 'He grabbed me around the throat . . . I got scared . . . and so I pulled out my gun and shot him.' His defence counsel suggested that Tommy's actions had been automatic. There was no time to form the intention of murdering Conabere.

The witness, an off-duty policeman, was an added bonus for the Crown, because all the action had already been caught on Tommy's own security system. Police who later attended the scene said they noticed that someone had chopped down one of the two large evergreen trees in the front yard of the Ivanovic home, resulting in the camera having an unhindered view of the street. It was revealed in court that while in custody Tommy had volunteered the fact that he'd had a camera installed, perhaps reasoning that the video would support his plea of self-defence. It didn't – the footage was his undoing.

This was Tommy's first stretch and he got the full whack. Before he imposed the fifteen-year minimum jail term, Justice

Philip Cummins told Tommy, 'Life is not cheap, nor should it ever be . . . Mr Conabere was a decent, law-abiding citizen who was trying to gain his motorcycle licence but dared to remonstrate with [you] about a driving incident. [This was] a wholly gratuitous killing . . . because your ego was offended.'

Others had a different view. Tommy's mother said in a statement that she had been sitting in the lounge that afternoon when she heard the two men arguing and then the shots. Tommy had come into the house as white as a sheet and in a shaky voice asked his sister Mary to call an ambulance. If killing came easy in the underworld, then maybe Tommy didn't fit in after all.

The christening of his goddaughter, Dhakota Williams, in late 2003 was the proudest moment of Tommy's life, even though he couldn't be there. Having delayed the festivities until Carl's return from prison, Roberta went all out, spending tens of thousands on the function. Money didn't matter: by this time they were awash with the stuff. It was a huge affair held at Crown Casino's Palladium Room, and every leading villain and his lawyer was there to celebrate with Roberta and Carl. His sister Meri read Tommy's speech to the throng and by all reports she did him proud. A man doing life takes pleasure in the briefest of moments.

Inside jail, Tommy, through his association with Carl Williams, had become something of an authority on the gang war raging outside, with other inmates seeking his opinion on the character and bravery of the various players. 'I have most of them asking me a whole lot of questions, on how I know the sketch of friends and so on. Most of the time I do not [comment], unless I see them to be in a good way of not coming back to the college. I spend time in letting them know that everything that shines is of course not gold.'

But he was still staunch to Carl, no matter the hard lessons he had learned. In July 2006, an informer would finger Tommy as the courier in a plot to smuggle a gun into Port Philip for the purpose of killing Lewis Moran. The Gunsmith told police that George Williams had procured a tiny .22 calibre pistol, a five-shot that wasn't much bigger than a credit card. George denied that this incident ever took place or that Tommy was part of it, but according to the Gunsmith it cost George five ounces of dope to bribe a bent member of the prison staff to get the weapon inside to Tommy. Tommy pulled off the pick-up and the gun was passed to another Williams associate in jail, who would assassinate Lewis. However, they couldn't get to Lewis because he was being held in the protection wing. Carl blamed Roberta for this. She had visited another inmate and told him to alert Tommy that the .22 was coming. She had made a hand gesture in the shape of a gun that was caught on video; that's why Lewis escaped, said Carl.

Later a tiny gun and some drugs were found in a cavity behind a vent in the cell of Michael Farrugia, an ally of the Williams family. Tommy got the Slot, but not for that – it was mostly on account of his loyalty to Carl. He would spend more than a year in solitary. They were working on him for confessions about Carl and it took its toll. He began suffering migraines and loss of balance, and they diagnosed prison-induced psychosis. In mid-2007, Tommy was in a concrete cell at the Melbourne Assessment Prison after another psychotic episode. They were leaning hard on him, but Tommy never rolled on Carl. He was staunch, perhaps the only one who was.

As we corresponded, I tried to understand what a life sentence in Barwon was like for Tommy. I told him that though his life seemed to be stuck in neutral he was actually still hurtling forward on his own journey. Sure, not too much changes in a prison cell, but the mind was an ever-changing world, full of choice and opportunity, and he could either use the time and resources in Barwon to transform himself and leave his cell as a whole man, or leave the best part of himself behind. In the timeless, formless world of jail, this was one truth he could hold on to. It could be said that Tommy's greatest foe lay within himself. He wrote back: 'I had a good read at your correspondence and your philosophy has really moved me.' He sent me the results from the catering course he was doing: he had scored top marks all round. I sent him back a dictionary.

'I learned a few new words from your letter. One was "foe". I never knew what a foe was. I thought it was a baby animal. One thing for sure, you keep me busy with the dictionary. As Jesus asked the Lord, how many are my foes? How many rise up against me? God will not deliver him.' He closed with a line that would surely resonate with all the players of this drama: 'A secret foe gives a sudden blow.'

Tommy would be there to the very end with Carl. He would witness that sudden blow from Carl's secret foe.

10 MONEY AND POWER

It was October 2004, and Johnny was heading back to where he had fought his personal war. As he swung his Commodore off the freeway onto the Western Ring Road, the familiar dead smell of the poultry works welcomed him like he had never been away. For once the sun was truly shining over Sunshine, glinting mockingly off a wire sculpture of the perfect suburban home strung up between the power pylons. He hadn't wanted to go back, but I had pestered him until he gave in.

A month before, out of the blue, Johnny had left a message on my answering machine. He said he had been in the underworld for fifteen years but was out now and ready to tell his story. 'Just another gangster wannabe,' I thought, but when I met him a few days later there was no doubt that Johnny was the real deal – the last man standing. His story, more than any other, would help me to untangle the threads of this war. His memories were like a road map of the gangland.

He was taking a risk. Three years before, if Johnny had caught anyone taking a reporter into Sunshine, both the journo and the offender would have paid dearly. Johnny and his mates – Andrew

'Benji' Veniamin, Dino Dibra and Paul 'PK' Kallipolitis – had always loved to 'play doctors' with 'dogs' and 'rats'. Torture was a thrill that neither drugs nor sex could match and disloyalty was always the best excuse.

On the outside Johnny had changed little. Cruising slowly down Glengala Road, he looked unchanged from his underworld heyday. He was a tall, handsome man with a sharp, almost triangular face. At one time those deep-set dark eyes used to narrow and glint, turning his face into a maniacal jack-o'-lantern, a perfect mask of evil. No wonder Benji nicknamed him 'Psycho'. The transformation in Johnny's heart had softened those eyes now, but the scars remained and every one told its story.

'People in Sunshine are going to call me a dog for talking to you, but I don't care. I know who I am and what I have done in my life,' he said as we drove. He ran his hand over the groove in his forehead. 'My head's still got a crack in it from where the jacks batoned me half to fuckin' death, fractured my skull, and all they got was my name and address. They musta battered me fifty times over the years, but at the end of the day I never ratted out no cunt. There's no one out here that ever did one day's jail because of me.

'And now all my mates are dead. Soon they'll forgotten, and nobody will learn anything from all the bullshit that went down out here. It's all going to start again, more mothers' sons lying in pools of blood. It will be just like us – friends killin' each other. I look back and ask: what was it all for?

'Money and power, mate, money and power,' he said softly, shaking his head. 'I would have taken a bullet for those guys, no questions asked. When they copped it, part of me died too.

'I'm not talking about no murders or any other crimes, you understand me?' He looked over his sunglasses at me, one eyebrow snapping like a whipcord. 'Anything else you might discover from other sources out here, well, that's your responsibility. I'm only interested in talking about my mates. And only to set the record straight. If you dick me . . .' He paused, remembering that he was no longer in the underworld. 'If you dick me, well, I'll never speak to you again,' he said, adjusting his grip on the steering wheel.

As we drove through Sunshine, Johnny marvelled at the changes. Where there had been paddocks just three years ago, rows of new houses, shops and supermarkets had sprung out of the ground. Sunshine was growing; new people were moving in. New bosses were running things now – the hydro marijuana houses, the stan-dover and the car rebirthing. Maybe there were some new rorts, but the new lords of Sunshine would all finish up the same way, Johnny said.

I asked him to drive past the houses where PK and Benji had lived, but he quickly declined. The dwellings were still owned by Kallipolitis and Veniamin family members, and the last thing Johnny wanted was to turn them into tourist attractions: already, one ghoulish entrepreneur had set up a bus tour of the famous sites of the war. So instead we drove out to Johnny's old place in West Sunshine, a modest brick veneer turned into a fortress with surveil-lance cameras, motion sensors and aluminium roller shutters on every window, bulletproof screens on the doors. 'I could turn day into night behind them shutters,' he said. But could he sleep well in there, knowing who might be waiting outside, I asked. 'Mate, I slept well, but I knew it wouldn't be forever.'

We drove out to Keilor cemetery where Benji had been laid to rest. Johnny ran his hand over the cold polished granite of the headstone, admiring the gold-inlaid epitaph and the compartment that held Benji's kickboxing trophies and his favourite 'No Fear' baseball cap. 'Awesome,' he repeated over and over, his voice trailing off. 'It's just awesome.'

It was a truly monumental resting place. Benji's black grave towered over those around it. He had always told Johnny this was how it would end up, but still Johnny couldn't help cursing him out. 'You bloody idiot, Andrew. You should have come with me, Benj,' he said softly, tears welling up in his eyes. 'You shoulda come and this would'n'a happened. It didn't have to end this way, man.' He looked up at the replica of Benji's tattoo on the apex of the headstone: two tribal bands around his upper arms that had been joined across his chest with a huge, striking scorpion. Under his expensive tailored shirt, Johnny bore the same tribal-band tattoo. It was fitting, he thought, that the centrepiece of Benji's tattoo had been a scorpion. In a fight, a scorpion just keeps stinging in a frenzy until either its enemy dies or the scorpion does. And that was Benji.

Johnny and Benji had got that first tribal band together. It was a pact sealing a friendship that had begun in high school. When their mate Dino Dibra tried to get in on the act, he found that Benji had ripped up the stencil so nobody else could have it. So Dino got two similar bands around his ankles and paraded up and down the Glengala Road shops in Sunshine in the rain, with his pants rolled up to his knees, showing them off.

Johnny already had an American eagle on his right arm and had been happy to stop at the tribal band, but Benji kept going with the ink. Eventually both his arms were fully sleeved with tribal designs that resembled flames licking his body. The tatts helped Benji to become the man he had always aspired to be. The respect and fear the ink inspired in others helped to quell the turmoil in his mind, and neatly covered the vivid, slashing scars he had inflicted upon himself with a razor in boys' prison.

Standing there in front of Benji's grave, Johnny could feel the pull of the underworld strong again. A few rows away lay the remains of two other childhood mates from Sunshine who had died on the one day, the first stabbed in a local nightclub and the second shattered in a speeding car en route to Adelaide. Who came to see them now except their families and a few staunch mates? By contrast, nearly six months after Benji's death his grave was still festooned with flowers and laminated tribute cards, and fresh candles were burning in lamps that were tended daily. Perhaps he would be remembered after all. Maybe Benji's last, crazy tilt at death would never be forgotten.

Johnny was doing it tough in the land of the squareheads. Working for a living was hard when you used just to take what you wanted and batter anyone who objected. Now everyone was Johnny's boss, and no one knew he used to be a somebody. What was his life worth now – the twelve bucks an hour he was picking up for sweating and straining on a removal truck? It was like being dropped in an alien world. Once he had walked straight into the VIP area in the best nightclubs in Melbourne, now he queued up with the rest of the punters. In the old days, the big men of the underworld would come up to him, kiss him on both cheeks and press free drinks on him. In ten years of criminal life millions of dollars had slipped through Johnny's hands, and now he was counting every cent. It was getting harder and harder now that his two kids were growing up.

Life had been so much easier when he'd thought there would never be a tomorrow, said Johnny sadly as we turned and headed for the car.

The suburb of Sunshine was hardly the land of opportunity and hope that its name suggested. It had been named after the Sunshine Harvester Works, which was the main local employer for years, and had been a dormitory suburb for the heavy industry that dominated the entire western suburbs in the post-World War II era. In that period it was the site of much of Victoria's manufacturing base, which thrived behind walls of tariff protection. In the 1950s and '60s families from a melange of different ethnic groups spilled out from inner Melbourne to pursue their dream of a brick veneer with a double garage on a quarter-acre block. Skull Murphy said you needed interpreters for sixty different languages just to operate in Sunshine back then.

Two generations of mainly European immigrants worked in the factories until governments in the 1970s and '80s tore down the tariff walls, forfeiting thousands of jobs that were never to be replaced. By the time Johnny and his pals hit high school in the early 1990s the prospect of future employment was looking bleak indeed. In any case, there were much easier ways of making money.

Though they were born here, kids like Johnny Auciello grew up rarely, if ever, mixing with 'Australian' kids, as they called them. He and his three friends Dino Dibra, Mark Mallia and Benji Veniamin were all from different ethnic and religious backgrounds: Johnny's family were Italian from Naples, Dino's were Muslims from Albania, Benji's were Greek-Cypriots, and Mallia was Maltese. They became the scourge of Ardeer High School, playground bullies sharpening their skills for a future in the underworld. Johnny got expelled at fifteen when the Ministry of Education gave him an exemption to go before his sixteenth birthday, and the rest followed soon after. At Charlie's pinball parlour in Sunshine, the boys began to hang around a Greek boy four years their senior, who would give them the opportunity to realise their dark ambitions.

If there was ever a criminal squire of Sunshine, it was Paul Kallipolitis. He's a figure often overlooked in the bloodbath that followed his death in October 2002, but if police get to the bottom of his life, they will find the wellspring of much of the mayhem.

In September 2004 there was a flurry of interest in PK when the Purana Taskforce applied in the Melbourne Magistrates' Court to question a suspect over PK's death – the Gunsmith, who was already in custody with Carl Williams over the June 2003 murder of Jason Moran and Pasquale Barbaro. By that time the others – Benji, Dino, Mallia and company – were becoming folk heroes and PK was slipping into the middle distance. There wasn't even a photo of him when the Melbourne press drew up their graphics of the victims of the underworld war. This just didn't seem right. PK had taught these boys how to behave if they wanted to be men of honour, and now he was being portrayed as a faceless silhouette. Then again, he was no 'redlighter' – or show-off – not like Benji and Dino.

When PK put on his two-tone calf-high snakeskin boots,

steel- capped and Cuban-heeled, there was no one in Sunshine who could touch him. In his younger days, at Charlie's, he would demonstrate his power by bending a no-standing sign with one thundering side kick. In his pomp, beefed up on the juice, no one could beat him in a punch-on. PK's father had put his three sons through martial arts training and only let them stop when they were wearing 1st or 2nd dan black belts. Paul went to a private school, St John's College in Braybrook, and averaged a couple of hundred winning fights there each year in addition to the cabinet full of trophies he won in organised battle.

In Greek, *kallipolitis* means 'good citizen', and that's what PK's father had hoped his three sons would be. PK finished an apprenticeship as a panel beater, but his destiny lay in the underworld and his ruthless dash dragged the rest behind him. He tasted power at a young age, and it was the most powerful drug of all.

PK and his crew – Benji, Dino, Johnny and Mark – would wag school and meet up at Charlie's or further along the street at Upstairs. From there they might cruise into the city or St Kilda to look for cars to fill orders for the rebirthing trade; the going rate was $1500 a vehicle. When they put in an appearance at school it wasn't in uniform but in expensive designer tracksuits and sunglasses, with $10000 gold chains round their necks. They were a team who had sworn to back each other till the end. You 'chopped out' your mates no matter what, whether it was money, drugs or a woman you had just met. You chopped them out or you couldn't call yourself a mate.

No one but the Sunshine police took them on, and the only jack they feared was a legendary local copper whom I will call Sergeant

Red. Red was 191 cm (6'3") and could bench-press 180 kilos (400 pounds). If he spotted under-age drinkers in 'his' pub he would grab them by the throat and suspend them with one meaty hand until back-up arrived. Red wasn't going to leave the pub for these junior shitheads. In his grasp, a little guy like Benji looked like live bait wriggling on a hook.

Dino thought he could take Red and continually cursed him out, challenging him to take off his badge and gun for a punch-on, fair and square. One day as Red was hauling him into the station on some minor matter, he decided he'd had enough of Dino's cheek. He stopped and released his grip on the seventeen-year-old boy. 'Righto, then. Fuck laying the charges – I'm going to lay some fucking knuckles on you, son. C'mon then,' said Red, taking off his side-arm and police hat. It was broad daylight in the main street of Sunshine and there were numerous witnesses, but Red stepped up to Dino and ripped off his gold chain. No one fucked with Dino's bling. He gave a good account of himself, but Red gave him a memorable thrashing. But even Red couldn't hack Sunshine forever. He left the force after some hoons blew up his car and promised it would be him next.

Sunshine police tried to beat the dash out of PK's crew early but they failed. Still, the jacks were not without a sense of humour. Once Johnny and Dino were busted with a few grams of dope while driving around in a car with a stolen engine and interior. The holding cells in Sunshine had a view of the car park, and two or three of the officers sat in the hot Commodore smoking Dino's pot through one of his bongs. 'It's pretty shit, Dino. You got ripped off, mate,' they taunted him. They never charged him for the dope.

Crime was an adventure, and getting caught was part of the fun. As minors, the boys could rack up lots of blues before they would ever be locked up. This 'play now, pay later' plan seemed a great deal for all the money they were making. They didn't care about the enemies they were making. As long as no one lagged them to the jacks, they could do pretty much what they wanted.

It started off small, like a running battle with a local service-station owner and his crew of Croatians. In one episode, Johnny, then aged seventeen, marched up to the counter cocking a left hook at Tony the servo owner only to find a six-inch blade sticking out of his hand. He and Benji flogged the guy properly, smashing him over the head with slabs of Coke cans. Meanwhile, customers were lining up to pay for their petrol. Benji waved them away, laughing: 'Hey, people, today's your lucky day. We're having a knockdown sale – nothing to pay today! Take as much as you want!' When the guy's wife wouldn't stop screaming, she copped a broken jaw though she was seven months pregnant.

There were moments of pure slapstick. One day Johnny and Benji were told to pick up a car from outside a house in Sunshine using a stolen spare key. When they tried the key, they realised that the car had a hidden kill switch and their key was useless. Rather than abandon the job and the $2000 they had been promised, they decided to push the vehicle home. A driver slowed down to ask if they needed help. 'No worries,' said Benji. 'We just ran out of petrol. Everything's cool, mate.' Unfortunately the helpful driver recognised his friend's stolen car, and soon a dozen men with machetes and baseball bats were giving chase. Johnny and Benji outran them, only to be identified from fingerprints they had left on the boot of the car. It was marginally better to get caught by police than by your rivals.

'I was taught one thing very early,' said Johnny. 'The jacks can hurt you, but they can't kill you. Your mates can kill you.'

The double garage attached to the standard villain's home in Sunshine made a perfect venue for torture. The favoured method was to suspend the prisoner by handcuffs from the top rail of the roller door. From there one could tenderise him at leisure with a baseball bat as he swung like a helpless piñata.

It was all stuff they had learned inside the Sunshine police station. The jacks would handcuff the boys to the old gas heaters concreted into the walls and go to work on them. Early on, they would be forced to slip a Yellow Pages directory up their T-shirts while the officers practised their baton work, confident that all the bruising would be internal. The jacks needn't have worried – the boys would always cop it sweet. Later, when the rules of engagement were established, the phone books were put aside and replaced by a flurry of kicks and elbows and baton charges.

Stupidity was no excuse for lagging a mate, as Dino later found out. Showing off was a much greater threat to the enterprise. Indeed, it could be said that one moment of redlighting set off a chain of events that led to the deaths of PK and Dino, not to mention a string of bashings and torture that went on for nearly eight years.

One night in 1994, Benji and Dino were cruising around Port Melbourne looking for a VN Holden Calais to fill an order. Rebirthing was an easy earner: you bought a wreck from an auction, then located another vehicle of the same make and model to steal and chop up for parts, and soon the wreck would be miraculously reborn. The Calais was an easy $1500 for the lads. It wasn't till they got it home that they realised they had stolen a jack's private car and there was an added bonus in the boot – a laptop computer containing a disk with the names and addresses of a number of Victoria Police's best informers and the home addresses of many jacks besides. There was information on just about all the dogs in Melbourne – and some brain-dead copper had left it in the boot of his car.

This was a valuable prize in the right hands. Johnny suggested that the Carlton Crew might pay $100 000 or more for this sort of intelligence, but Benji had other ideas. Rather than deliver the car, they decided it would be more fun to burn it, which they duly did, but not before enjoying a little live theatre. Using information from the stolen laptop, the next day Benji and Dino drove slowly past the home of one of their least favourite jacks with techno music blaring. The officer was out mowing his front lawn, and they slowed right down and gave the royal wave to him and his wife and kids, who were sitting on the verandah.

It didn't take long for the jacks to join the dots. Dino and Benji were hauled in and thrown into a police holding cell. Dino always liked a chat and began to mouth off to a heavily tattooed man with long hair who was sharing the cell with them. Benji kept quiet but Dino was off, and before long he had cheerfully confessed that they had stolen the jack's car. Their cellmate turned out to be a police informer who had been put in the cells to trip up the lads.

When Benji was sentenced to twelve months' jail and fined $2574 but Dino got off with a lot less, it was suspected that Dino had sold Benji out. Under pressure from the police, he had called several people from the jack station, pretending that he was at a payphone. The following day sixteen homes around Sunshine were raided. He and Benji had been equal partners in the exercise, but Dino got off with half the sentence Benji copped. On top of that, the cop's insurance company sued Benji for burning the car. He never paid the $30 000 award against him but the injustice burned in him for nearly two years. He still socialised with Dino, but the cycle of paranoia and revenge had begun. 'Don't worry, Johnny,' Benji would say. 'Every dog has his day, and Dino's is coming. One day I will expose him. Leave it to me.'

One night in March 1996, Benji summoned Johnny to his house to tell him that he was ready to publicly declare Dino a dog. It was time to pop Dino. 'Good,' thought Johnny, then he said, 'Benji, if you declare someone a dog, you have to back it up. If you don't, then *you* are the dog and you will be dealt with.'

Benji assured Johnny that Dino would have the chance to defend himself before any action was taken. Even in the ganglands you had that right. Benji convened what he called a 'kangaroo court' on his back verandah. As he outlined the case against Dino he strutted around like he had seen barristers in real court do. 'I put it to you that you acted like a fucking dog and a rat, and there's nothing to stop you doing it again. You tell me why I shouldn't fucking put a few in you, Dino,' demanded Benji.

Dino pleaded his innocence, and when that didn't work he flew into a rage. 'Who do you think you're fucking dealing with now?'

Dino shouted. 'If you think I'm a fucking nobody now, you're wrong. I'm a somebody now, and everybody knows it.' He proceeded to claim that he was as powerful as Carlton boss Alphonse Gangitano – an extraordinary boast for a guy barely past twenty. 'And anyway, Al's just a fucking dog and a rat. He pays the jacks so they leave him alone. And you wanna be his mate, Benji. What does that say about you?' he raged.

Benji would soon be sweet with the Carlton Crew, and Dino was going to fuck it all up for him. Already he had been making a fool of himself around the senior heavies of Carlton, seeking them out at their favourite bars, hassling them to share big lines of his coke and bragging about his exploits in Sunshine. More dangerously, he had taken a shine to some of the women who orbited Gangitano and the boys. One night he had pulled a wad of nearly $20 000 from his pants and waved it in their faces, saying, 'I can buy every one of your bitches with this, and there's plenty more where this comes from – trust me.'

On the coke, Dino behaved like he had a big red light on his head. If he was refused entry to a nightclub he would pull out a gun and threaten the bouncers, promising he would put a contract on them. Off the coke, he was the lovable old Dino who Johnny had known since they were ten. He wasn't a killer – it wasn't in him. He just liked to talk big. As Dino told one newspaper, 'I've seen *Reservoir Dogs* too many times, mate.'

Johnny told me, 'I would put my life on the fact that Dino was not a killer. He got other people to do his dirty work, but even then he didn't want to kill anyone.'

One night under the influence of coke Dino became obsessed

with the idea that two guys who had been cruising the street near his house all night were in fact preparing to kill him. Rather than step outside with his own gun, Dino summoned another associate to intercept the guys. While Dino sat in his car and looked on, the associate put half a dozen slugs into one of the men. It turned out the two guys didn't even know Dino: perhaps he wasn't as famous as he thought. His mate got nine years' jail for attempted murder.

It's lucky Dino wasn't a man of his word, or half the underworld would have been off by 2000. Most of his rap sheet was taken up with driving offences, a few assaults, nothing impressive. His greatest thrill in life was to lead the jacks on high-speed pursuits. He had a friend with a rental business who was foolhardy enough to let him hire exotic cars such as Lamborghinis and Ferraris. The cars invariably came back with smoking gearboxes and thrashed engines. With a head full of coke, Dino would take to the highway or just throw burn-outs in the car park of the Glengala Hotel for the enjoyment of his associates.

That night in March 1996, Johnny believed they had no choice but to kill Dino. 'Listen, Benj, you just pop him in the leg and he'll build himself up and save every penny to get you knocked. He has to go.'

In 1505 Niccoló Machiavelli wrote in his classic tome of intrigue and diplomacy, *The Prince*, that: 'If an injury has to be done to a man, it should be so severe that his vengeance need not be feared'. It didn't take a scholar to predict what would happen next if Dino were not dealt with. But Benji hadn't yet made up his mind. Dino was already making serious money from his hydroponic dope crops. Later he would finance others such as Rocco Arico and

Mark Mallia into the business, buying them shacks for their crops and arming them with pistols. He was building his own army. It was a huge dilemma and probably the last time Benji thought twice about killing someone.

The next day Dino was again called to Benji's, and the interrogation recommenced – this time over a 9mm. Dino was shocked. He had never imagined his two brothers would set him up like this. In the kangaroo court Johnny vented his frustration on Dino. He had always known that one day this would all come to guns and blood. He'd been prepared to die young, but never thought he would be at war with his childhood mates.

Johnny begged Dino to confess that he had set Benji up, to clear the air, but Dino refused. He protested his innocence, rising to his feet to remonstrate. 'You sit the fuck down and shut your big fucking dog mouth, Dino,' Johnny snarled. He felt his entire body trembling with anger, sweat pouring out of him like it always did at these moments. 'What are you doing, Dino? What's happening here? We should be out taking on other crews and putting holes in them other fuckers, not fighting among ourselves. What's going to happen to our crew if this shit sets in? You tell me, you cocksucker. We could be anything if we stay staunch to each other, anything at all – even the top team in Melbourne. From there we can take on any crew in Australia. But instead we're gonna end up just killing each other.'

It drove Johnny almost crazy that Dino stuck to his story that he hadn't lagged Benji. 'Be it on your head, my friend. Your life is in Benji's hands now.'

Johnny wanted to get the whole thing over with. He was already feeling like he had been dragged into someone else's business. He hadn't signed on for this. 'Fuck this questioning shit, Benji. Either you do something – pop the cunt or get the baseball bat – but you gotta leave him in a pool of his blood or just fucking let him go.'

'Let's go for a drive,' said Benji, tucking his toy into his pants. Johnny grabbed Dino and pushed him out to the car. They sat either side of him in the back seat, toys in hand, as another man drove them along Glengala Road. *This is where it started*, thought Johnny. It had seemed a short journey – from hanging out at Charlie's playing pinball to sitting in the back of this car leaving the Glengala shops behind, driving out of Sunshine to the farms with Dino's life in their hands. The boys were all grown up and still they were playing with their toys.

Dino turned back and forth to Johnny and Benji, the hurt and betrayal shining in his eyes. 'Johnny, wha—? What are you doin', man? We're brothers. How can you do this to me, Benj? I was going to go home to get my toy but then I thought, no, these blokes are family, they wouldn't do this to me, so I left my toy behind. Looks like I shoulda fucking brought it now, doesn't it?' It was like a shiv straight into Johnny's heart. Trust Dino to try to pull that shit. It was true they had been mates since Grade Four, but Dino had done the wrong thing and now he had to pay. That was the code, and if Dino got away with it, where would it end?

Benji was still working out whether he would kill him and Dino didn't seem to realise that his life was hanging by a thread. 'C'mon, Benj, you can't pop me out there in the farms!' cried Dino. 'You know I'm fucked if you leave me out there.'

All this bleating and moaning was taking its toll on Benji. As they reached the city limits, he decided to give Dino a second chance. He knew he would regret it, but Dino's begging had softened Benji's heart for an instant. He turned the car around headed back into town, still not sure what to do with his noisy, maddening hostage. Dino implored Benji to take him into Footscray and shoot him there, but just in the legs. Benji agreed to shoot him across the road from the Western Hospital.

Johnny felt like he was stuck in a gangster comedy movie. 'What sort of bullshit is this, Benj? It's fucking VIP service for this dog,' he said, in favour of a quick and clean execution in the farms.

Dino looked hard at Johnny, but said nothing and turned to Benji again. 'Thanks, Benj, you're a real mate. You know I'll cop it sweet. That will be the end of it. You know I love you, man,' he said, firing another poisonous look at Johnny.

'I hope you know what you're doing, Benj. You do this and you'll be looking over your shoulder for years, mate – trust me,' said Johnny.

When they got to the hospital, Benji and Johnny dragged Dino out of the car and without further ado put two shots into his left leg, breaking it in two places. Dino was sprawled on the verge. 'Just tilt the toy a couple of inches higher,' thought Johnny. 'Just one more into the head, and all the problems will be solved.' But the shots had been heard, and lights were flicking on in the block of apartments behind. Benji pulled Johnny away and into the car.

Dino was resting comfortably in hospital when Johnny and Benji turned up at his bedside a couple of days after the shooting. Benji drew the curtains around the bed and Johnny said, 'Now, Dino, you're gunna cop it sweet, aren't you, bro? You're not gunna lag us again, are you, you fucking dog?' He grabbed Dino's broken leg and gave it a savage twist. Dino cried out so loud a nurse came running. 'Mr Dibra – uh, would you . . . like these people . . . to leave?' she asked, gesturing to Johnny and Benji, who were now innocently arranging the flowers by the bed.

'No, no, not at all. They're my mates. That's fine,' said Dino, wincing, 'but just leave the curtains open, if you wouldn't mind.'

Four days later and hobbling on crutches, Dino was ready for revenge. He and an associate paid a visit to a friend of Johnny's. With his .357 magnum down the poor fellow's neck, Dino suggested that he invite Johnny over for a bong or two the following day. When Johnny turned up, Dino and his mate grabbed him, pistol whipped him to a pulp and threw him in the boot of their car. They drove around for what seemed like ages to Johnny. Thinking hard about the sawn-off shotgun in the front of the car, he made a solemn pact with God. 'Dear God,' he began, holding tight to the crucifix he wore around his neck, 'if Dino is going to pop me, please let me die. Just don't let me lose my legs, please, God.' He had worn the crucifix just as jewellery, but now in the darkness he squeezed it hard. The idea of being a gangster on crutches appalled him. To be maimed would render him useless, and he was a proud soldier.

When Dino opened the boot and dragged him out, Johnny looked around him in utter desolation. They had taken him to a lonely dirt road in the middle of paddocks far from town. At least Benji and Johnny had dumped Dino where he would be found. Johnny could see nothing: no houses, no shops, nothing. Summoning all his courage, he calmly told them to get on with whatever they had come to do. But Dino didn't want to, even though Johnny had done it to him. He was having second thoughts. His mate became impatient: 'Dino, if you're not gunna fuckin' do it, then I'm gunna shoot you, you understand?'

Dino shrugged his shoulders apologetically and blasted Johnny's right leg with his magnum, knocking Johnny on his arse. The other shooter pressed his sawn-off shotgun to Johnny's other leg and pulled the trigger, shredding the limb. Remarkably, the magnum and the shottie didn't break Johnny's legs. Then Dino and his mate had pistol-whipped him soundly, opening up his forehead.

As the car drove away, Johnny shouted after it in impotent fury, continuing to rage and scream until the tail lights disappeared in the distance. Somehow he got to his feet and staggered down the road, propelled only by his anger. His left leg gave way and he fell backwards onto the dirt. He took off his expensive silk shirt and wrapped it around his legs and wondered what to do next. Then it began to rain. Far off on the horizon Johnny could see the grey smudge of the city skyline. He prepared himself to die, wondering why he could feel no pain in his legs.

But fate was not finished with Johnny yet. A few kilometres away a bushfire was steadily burning its way towards the dirt track where he lay. Through the delirium of shock, he heard a siren in the distance. A fire engine that had been dispatched to the mysterious blaze came barrelling over the hill, nearly running Johnny over. The driver stamped on the brakes and slid to a stop, sending a shower of gravel and stones flying at Johnny, as if the shotgun pellets and a .357 magnum in his legs hadn't been enough.

Johnny was a sight. His face was covered in blood and his jaw was grotesquely swollen. 'What's happened, mate?' said the driver.

'I've been fuckin' shot. Call me a fuckin' ambulance, you imbecile!'

'So do you know who did it? It wasn't those two blokes I saw in the HT down the road about fifteen minutes now, was it?'

That would be all he needed – to lag Dino would put a nice gloss on the whole affair. Johnny backs up Benji in a matter he has nothing to do with and ends up becoming the dog of the day. 'No, no, mate. I think it was some Asians. I never saw em before,' said Johnny, realising what a delicate position he was in.

There was no other way in or out of the area, so why hadn't the blokes in the HT stopped to give Johnny a helping hand, the fire-man asked. 'I don't know! Too many fuckin' questions. Just get me an ambulance, will ya? PLEASE!' Johnny roared. 'And make it a chopper, will ya?'

Soon twenty police cars were on the scene. 'Oh, fuck me dead – is that you, Johnny?' said a voice from one of the cars.

'Jesus, if we'd known it was you, we wouldn't even have come,' said another of the jacks. 'Well, well. After what you and your mates have done to us over the years, you finally got something back. How delightful. If you think we're getting the chopper here for you, then fucking think again.' Dino had also told the jacks it was the Asians that had shot him, leading the *Herald Sun* later to describe the tit-for-tat shooting as an underworld power struggle. No one but a few cops put the double shooting together with the police disk.

An hour later, an ambulance dropped Johnny at the Western Hospital, the same place where he and Benji had shot Dino four nights earlier. He woke up from six hours of surgery with 25 per cent of the muscle gone from his left leg. A nurse came to check on him. 'It's such a coincidence,' she said. 'Four days ago another young man was in this very same bed with gunshot wounds in his leg. Imagine that!'

'By any chance, that bloke's name wasn't Dino, was it?'

'Why, I believe it was,' exclaimed the nurse.

'If he comes to visit me, you'll tell me first, won't you?' said Johnny.

Less than a month later Johnny was amazed to learn that Benji had been seen driving around Sunshine with Dino, laughing and smiling as if nothing had happened. Johnny was furious. 'So what was all that about then?' he demanded of Benji. 'You call the bloke a dog and we shoot him, then he comes and fucking shoots me, and then you're mates with him again two seconds later. Benj, what was the purpose?'

'Fuck off, Johnny. I wanted to make an example of him,' said Benji defensively. 'Now it's over.'

But it wasn't. Just as Johnny had predicted, there was talk around Sunshine that Dino had bigger plans for his revenge against Benji. When the time was right he would pay someone to knock him. In the meantime, Dino would carry on as if nothing had happened.

This was common in Sunshine. Dino was always feuding with people but still maintained functional relationships with them. His cousin 'Rezza' was a case in point. Rezza was a notorious junkie who was forever ripping Dino off to feed his habit. Dino would hear that Rezza was dropping his name in nightclubs, threatening people that he would get his 'bro Dino to put one in ya'. On more than one occasion, Dino had given Rezza a severe beating for his thieving, but he was still prepared to give him credit on dope and coke. He even paid Rezza to drive him around like a chauffeur. The only problem was that whenever Rezza saw a cop car, he had a tendency of jumping out of the car and running away, leaving Dino sitting in the back.

One day Rezza came to Dino saying he had a bloke who wanted a pound of dope. 'And if he likes it, Dino, he reckons he'll take ten pounds. But he wants the dope first.'

Dino was immediately sceptical, but a bloke who buys in pounds is not someone you dismiss lightly, and besides, he always knew where to find Rezza. He laid a hand on his cousin's shoulder, squeezing ever so slightly, and said quietly, 'Now, Rezza, I'll give you the dope, but you know what's going to happen if you dick me, orright?'

'Yeah, yeah, sure, Dino. I'm not gunna dick ya, mate. You're family, mate. I'll be right back with the money, you'll see.'

A week later Rezza and the money were nowhere to be seen. Dino wasn't too concerned: Rezza always turned up eventually. Then a letter came in the mail, postmarked Surfers Paradise, Queensland. Inside was a photograph of Rezza sitting on a banana lounge under a palm tree at a beach resort. He was snuggled between two buxom girls in bikinis, pulling on a bong and giving the thumbs-up sign to camera. On the back he had written, 'Thanks for the money, Dino. Having a grouse time up here. See you some time, but not very soon', or words to that effect.

This was going too far. Dino showed Benji the photograph and immediately a sly smile broke out on Benji's face. 'Dino, I know where that place is, mate. I recognise it. I know where the little cunt is.' They set off to drive to the Gold Coast. It was a nice chance to get out of Melbourne.

When they caught up with Rezza at the hotel, he was thunderstruck. 'Why didn't you invite us on your holiday, Rezza?' asked Dino. 'That's not very nice of you, considering it's my money that's paying for all this, is it now?'

They tied him up and bundled him into the boot of their car and set off for home almost immediately. Occasionally they stopped at a drive-through and fed Rezza a burger and fries through the back seat, which folded down. It was a jolly holiday until Benji noticed smoke coming out of the front of the car. When Dino got the bonnet open, the engine was in flames. Always a quick thinker, he remembered that his father kept a jerry can of what he was sure was water in the boot. Pushing Rezza aside, Dino grabbed the jerry and then splashed it on the flames. The can was actually full of petrol, and Dino was now on fire – or, more correctly, his very expensive, highly synthetic trackie pants were searing his newly waxed legs.

History does not relate why all three were not incinerated at that moment. It might have saved everyone a lot of pain and suffering. When they managed to put Dino and the engine out, it was looking bleak for Rezza. 'Rezza, you cocksucker, when we get you home you are going to pay for this,' said Dino, wincing as he peeled sizzling flaps of tracksuit off his thighs.

They gave it to Rezza for nearly three days in a Sunshine garage. He shat himself so they dragged him into the bathroom and hung him up in the shower by a dog collar. He was ordered to clean himself up so they could play another round of 'doctors' on him without getting their hands dirty. Finally they got bored and decided to go to the casino. On their way out they lobbed Rezza into the dog's kennel, bound, gagged and wearing nothing but the collar. Someone dropped by the next morning and, hearing whimpering sounds from the kennel, found him. The pit bull, perhaps confused as to why Rezza was wearing his collar, had spared him.

A couple of months later Rezza turned up again as Dino's driver, minus a few more teeth. Maybe the photo with the bikini girls was worth it. You be the judge.

By 2000, Johnny was still very much at war with Dino. He hadn't spoken to him in nearly three years, unless you counted the occasional encounter at a nightclub where he would challenge Dino to a punch-on but Dino would refuse to come outside. Instead he would just mouth death and destruction, talking about how he was going to kill Johnny's family one by one. There had been a mediation, at which each was represented by two very influential players from opposite sides of the community. If Johnny and Dino had gone back to fighting after that, it would have been terribly embarrassing for their patrons – neither patron wanted to step on the other's toes. So Dino and Johnny stuck clear of each other.

Then one day Dino asked Benji to choose: 'I don't want you seeing Johnny no more. I know you're seeing him here and there, doin' this, that, behind my back. It's gunna stop, you understand? I don't want to hear Johnny's name no more.'

Benji was incredulous. 'Listen here, you fucking dog. You don't tell me what I do, where I go and who I fuck, do you? I want you to know, just for your information, that I'm in different hotels every night with Johnny, having fun with girls and mates, and we're all laughing at you, you fucking idiot. How long is it now that you've been saying you were about to kill Johnny, eh? How long, buddy? And here he is still walking around, still going up and down Sunshine, and what are you doing about it? All you do is talk, buddy. So what the fuck is going on?'

Dino was lost for words. Benji had a point. 'Wait till you have an enemy who is actually not your friend – what will you do then?' asked Benji.

One spring evening in October 2000 Dino was leaving a friend's place, a shack in West Sunshine with a sofa and a fridge. He had been to a barbecue with his family in the afternoon and had popped in to regroup with his crew before going out for a night on the town. At 9.15 p.m., he was the first to leave. As he strode over to his rented Fairlane parked out the front, a car screeched to a halt alongside. Three men in balaclavas jumped out and opened fire on Dino. In the first volley he took at least five shots in the upper body and sank to his knees in the driveway, but the shooters continued to blaze away, one even going back to their vehicle to reload. No one else was hit, and there was no need to get an ambulance as Dino had been shot more than a dozen times and was clearly done for. Eyewitnesses thought they heard one of the shooters speak with a Russian accent. Strangely, when the bystanders tried to take shelter in the house during the shooting, they couldn't open the door. When they forced it open they found that Rezza had been bracing his legs against it to keep it shut. One of the witnesses remembered Rezza earlier taking a call in which he had overheard him clearly saying, 'He's here' and 'There's five of them'.

Carl Williams was one of the first to call Dino's parents, about half an hour later. Ramiz and Violetta Dibra had been cleaning Carl and Roberta's place in Taylors Lakes for the past year and they got on well. But tonight there were no pleasantries. Carl asked whether it was true that Dino had been shot outside their home that night. No, they were at home themselves and had just left Dino two hours before. Surely Carl was joking, said Ramiz.

'Uh-huh. So it must be lies then,' said Carl, hanging up abruptly. It took the Dibras nearly four hours to learn that their son had died that night.

The rumours soon started flying around Sunshine. A few days after the murder Johnny heard that people were saying that he, Benji and PK were the men in the balaclavas: they were being framed with the murder of their oldest friend. PK was outraged and made it known that he would deal with whoever was spreading this vile accusation. The name he came up with was Rezza. They found him over in another shack having a cone or two with mates. The rest of them dropped their bongs and fled as PK and Johnny burst into the place armed to the teeth. Rezza tried to flee too but Johnny grabbed a handful of his hair and upended him. He was surprised when a great clump of Rezza's forelock came out in his hand.

'Shit, PK, I think I've fuckin' scalped Rezza,' said Johnny, dropping the bloody clump onto the carpet.

'And now it's time to gut the cocksucker,' hissed PK, the veins in his head throbbing so hard it made him feel a little faint.

It was a short interrogation and conviction. Everyone had fingered Rezza as the source. PK plunged his hunting knife so far into Rezza's backside that it collided with bone. Again and again PK plunged the knife in and twisted it with all his strength, trying to drive it in up to the hilt, but it lodged fast against the bone. It was bent like an S when he pulled it out.

Johnny tried to get PK out of there. There was no mileage in knocking Rezza. Killing Dino's cousin to prove they hadn't killed Dino made absolutely no sense, Johnny said. But PK was intent on extracting a confession.

Johnny finally managed to calm PK down, but the battering only heightened the rumours that they'd killed Dino. Now there was word that every local Mafia team was after them. Dino had made a thousand fast friends across town, and three separate groups – the Albanians, the Russians and some miscellaneous Italians – had issued contracts.

It was nothing that PK hadn't seen coming. One afternoon in his backyard a year before he had told his mates they were all marked for death. The only unknown was which of them would cop it first. 'We've done so many bad things to so many bad people that something is bound to come back to us sooner or later,' he'd told them solemnly. They had all passed the point of no return. Perhaps PK already knew that their enemies were standing among them.

Within four years all but one man at PK's house that day would be dead, all of them murdered by people they'd known and trusted.

As the paranoia levels began to rise in the late 1990s, it was standard for the lads to go around tooled up 24/7. Benji had four or five 9mm toys stooked around his house and in the garden, so he was never more than five metres from one if he needed it. There are probably a couple still stashed in that garden today, wrapped up in rags and plastic bags, oiled up and loaded ready to go. PK generally liked to deal with his enemies with fists and feet, but if they still wanted to rumble in his jungle, he had a choice of two 9mm toys always fully loaded and ready to rock. His favourite was a gold-plated 9mm just like the one he had seen in the hands of Samuel L. Jackson's bible-quoting hit man in *Pulp Fiction*.

Benji was a 9mm man, too. He had field-tested one in his back-yard and been pleased that the rounds could go right through two and a half Yellow Pages telephone books, no problem. The only drawback with the 9mm was that it could go to pieces when used to pistol-whip someone, or it might jam the next time you went to fire it. A .357 magnum or a .38 was a better all-round weapon, but cannons like that were a little too bulky to wear under casual clothes. You didn't want others knowing you were tooled up until you were ready to use it, and besides, it could spoil the line of your clothes. The boys liked their clothes: tight-fitting Bonds T-shirts that showed off their physiques, tailored jackets and trousers, and 400 grams of solid-gold chain around the neck to finish it off. A line or three of coke and they were ready for anything.

The clubs around Sunshine – the old Hot Gossip or Bombay Rock – were their favourite haunts. The heavy bass-laden gangsta rap, full of hate and easy money, seemed like a soundtrack to their lives. They walked in for free, and any bouncer who tried to challenge them quickly got bounced himself. Not that Benji wanted to go – he would wait to be chopped out with a willing female at a hotel later on.

If, police sources suggested, Carl Williams was an up-and-coming force in the drug scene of Melbourne's western suburbs at the time, he had to have been friendly with PK or it's unlikely he would be walking today. A couple of dozen dealers of various commodities – from methylamphetamine to ecstasy and coke – paid PK a cut of their turnover, or they didn't do business in Sunshine. It was not unusual for him to pick up $100 000 in a day's dealing while never leaving his fortified home in West Sunshine. He was no redlighter. He kept it all low key: no Porsches or BMWs for PK. His pride and joy was a bone-coloured '79 Kingswood with matching velour interior and Statesman wheels and trim. Benji might have had a $130 000 Boxster and then a BMW 330i with 'ALLHOT' plates, but PK had the Kingswood, with 'CORUPT' on the plates. It was his one concession to his growing fame in Sunshine.

In this crew you were judged on two things: how staunch you were and whether you chopped out your mates. PK had chopped out more than any of them. He once put his life on the line over a $50 foil of speed. A rival dealer, Mark Walker, had ripped off a mate of PK's with speed that had been jumped on (cut) so much it was useless, then dissed PK on the telephone when he'd tried to sort it. It wasn't PK's fight, but the slur could not go unaddressed. Walker and PK arranged to meet at a lonely bush location. PK came without his toy, fully intending to punch on with Walker. When he flogged him like he did everyone else, Walker pulled out his own toy but hadn't the heart to kill PK. It was a huge mistake to pull a toy and then not have the dash to use it. PK wrestled it from him and put two slugs in the back of his head. He got eighteen years' jail, but on appeal the sentence was reduced to four despite the fact that he had dispatched Walker on his knees, like an executioner. Using Walker's gun made it self-defence.

In jail, enemies tried to test PK out and he overcame them with a vengeance. One day in the Pentridge mess hall three rivals set him up. One distracted him as he was eating, while the other two crept up behind him with a pillow case full of cans of Coke. They put him in the prison hospital, but it was only a temporary victory. When he got out, he caught up with them and delivered his revenge. The story goes that after two of the men were left paralysed, the other lost his taste for the fight.

The stories of PK's dash spread far and wide and when he got out of prison in 1999 his reputation was unassailable. Benji was at the gates of Pentridge to pick him up when he got out. He gave PK a Nissan 300ZX and set him up with some cash and all the necessary gear for a hydroponic crop of dope. Within three months, PK had $40 000 and was on his way again.

It was common knowledge in Sunshine that PK's mate, the man he had gone to the wall for, had cracked under interrogation by the jacks and lagged PK for Walker's killing. The kid's mother came to PK and begged for her son's life and PK was gracious enough to spare him. He gave the fool twenty-four hours to get out of Sunshine or face the consequences, and he wisely agreed. He didn't return till after PK was dead and gone.

For more than a decade they had lived like kings, but now, after Dino's death, there was a new edge to things. Johnny and PK were doing exactly as they pleased, never paying for anything, walking into every club and battering anybody who looked sideways at them. There was something extraordinarily exciting about torturing a man, tying him up and beating him with a baseball bat and then interrogating him, then beating him some more. It was even better if you ran through a guy's house and took him down right there, on his own turf. To hear a hated foe squealing and whimpering for mercy was better than sex, and these lads loved sex nearly as much. Very nice middle-class girls were more than happy to accommodate them. It was hard and rough, frequently punctuated by violence and degradation, but no matter how rough it got, the girls always came back for more. The boys would taunt them, making them scream out that their nerdy squarehead boyfriends could never fuck them like that. The team produced some of the best amateur porn videos ever to hit Sunshine. They had more money than they could spend, and they definitely tried hard to spend it. They could chop out girls and drugs for their mates in the best hotels in town every night of the year, and still there was cash to stash in stooks all over Sunshine.

But the paranoia was rising in PK. He was doing $400 a week of HGH (human growth hormone), courtesy of a crooked chemist who would dole out the stuff for a hundred bucks a script. HGH and a lot of coke on the side made PK tetchy and paranoid, especially when he couldn't satisfy the ravenous appetite for food that the HGH gave him. Associates were well advised to head for the nearest drive-through when the poisonous rage and hunger began to rise in him. One day some punk was stupid enough to stick his fingers up at PK as he drove past. PK stopped and chased the guy down, then dragged him back to the car, wrapped his head in the seat belt and gave him a flogging he would never forget.

Somewhere along the way Johnny lost his heart and found his everlasting soul. In late 2001, the deep, horny thrill he got from crime and mayhem was ebbing, evaporating even. His dash was gone. As he drove around Sunshine in Benji's Beemer on their way to do someone over – maybe some fool who hadn't paid his debts – he actually felt sorry for the intended victim. He thought about Dino and the rest of them who had bought it. And for what? They had sought to rule the world and ended up whacking each other. *Tony Montana would have been proud of us, you bunch of dumb fucks*, he thought. He had forgotten who he was supposed to be in the scene, though he certainly looked the part at 188 cm (6'2") and rippling with lean, cruel muscle. He had recovered quite well from Dino's kneecapping and had just the slightest trace of a limp. *Thanks, Dino*, he thought. *Any lower and I never would have been able to run again.* Dino had been very considerate, really.

As Johnny explored this new sympathy he was feeling, a deep remorse enveloped him. When torturing a guy, he had used to hear a little voice just behind his ear, saying, *Give it to him some more. Go on – the dog fucking deserves it. He hasn't had enough!* Now a new voice was nagging at him, but from deep inside his head. He tried to ignore it – maybe it was just a side effect of the crack that was still open in his forehead – but it kept nagging, telling him there was still time to change his ways. This was a dangerous thing for Johnny – he knew that if anyone saw the pity in his eyes for the people he was standing over, pretty soon someone would be standing over *him*. People were so scared of Johnny and Benji that they didn't have to carry out much actual violence any more. If they got involved in a blue in a nightclub or on the street, the story would get back to Sunshine by the morning, embellished and exaggerated. In the past Johnny hadn't worried about this – it was good for people to be scared – but now he was the one getting scared. He had to get out, get away, so he could understand what the new voice was saying to him.

Little by little Johnny realised that the voice was God, and He was telling him that he could indeed be saved. He found a pastor and began to pray, and the more he prayed the better he felt, as if a weight was being lifted. Johnny had always assumed that he would follow Dino and the others into the cemetery, but now another path was opening up. He resolved to keep the messages from heaven to himself, at least until he could sort out whether he'd been touched by God or was just going crazy. He decided to come straight out and tell PK that he had had enough of this life and was leaving the crew. Johnny's mother had fallen ill with severe diabetes and already he was alternating between being a gangster and caring for her. The contradictions in his life were doing his head in. PK took it well on the surface, but Johnny knew this was never a clue to his true feelings. He had seen PK forgive an enemy and then, five minutes later, plot his demise.

Some people around Sunshine said Johnny was leaving his mates in the lurch – after all they had done for him. It was time for him to get out of Sunshine before the paranoia took over and someone shot him for fear that he had turned informer. So he drove to Adelaide and spent the next three months hiding out.

From relatives, Johnny heard that PK had offered a bounty of $10000 for anyone who could tell him where Johnny had gone. PK made it clear that he didn't want to hurt Johnny, just that he needed to know that he wasn't going to sell him out. Johnny knew that PK would find him eventually, so one night he drove back to Melbourne and knocked on the door of PK's shack, which was in a location known only to him and Benji.

PK answered the door packing his two 9mm pistols. 'Johnny, where you been, man? I've been worried about you,' he said, lowering the pistols and motioning Johnny inside. 'I've heard stories about you, man. Now you better tell me what's going on with this religion shit, mate. You can't just leave the underworld like that, just leavin' us in the lurch, you know what I mean? And all over a book, Johnny, all over a book.' He put the two 9mms on the table and offered Johnny some tea, which he prepared as he listened to Johnny's story.

Johnny could see the hurt shining in PK's eyes as he tried to tell him it was more than a book – the Bible would lead them out of the wilderness of the underworld; it wasn't too late. PK shook his head sadly, but said that whatever Johnny chose in life he would support, and anyone who said Johnny had run out on them would answer to him. As PK swore violence and death upon any who criticised Johnny, the tears welling up in his eyes, it occurred to Johnny that even a man without mercy or conscience could feel alone and vulnerable. Even PK needed his mates to survive, and they were now thin on the ground.

Then the subject was dropped abruptly. 'You know, I've got this new drug, mate. It's pure MDMA,' PK said, looking hard at Johnny. 'It's like the stuff Hitler's SS blokes used to give their prisoners to make 'em tell the truth. Truth serum – the most powerful one in the world.'

He kept talking and talking about the MDMA, making Johnny irritable. What did this have to do with him?

Then the room started spinning and pulsing, and Johnny began shaking as if he was in an earthquake. 'PK, the tea – you fucking drugged it, didn't you, you bastard!' he said. He hadn't touched drugs for months and PK had given him enough to knock a horse.

'Sure, mate,' PK said. 'I just needed to find out the truth, Johnny. Are you hanging out with somebody else or are you really in the arms of the Lord? You had better tell me, because if I find out later, you know what's going to happen, don't you, Johnny?'

The interrogation lasted several hours, until Johnny's paranoia and hallucinations had receded enough to let him get off the couch. PK was satisfied that he was still staunch, even though he still couldn't believe that Johnny would turn his back on all the things they had created.

PK's words – *And all for a book, mate* – rang in Johnny's head. He began giving his testimony in church, speaking about his life of crime with Benji and PK while the congregation listened in rapt amazement. His pastor gave him a tape purportedly made by a reformed US wise guy named Tom Papania, telling the story of how he'd got to the top of the Gambino crime family. (Later I discovered that some people regard Papania's claims sceptically and believe that he was no more than a petty crim. Perhaps Johnny is more authentic than his spiritual mentor.)

Three weeks before PK died in October 2002, Johnny went to warn him that he had seen his death in a vision. Dino had been murdered almost two years earlier to the day and now it was PK's turn, Johnny told him.

'Take off, Paulie. Get away,' Johnny pleaded. 'Bro, you've always wanted to go and live in Cairns where you can fish all day on the Great Barrier Reef. You've got two kids, mate. They're growing up now. Mate, you can raise 'em in the tropical sunshine, under the palm trees, bro . . . not here in fuckin' Scumshine. This is your chance, mate. Take it and make tracks. This is not your destiny.'

But PK was determined to deal with the threats one by one or go out with his 9mms blazing. The bleak plains of Sunshine had become his prison.

By now the threats, both real and imagined, were coming thick and fast. There were only two or three people who were allowed into PK's house through the cameras and the triple-locked door and the security screen. One of them was Benji. When PK's sister-in-law and brother went to his house that October morning they found the fortress had been left unlocked. In the bedroom PK was sitting on the floor with his back against the bed. It was only when they got close that they noticed the two neat entry wounds in the right side of his head. Less than a metre from where he sat, police found a fully loaded 9mm pistol tucked into the mattress.

Police say PK didn't forget his mates, even if one of them had betrayed him and probably murdered him. An old assault case came to court after his death: several members of the team had battered some poor soul after a nightclub row over a girl. Police said they had flogged him and run him over in a four-wheel drive, leaving him paralysed and barely alive. It came to light that the late Paul Kallipolitis had taken the rap for everyone. In death, PK was still chopping out for his mates.

After PK's death, Johnny thought back to that night in 1994 when

Dino and Benji had made their fateful decision. If they had sold the cop disk and delivered the Calais, how different things would have turned out. Dino and PK would probably be alive, and he wouldn't have this limp from the gunshot wounds Dino had inflicted.

Ever since Dino's murder, Benji had been saying about once a week that they were terminal, even making a joke of it. One day in the summer of 2001, he and Johnny had been cruising along through Sunshine when suddenly Benji pulled a face as if he had smelled something horrible. 'What's that fuckin' smell, Johnny?' he said.

'I don't smell nothin', Benj,' replied Johnny.

'There's sumthin' off in this car, Johnny,' said Benji. 'Sumthin' smells real bad, like it's past its use-by date.'

Johnny was getting irritated now, trying to smell what Benji was talking about. Then Benji said, howling with laughter, 'It's you, Johnny! You're off, you've passed your use-by date, you're a dead man walking!'

Sometimes Benji could make a bloke so mad he wanted to strangle him, but Johnny had to admit he had a point this time. In that year after Dino died, Johnny had expected a bullet at any time. The suspicion alone that PK, Benji and Johnny had been Dino's killers had sparked all this off. There were people using Dino's death to set friends against one another, and maybe that had led to PK's death.

Some time after PK copped it, Johnny asked Benji why he hadn't gone out to avenge his friend's death. Benji couldn't answer. That sort of awkward question was hanging in the air all over Sunshine. Gossip and rumour were masquerading as fact.

Of all the suspects in Dino's murder, Johnny had been the only one to survive. One day as we sat in a cafe I looked him hard in the eyes and asked him straight out: 'Johnny, don't take offence, but I feel I have to ask you this. Did you kill Dino?'

Looking hard back at me, he said, 'It's like I told the jacks – I was home that night with the missus. We got some videos and some Scotch and we stayed home all night. I can even tell you what we watched. My conscience is clear. My alibi checks out, mate.'

'I'm not talking about alibis, Johnny,' I said, emboldened by a second coffee and nimming furiously under the table. 'I'm asking what actually happened to Dino. Because if you did, then it makes a lie of all the stuff you told me about Jesus and your journey out of the underworld. It just destroys everything. I need to know whether there's anything else you want to tell me.' Benji and PK had always suspected that Johnny's faith was a sham, that he had fooled all the pastors and the jacks and they had swallowed it like every other rort the crew had pulled. And now here I was doing the same thing.

Johnny paused. He looked down and around the cafe. Just for a moment it was like he was back inside Sunshine jack station, preparing to supply Sergeant Red with his address and date of birth. Then he fixed me with his dark eyes. 'That doesn't change anything, mate,' he said softly. 'I know what I have done and what I haven't done. I can tell you that I didn't kill Dino, but at the end of the day God sees everything.'

And what a story He could tell, I thought.

11 | STAYING STAUNCH

It was 10.15 a.m., early February 2004, and I was running for the County Court in Melbourne. I was late and had forgotten to book a camera crew for today's star appearance.

I got there only to find there was no media scrum, no gangsters – nothing. Perhaps I was at the wrong court, I thought. I sat in the corridor outside Court 12 to ring the news desk. I was at the right place, the news editor told me, but the pack had apparently descended on the Supreme Court across the street for an appearance by the Raptor on the Mick Marshall hit.

Carl Williams and his team – Dad, Mum, Roberta, their three-year-old daughter Dhakota, and at least two others – ritually showed up for the Raptor's court appearances. These occasions became 2004's most familiar media events. Carl would make the walk of shame through the cameras, smirking to his companions, occasionally leering crudely at the female reporters he fancied, but always refusing to answer questions. Still they would stick microphones in his face and fire away, 'How's it going, Carl? How's the family holding up?' trying the friendly approach, or, less prosaically, 'Did you kill Jason? Do you think you are going to be next?'

Nothing raised a flicker in Carl: he just kept sauntering along the footpath, a dull glint in his eye.

This day, though, instead of supporting the Raptor, Carl and Roberta had business at the County Court – a hearing on their drugs charges. Such was my panic to get Carl to say something in my television story that I had planned to bring my own film crew that day, even if it was only to get a polite brush-off. I had just discovered that the ABC's *Four Corners* had jagged a few comments from him months earlier and a producer with a camera crew had later wangled her way into his daughter's christening. In desperation I planned to ambush Carl on his way into court.

I sat there in a deepening funk, wondering again what this whole exercise was for. Then I noticed the stocky little man in the baseball cap seated at the other end of the bench, doing his best to avoid eye contact with me. Andrew Veniamin could tell right off that I was a reporter, having heard my call to the news desk and seen my fumbling of notebooks and my cheap suit. He threw me a withering look of disdain, but wasn't about to forfeit his seat because of one reporter. He was just kicking back as if he was at the mall, shooting glances at the pretty young solicitors pushing their trolleys of briefs in and out of the courts. We were waiting for the same man, but for different reasons. I was doing my best to get an interview with Melbourne's newest gangland celebrity, while Veniamin was waiting for his friend Carl Williams.

Such was his own public profile now, Benji's name struck fear into the hearts of young children and mobsters alike. Here, sitting on a bench in a corridor outside court, he looked anything but Melbourne's most prolific hit man. He was small and lively, no more than 168 cm (5'6"), with dark, impenetrable brown eyes that darted away from inquiring gazes. It was only his strong, thick hands that betrayed the cruelty of which he was reputedly capable. He had full, generous lips, and a broken nose from the many fights he could never walk from. A training jacket and tight-fitting T-shirt concealed the tattoos that covered his arms like sleeves.

I introduced myself and he reluctantly extended his hand. For all the power in the grip, the hand was baby smooth. 'So where's the summer gone?' I asked him, gesturing to the steel-grey skies outside.

'Yeah, it's just a memory now, mate,' he said softly. We talked of his holiday with Carl and the family on the Gold Coast. It had been nice to get away from the madness in Melbourne for a while, he said.

'But now it's all back on again,' I said.

'Well, what can you do?' he said with a cheeky smile, as if discussing forces of nature far beyond his control. 'It's like a movie. We just don't know how it ends yet.'

Carl and Roberta swept out of court, lawyers in tow and deep in conversation. Benji and I followed a step behind. For once there was no media phalanx waiting for the Williams team outside. Perhaps Carl and Roberta were disappointed, having anticipated another chance to parade their defiance for the cameras. The entire family stood around chatting for a full half-hour, waiting for nothing in particular.

This meeting with me was as close as Benji would ever come to a media interview. He thanked me for clearing up the question of his supposed employment with Carl. Smiling and laughing, he denied he was a bodyguard. Yes, he was a gunnie all right, but the idea of being hired muscle for Carl was demeaning. He'd always been a player in his own right – a force to be reckoned with. 'Look at me – I'm small. I couldn't hurt anybody.' He puffed out his barrel chest comically and pointed at Carl. 'Look at him. This big fella's about 120 kilos. What am I going to do?' he chortled, slapping Williams on the back.

I had one chance, so I put it on him hard for an interview. I asked him if he had the courage to come on television to deny he was a killer, to tell his story. That started Carl laughing, and he came over and pushed Benji playfully. 'Yeah – what sorta body-guard are you anyway, little bloke like you? Yeah, you go on telly and tell everyone about our holidays, won'tcha? You gotta get a bit of ex-x-x-xposure, buddy.'

Benji was on the spot now and he stuck his hands deep in his jean pockets. I was losing him quickly even as he was working out a time and venue for an interview. Carl had lost interest in the joke and was playing with his daughter. Benji looked away at the traffic and the flirty secretaries in their white shoes out for a smoke. He was polite and smiling as he let me down: he would call me back, or maybe Roberta would.

My pitch was dead. There was nothing to lose, so rather than thank him in advance for the call that would never come, I just looked him in the eye and said, 'Yeah, thanks for that – but no, really, do you have the courage to come on television and talk about this stuff?'

Just for a moment the smile left his face. 'Of course I have the courage,' he said coldly, his lips tightening. To press on would have been to invite offence.

Benji and Carl's relationship had moved to a new plane since their trip to Queensland two months earlier. Given the events of the past three years, Benji had never expected to be alive now. Despite his bravado, the tension was taking its toll. The Fight Doc had diagnosed stress-related stomach ulcers and pancreatitis, and Benji frequently couldn't sleep without tranquillisers. At age twenty-nine, his health was so dodgy that the doc had signed off on the form that allowed him to draw a disability pension.

Despite this, he had a look of rude good health. In the last couple of years he had put on eight kilos through a legitimate therapy routine of human growth hormone and a five-kilometre daily run. The Fight Doc had actually rebuilt 10 per cent of the muscle and bone Benji had lost in a motorbike accident on Glengala Road in 1998. The doc couldn't do much about the big scar on Benji's hairline, sustained in 1999 when, not wearing a seatbelt, he had crashed through the windscreen of the car he was driving. Even on a disability pension, Benji was indestructible.

It had been a busy period of killing and plotting, and staying ahead of the plods from Purana, so to be holidaying in luxury with most of their enemies dead had made him and Carl feel euphoric.

And now that Jason Moran was dead, Carl could even begin to trust Benji again. With the Moran brothers and the Munster gone, the list of employers for Benji's freelance killing services was now short. Lewis Moran was too cheap; only Mick Gatto and Mario Condello remained and they no longer trusted Benji after the murder of the Munster. The Raptor and Goggles were both in custody for the Marshall hit, so Benji was now number one with Carl. But George Williams never trusted him: he believed Benji was there to kill his son.

In Surfers Paradise, they got drunk together at lunch – not that it took much alcohol to get Benji rocking. He was not a drinker, and keeping up with Carl nearly laid him out. He put his napkin on his head and sang at the top of his lungs until the party was forced to leave the restaurant. Out on the strip, Benji took off his T-shirt and waved it at the passing cars like a demented matador. Roberta captured the whole thing on her video camera, even the moment when Benji looked down the barrel and raised one finger and shouted that he was number one.

In Benji's company, Carl came alive again, laughing and enjoying himself like the old days. It didn't matter to Carl when people said Benji still had a contract on him, or that his new friend had romanced his wife. Friends were always much more important to Carl than women. As he would write to me from prison a few months later: 'A good friend is hard to find, hard to lose and impossible to forget.' There was no doubt that Carl loved Roberta, in his way, but Benji was much more important to his survival. Carl had another life that Roberta would never be invited into.

That day in court the Williams' lawyer, Theo Magazis, had handed up two separate new addresses for his clients. I caught Roberta at the lifts afterwards and she dissolved into tears. It seemed that Melbourne's number-one gangland crime couple was no more. The pressure had forced them apart, she said. Police were listening to every minute of their lives; their homes, cars and mobile phones were all bugged. 'I have to lip-read what the kids are saying because they don't want to talk inside the house,' she said tearfully. 'I've had enough. I just want this all to go away.'

Roberta was moving into a rented house in Moonee Ponds

until the renovations on her new home were completed, while Carl took up residence in a high-rise apartment in the Regency Towers building, next to the Marriott Hotel complex in the city. His new flatmate would be Andrew Veniamin. It was now well-known that it had been Benji who had killed Carl's then best friend, Dino Dibra. Carl still had a smiling portrait of himself and Dino by his bed. One of Carl's greatest skills was his ability to compartmentalise his life. There was still work to be done.

As Benji's reputation steadily grew in the underworld, he would say that he had many associates but only a handful of friends. His true friends were the boys he had grown up with in Sunshine, and the rest of his relationships were strictly business. But in the end, it was Benji's friends who had the most to fear from him.

A lot of him was always the good Greek boy – he kept his criminal life away from his family and would say there were things about his life they should never know. It was just better that way, he said, safer for everyone.

According to Johnny, Benji boasted that his father had registered his second-born son with two different surnames. One birth certificate bore the name 'Andrew Veniamin' and the other 'Andrew Benjamin'. From day one, the boy had two identities. 'They must have known he was going to be a crim,' one former policeman told me. Though Apollo never explained why he had done it, Benji was thankful for the dual identities. He had driver's licences in both until he maxed them out with fines and demerits. Then he didn't bother with a licence at all.

Helen was much like her little brother: defiant and disrespect-ful of authority, outspoken when crossed and quick to anger. They were both completely incapable of walking away from a fight. Steve was a year older than Andrew, though he looked like his twin. He had a totally different personality – quiet and self-contained – but like Benji was staunch in defence of his family.

By his early teens, Benji was a law unto himself. One day he was in the milk bar at the Glengala shops in Sunshine when the owner accused him of shoplifting, slapping him hard across the face and throwing him out of the shop. Benji went straight home and picked up a baseball bat, then returned to the shop and set about smashing everything he could.

Apollo saw a lot of himself in his rebellious son. He had emi-grated from Cyprus in 1970 and worked for years as a welder at the Sunshine Harvester Works. He too had found it hard to turn the other cheek, and though he was quiet and industrious he had gained a reputation as a man to be reckoned with. Even when the boys became teenagers steeped in martial arts and testosterone, they thought twice before crossing their father. One night when Benji was about seventeen, he and Steve decided they would test their father and attacked him simultaneously. After a short, thun-derous struggle, Apollo laid them both out cold.

Apollo and his wife, Marianna, tried hard to raise their children in the Australian way, but culture and tradition ruled at home. They were sent to Greek School every Saturday to learn the language and customs of their Greek-Cypriot heritage. Steve and Andrew were both altar boys at St Andrew's Greek Orthodox Church near the Glengala shops.

In his early days in PK's gang, Benji came in for special treatment from Sunshine police because he was small. This created a passionate hatred for jacks that burned in him till the end. He couldn't understand why he copped so much when the entire crew was in on a gig. PK would patiently explain to him that it was because police thought he was the weak link. 'You're small, and they expect you to buckle under the pressure. But you won't, will you?' he would say.

Benji certainly earned his reputation for staunchness. At seventeen, he and several older men hijacked a truck as it prepared to unload a delivery of cigarettes at a newsagent. Benji was the only one not wearing a balaclava. The crew parked the truck at his place and hid the booty under the house ready for collection the following day. When the jacks picked him up, he refused to name his accomplices. The magistrate told him if he dobbed in his mates he would receive a non-custodial sentence, but still he refused, so he was sent to Turana Youth Training Centre.

Even back then Benji had more heart than anyone. He would take on all comers, but not PK. There was a deep, merciless intelligence in PK that unnerved Benji and the others. PK could keep his anger in his heart, forgiving his rivals while quietly biding his time. Benji's rage, in contrast, boiled over into immediate threats and, soon after, violence. He set out to prove that he was just as staunch as the rest, and after twenty-odd beatings the jacks stopped battering him – because it did no good. Their violence made him what he was.

Benji built himself a name for ruthless cruelty. Business associates were owed no loyalty – they would probably double-cross him eventually, lag him out like the rest of the dogs in the underworld. Benji never took drugs – he tried speed once and hated it – and hardly ever drank. He looked down on anybody who took the stuff on which his livelihood depended, including PK. If the boys were pulling a few lazy cones, Benji would niggle away at them, calling them 'bong junkies'. Even when he was involved in selling ecstasy, he would threaten to shoot any of the younger boys who dipped into the company inventory for recreational purposes.

The only drugs that interested Benji were steroids and human growth hormones, which turned a small man into a fighting power-house. The rage that came on with the juice was useful, too. As a kickboxer, his success lay in his lack of fear. He would take on any-one, and often kicked the arses of much bigger opponents. When Benji was in his early twenties, a local trainer renowned for pro-ducing champions took him on the proviso that he left his guns at home; it was one of the few edicts Benji ever agreed to. However, the reckless ride on the motorbike in 1998 left him with a smashed knee, ending his fighting career.

Local police sources said that most of Benji's business in his young days was in rebirthing cars or growing hydroponic marijuana crops under lights in houses around the west. On one occasion he took a liking to the girlfriend of one of the 'sitters' (associates employed to look after a crop). Benji had a devastating charm that few Sunshine girls could resist. He duly bedded the girl, and while the sitter was understandably upset at this casual betrayal, he knew enough about Benji's dash to keep his mouth shut. Unfortunately, a few weeks later in a bar he complained in company that it had been a 'doggish act'. It wasn't the same thing as actually declaring someone a dog, but it was enough for Benji. The word went out all over Sunshine that he was in a rage looking for the sitter to put a couple of bullets in him. It's said that when he couldn't find the sitter, he drove around to the bloke's parents' place and demanded they pay him a $20 000 fine or he would put their son off. Terrified, they took out a bank loan to pay Benji. Still he wasn't satisfied. A week later he hadn't found the sitter, so he went back to the hapless parents and demanded another $20 000. But there was no more money, and no more credit to be had from the bank. Benji ran outside and put a couple of clips from his 9mm into their car and their house. Eventually he caught up with the sitter and shot him in the legs and buttocks.

Benji did have a sense of justice, however distorted it might have been. One day an associate's sister complained that someone had run into her car and driven off without stopping. She had the licence plate and was preparing to go to the jacks to lodge a complaint, but Benji had a better idea. Two weeks later he came around and picked up the girl, taking her to the address of the offending motorist. She waited while Benji went inside. Police believe that he dragged the terrified man out at gunpoint and, right there on the street, shot him in the groin. Even though details of the incident were widely known in underworld circles, police could do nothing, because the victim never complained. Perhaps he knew what would happen if he did: no place would be safe from Benji's vengeance, and no one would be prepared to protect him. Only PK had any control over Benji.

Benji was getting too big for Sunshine. He yearned for the bright lights and fresh fights he would find in the city. As the new millennium dawned, he was running with the boss of the Carlton Crew, Dominic 'Mick' Gatto. Years earlier, in his parents' garage one afternoon, Benji had told the boys that one day he would be a member of the Carlton Crew. It was his solemn vow, a life's ambition. He said he took up kickboxing partly because you got to meet big shots like Mick Gatto and Mario Condello that way.

On a big title-fight night the kickboxing venues were like a four-sided parliament of villains. Each crime group – the Carlton Crew, the Russian and Albanian mafia, the Asian gangs, outlaw bikies – had their appointed place in the front rows. They would come and greet each other with great ceremony and then retreat to their seats for the night's entertainment, regarding each other warily. This was the theatre Benji signed on for, the big stage alongside the most powerful men in town. One day he promised he would sit there next to Mick, but first he had to find a way to get close to the man, who was as yet unaware he was about to get a new protégé. Benji made the supreme sacrifice for his ambitions and actually worked a legitimate job. A cousin of a well-loved senior Carlton man ran a souvenir factory from a Sunshine garage, and Benji signed on to work for him, reasoning that this would get him close to the powerbrokers of Lygon Street. For eight solid months he assembled copper souvenir maps of Australia, sticking on little clocks and tacky decals of emus and kangaroos. The strategy worked perfectly, and he began to meet the right people.

Mick could see a lot of himself in the cheeky little upstart from Sunshine. He admired his dash and could see a future for him in the various businesses he himself was running. For Benji, Mick was a big step up in class. For the first time he was being introduced to people of quality from the city, big business people who employed Mick to do certain delicate jobs for them. Benji began to run errands for Mick, such as seizing the motor vehicles of blokes who wouldn't pay their debts. He began driving around with a pink slip in his glove box to facilitate the efficient transfer of ownership of the vehicles. Benji was enamoured with Mick and his stylish gangster ways. The big fella was a thorough gentleman, Benji would say. In return Mick loved Benji like a son, drawing him very close, much closer than he should have.

One night Benji was on his own in the city, looking for mischief as always, and decided he would take in a girlie show at the Men's Gallery strip club. As usual, he was dressed in jeans and a Bonds T-shirt that showed off his muscles. The bouncer objected to what he was wearing and refused him entry, but Benji just pushed past. Two or three bouncers then grabbed him and threw him out, giving him a few elbows and fists to go on with. As it happened, Mick was having dinner close by in the city. When Benji called him, he and his dinner companions dropped their forks and raced to the scene. Within five minutes they were striding into the club. Without a word Mick and the boys laid into the hapless bouncers. Mick punched one of them so hard he flew through the air and landed in a heap among some tables, breaking a leg. No charges were ever laid, and later the club owner apologised to Mick and Benji for the 'misunderstanding'.

Benji was flying higher than he could ever have imagined. His father, Apollo, could see what was happening but was powerless to intervene. 'Just as long as you know that you are going to hell for the things you are doing,' he would tell Benji. Apollo loved his troubled son deeply just the same, for his was a forgiving God who was always ready to redeem the most wicked of sinners. Apollo even forgave Benji the time he lost it and, in a screaming rage, put a gun in his father's mouth and threatened to blow his head off. The jacks were called, but Benji was never charged – how could Apollo bear witness against his own flesh and blood?

By early 2002 it was all getting too confusing out in Sunshine. Benji was playing both sides of the fence. He was hanging out with Mick and the Carlton Crew, whose intimates controlled the neighbouring turf to PK's. Meanwhile, he was getting much closer to Carl.

A multi-cornered summit was held to discuss the fallout from Dino's death. Benji stood in the middle playing referee, but nobody could tell whose side he was on. 'Where do you stand, Benj?' asked PK all of a sudden. 'You're all over the place, little man. One minute you're with the Carlton Crew, the next you're running with Carl Williams, and then you come over to my house and tell me you're my friend. You said it yourself – you've only got associates.' For Benji, loyalty was a minute-to-minute proposition. As long as you didn't try to be his boss, you would have his undivided attention.

There was tension building. Benji had begun standing over people. He was a law unto himself and a threat to everyone. By the end of the year PK would be dead and Benji would have jumped the fence again, throwing in his lot with Carl Williams and the Chief Executive. The atmosphere in the ganglands was turning more toxic by the day.

Benji was a little disturbed when he heard about Johnny testifying in church about his life of crime. In late 2003 he came upon Johnny by chance one day at the Bridgestone shop in Flemington, where Johnny was having a wheel alignment on his SS Commodore. They chatted for an hour and a half. 'Are you talkin' about us in church, mate?' Benji asked.

'Er . . . yeah, sure, Benj,' said Johnny awkwardly. 'It's part of my path to spiritual redemption, showing others where I have come from.'

Benji had a grave look of concern. 'I know you've found the Lord and all, but I hope you aren't talking to Him – and the other people who might be listening – too much about us.' They laughed at the thought of getting busted like that. 'You go and testify – just leave the names out, right?'

Johnny tried hard to get Benji to see what his faith had done for him, to persuade him that his destiny did not have to be a violent death. He told his friend that he had given away a car worth $50 000, a 400-gram solid-gold chain, and tens of thousands of dollars he had made through crime – he couldn't keep all this stuff, having left the underworld. There was no need for money when you would be dancing on a lake of fire in hell for all eternity, he reasoned. He had risked his life to get the stuff and now he was giving it away.

In early 2002, a few months after Johnny had left the underworld, his mother's health had deteriorated rapidly, her chronic diabetes sparking a terminal case of cirrhosis of the liver. For months Johnny nursed her as she gradually faded before his eyes. In July, she was admitted to hospital and the doctors told Johnny she had only twenty hours to live. Even his pastors told Johnny to prepare for her death, but he refused to accept it. As she teetered on the brink, he prayed with all his heart and soul and miraculously she stabilised. He had another three months with his mother until she died on 26 August 2002. No one, he told the doctors, had the right to call an end to someone's life. That was God's will and His alone.

His mother's dying wish was to see her wayward son become a regular churchgoer, and despite all his sins he had achieved that. That first year of his life in the church, he told Benji, he had read the Bible seven times, memorising dozens of verses that he felt must have been written especially for him, so deeply did they touch him. He read the Old Testament, too, with its vengeful doctrines of 'an eye for an eye and a tooth for a tooth'. He realised that as a gangster he had been living his life by a code out of the Old Testament – he had played God in wreaking vengeance on his rivals. In the New Testament he read that he could forgive his enemies and turn the other cheek.

At first Benji thought Johnny had gone completely crazy. At the time of their conversation, Benji had recently hooked up with Carl and the money was flowing like never before. Carl had given him a $20 000 gold chain for his birthday and there was much, much more to come. Benji was tired of doing what he was told and following all the rules. Life with Mick had been exciting – the Carlton Crew had taken him to the heart of the underworld and shown him how Melbourne really operated, how the biggest property developments could not be built without Mick's involvement, how big-time entrepreneurs didn't make a move without Mick's say-so, how some of the best people in town sent Mick Christmas cards every year – but he wasn't going to kiss the ring any more. With the Chief Executive and Williams, you could be what you wanted to be.

He urged Johnny to come and meet Carl. 'I'm telling you, Johnny, once you meet Carl, spend just a little time, you are going to want to come back. You'll be begging to come back.' Benji had already recruited a couple of Sunshine boys to the big city crews. One of them, Chris, was just eighteen years old when Benji plucked him off the street, a skinny redhead kid from Sunshine. Benji had introduced him to Carl and Roberta and now Chris was a part of the team. 'There's always a place for you, Johnny. C'mon, buddy, you've still got this in your heart, you know.'

Johnny refused point blank, but not because he had anything against Carl. He knew Benji was right on that score. A few days with Carl and he would be right back into it – the girls, the drugs, the batterings and the funerals. Only this time Johnny knew he would be the one in the casket. Watching his mother die had reaffirmed not only his newly found compassion but also his desire to live. There were still some legal matters to deal with – a charge for assault and another for a 25-kilo crop of marijuana – but it seemed the Lord didn't want Johnny to go back to jail. He beat the assault charge and received a suspended sentence for the marijuana, and an old blackmail charge was dropped before it got to court. Now a free man in body and soul, Johnny thanked Jesus (and his barrister, Dan Causovski) for his deliverance.

Despite all of this, when Benji saw the SS Commodore Johnny was driving that day in Flemington, he concluded that Johnny had returned to the underworld: 'I knew you was bullshitting us all with that Jesus crap. You're back in, aren't you, Johnny?' He laughed and slapped Johnny on the back. 'What are you doing, eh? You back with some of those Carlton blokes? I knew it, Johnny. Once a soldier, always a soldier.'

'No, Benj, I bought the car with the inheritance money from my mother, mate. I don't do that shit no more,' said Johnny. 'I'm a soldier for Christ now, Benj. Now that PK's gone, there was no way I could go back into the underworld. I've changed my life.' Benji looked disappointed. By now there was no one except Carl whom he regarded as a true friend. To have Johnny around would have made it like the old days. 'You know I was praying for you all the time you was inside, mate. My whole church got down on their knees for you, Benj.'

While Benji was in jail on racketeering charges in 2002, Johnny had asked his entire congregation to pray for his old friend, and every night for months he had prayed for Benji at home. 'Dear Lord, please help Benji to see the light, to repent his wicked life and allow Jesus Christ to come into his heart before it's too late,' he would say. 'If he killed PK and Dino, may God save his immortal soul.'

A strange, wistful look passed over Benji's face. 'That's funny you should say that, Johnny, 'cause when I was in the nick I picked up a Bible – that's the one thing there's no shortage of inside, mate. And I start reading it and pretty soon I'm reading it every night. I read the whole fucking thing, mate. Then I read it over again . . . And you was praying for me at the same time. Really?'

'Yeah, sure, Benj. We lit candles for you, mate, and everything. It's the power of prayer, mate. Have you accepted Jesus Christ into your life as your personal Lord and Saviour?'

'Johnny, something has happened inside me, but Christ hasn't done for me what he's done for you and I don't think He's ever going to. My path in life is already set, my friend. It's too late to turn back,' said Benji.

'No, Benj, it's never too late to turn away from this shit. You've just got to believe, to have faith that you can change. We've done wicked things, but there's always time to repent before the Lord.'

Benji thought for a moment. He remembered how he had asked his sister, Helen, to light candles for him at St Andrew's while he was in Turana. It had meant something back then – like there was hope for him. Maybe God *could* take this awful rage from his heart and leave the rest of him to begin again. 'But them pastors, Johnny, they don't know what we've done. They just go "Sure, you can be saved", like it's some kinda ordinary sin, but they don't know what we've done. I'm going to get to the gates of heaven and they're gonna say, "Wrong place, you dumb fuck. What makes you think you could ever come in here?"'

Johnny told him the story of St Paul, who had journeyed to Damascus with the murder of Christians on his mind. 'Benj, he was almost at Damascus and a divine light hits him and knocks him off his horse, then when he comes to his senses he's converted. He even stays in a house on a road called Straight Street in Damascus. Then he writes a whole lot of the Bible, Benj. You know what I'm saying – a murderer wrote a shitload of the Bible. So why can't you be saved, too? You've just got to be convicted with the Truth.'

'No, Johnny, I've lost none of my heart,' replied Benji. 'I am really happy for you that you have found the Lord. Perhaps that was your destiny all along. But this is my destiny and I have gone too far to turn back now. Like Paulie said, I've gone past the point of no return.' Like many of his mates, Benji was a John Gotti fan. The legendary New York boss had killed and schemed his way to the top of the Mob and provided a perfect role model. 'If they don't put us away for one year or two – that's all we need. If I can get a year run without being interrupted . . . Put this thing together where they could never break it, never destroy it. Even if we die it would be a good thing.'

Benji was on his final run, and he was primed for it. Yes, there was a place in his heart for what he had read in the Bible. He had memorised Ezekiel 25:17 just like he had heard it in *Pulp Fiction*: 'The path of the righteous man is beset on all sides with the iniquities of the selfish and the tyranny of evil men. Blessed is he who, in the name of charity and good will, shepherds the weak through the valley of darkness, for he is truly his brother's keeper and a finder of lost children. And I will strike down upon those with great vengeance and with furious anger those who attempt to poison and destroy my brothers. And you will know that my name is the Lord when I lay my vengeance upon thee.' It wasn't really Ezekiel 25:17, but a blend of biblical verses that the *Pulp Fiction* hit man, Jules, had twisted to his own purpose. In the movie the lines build to a furious crescendo, followed by a volley of murderous gunfire. Benji would play it loudly as he showered and dressed, psyching himself for the night's work ahead. A small man stood tall as Benji slipped his toy down the front of his trousers and went on his way.

Meanwhile, if his enemies got in first, he would have a send-off to remember. In late summer 2004, he and Roberta paid a visit to Tripodi Funerals on Sydney Road in Coburg. This firm handled most of the big Italian funerals of Melbourne, including the send-offs of many Carlton Crew elders. The staff were surprised to learn that Benji was planning his own funeral, right down to the casket. He chose the best Tripodi had to offer, a massive bronze number finished in black and gold and with a silver bas-relief of Leonardo da Vinci's *Last Supper* fixed into the inside of the lid. The bill for this alone came to $17 000. To make sure he was happy with his purchase, Benji clambered into the casket and lay there, declaring it a perfect fit.

'I've got two, three years left max, Johnny. I have told my parents that, too. I'm not going to let up. I'm going to take down as many of the dogs as I can,' he said, a look of pure rage passing across his face. Anyone who got in his way from here would be fair game. And Benji would stand by Carl, even if the relationship was purely commercial: in return for his protection Benji would get half of whatever money Carl had left from his drug trafficking.

FRUIT AND VEG FOR LIFE

On the morning in May 2000 when the boss of the markets Frank Benvenuto was murdered, Victor Peirce was at home in Port Melbourne with his wife, Wendy, watching a quiz show on television. He liked to watch wildlife documentaries on the ABC or the news, but Wendy liked her quizzes, so he put up with it. Anything for the quiet life. Wendy could 'air-raid' like nobody's business, kicking up a big fuss when she was crossed, and she could fight like a man. He hadn't nicknamed her 'Witch' for nothing.

Victor used to joke that Wendy was lucky he hadn't put a bullet in her after all these years. But she had been staunch – except for the time she had nearly sent him down for murder over Damian Eyre and Steven Tynan, those two young police officers he and his mates had clipped in Walsh Street, South Yarra in 1988. She claimed she only agreed to testify against Victor after the jacks put her under extreme pressure. She never planned to go through with it.

Victor's mother, the legendary crime matriarch Kath Pettingill, had told him that if he ever married Wendy he wouldn't have a mother, so he and Wendy had never tied the knot. Victor was a conventional man who liked a house in good order and well-mannered, respectful children. There had been many other women along the way, but Wendy had been there through thick and thin. She had raised their four kids, Victor junior, Chris, Katie and Vinnie, while he was in and out of jail for all the stick-ups in the 1980s and through the Walsh Street era, when Victor was the most hated man in Melbourne. She had been there when he got out of jail on drug-trafficking charges in 1998. He had spent the best part of two years since then at home on the couch, trying to picture a life without crime, and the business of the house had gone on around him. The Peirces had been through the sweets and the sours together – and Wendy could be sour indeed. If you went to kill her, you wouldn't want to miss.

Victor's mobile phone was ringing. The caller ID showed it was his boss, Frank. He answered, but there was just a gurgling sound on the line, no words he could make out, then nothing. He hung up and turned to Wendy, saying, 'It's Frank. It sounds like he's in trouble.' He tried calling back, but it rang out. Ten minutes later the phone rang again, and this time it was Rose, Frank's sister, with the news that Frank had been shot dead in his car in the driveway of his Beaumaris home.

Victor and Wendy were shattered. Frank and Rose had been very good to the Peirces for a lot of years. When Victor and Wendy were both in jail, Rose and her husband had taken care of Katie like she was their own. Frank had visited Victor regularly in jail when he was doing a six-year stretch for drug trafficking, and had given him a job when he got out in 1998.

Victor had intended to go back to his first love: armed robbery, and bank stick-ups in particular. To the police that study them, every career criminal has his own speciality as individual as a fingerprint, and Victor Peirce was a stick-up man. He thought about getting some of the old team together for one last tilt at the big money. He loved the whole caper – the planning, the teamwork, getting dressed up in six layers of clothes to disguise his appearance, the adrenaline of pulling off a big heist. But while he'd been in jail the age of the stick-up had passed into history. New security grilles inside banks and quick-response alarms that brought the jacks down in minutes meant that there were few with the dash to take on the job now.

Victor was one of the last of a dying breed. He was a criminal legend in Melbourne, having beaten charges that he had participated in the murder of the two police constables in Walsh Street in 1988.

In 1998 he was tired of all the questions from the young turks about Walsh Street and the interest his profile had drawn from the jacks. All he wanted to do was get back to knocking over banks, but most of his old crew had gone out of circulation years ago, shot dead by police or each other, doing life in jail or simply too old to be terrorising pimply-faced bank tellers. Barely into his forties, Victor was already a museum piece, his prison tattoos a testament to one of Melbourne's most notorious eras. So Frank took him on as a bodyguard.

Frank Benvenuto had long been regarded as the Godfather of Melbourne's fruit-and-vegetable markets, but a boss like him could never really relax, such was the high-stakes competition. There have been plotters and schemers down at the markets as long as there have been tomatoes and beans. You needed to put the fear of

God into your rivals to keep them in line, and that was part of the reason for having Victor around. Peirce is reputed to have opened fire with a machine gun at the Footscray markets early one morning during one of the regular conflicts between rival factions – or maybe it was just for fun. There was enough intrigue to keep everyone amused.

Though he was loyal to Frank, Victor was his own man and refused to pay tribute to the haughty old Italians who ran the rackets down at the markets. On one occasion, a very senior boss extended his hand for Victor to kiss; Victor took a long look at the pudgy, hairy hand with its glittering pinkie ring and promptly turned his back. 'I wasn't going to kiss the bloke's hand – fuck that,' he told Wendy.

One time another operator at Victoria Market had come to Victor with a proposition that he might kill a rival in return for fruit and vegetables for life. Sure, Victor was a vegetarian, but this was ridiculous. Cash got people killed, not cauliflowers. No one would ever accept a contract like that. Besides, the way people were dying in Melbourne, such a deal for life might not amount to much – maybe just enough for a salad.

It was a time of turmoil for Frank Benvenuto. Early in 2000 he had endured a very unpleasant introduction to one Andrew 'Benji' Veniamin. Frank had been in dispute with a guy running transport at the markets and things had got nasty. One morning at the markets Benji had accosted Frank, pressing a 9mm into his guts. He had taken Frank into the back of a car and suggested very strongly that he lay off his friend or he was a dead man. Frank had taken it badly. Who was this little upstart from Sunshine anyway, he raged.

At the age of fifty-two, Frank had survived some of the bloodiest chapters in the history of Melbourne's Mafia. He would deal with this threat by and by, but for now everything would be kept quiet. Frank would have the little punk capped when he least expected it. But for now he sought him out in friendship: he could use a man like Benji and his talent for killing.

Victor told Wendy he was certain that Benji had knocked Frank. Robbery certainly wasn't the motive: there was apparently $60 000 cash in the boot of Frank's car when he died, and it wasn't touched. Victor was also sure that the killing would not end with Frank. Benji would be expecting some blowback, and the best form of defence was always attack. Victor was ready for anything.

It seems every crim in Melbourne has their own pet name for a gun. For Victor it was a 'bizzo', and he had lots of them stooked around. Some were stashed on Crown land close to home, buried in parkland or the night-cart lane behind his home. He liked to have one in the house, too, for emergencies. Using his trade skills, he made a stook hole behind a skirting board in the laundry. Whenever he went to his car from their home, he observed a strict protocol: Wendy would stand in the doorway, a bizzo loaded and cocked, watching the street while Victor, with his own in hand, would unlock the car door and slip behind the wheel. It was a routine he had followed since Walsh Street, and it had served him well.

Police discovered that two weeks after Frank's death, Mick Gatto had broken the stand-off. He had rung Victor to say that Benji wanted to meet to discuss the issue. He told Victor that Benji had no quarrel with Victor himself: the killing of Frank had been purely business. Mick's role in the meeting would be solely that of mediator. There was no hard evidence linking Mick with Frank's murder, but there were plenty of stories.

The meeting was held in a small park in Port Melbourne one wintry afternoon. Victor came with his .45 stuck down the front of his trousers and a .38 down the back for good measure. No doubt Benji had his own 9mm tucked into his tracksuit pants. He turned up with Mick, and after minimal pleasantries it was down to business. Benji asked Victor straight out whether he was going to avenge Frank's death. If so, how, and when was this going to end?

Benji was nervous. Even he had the good sense to respect the criminal legend standing before him. How many heads in Melbourne had beaten the rap on three murders and five armed robberies? Maybe it would be better just to end it all quickly now, in a death-or-glory shoot-out. The last thing Benji wanted was to be hunted down by a pro like Victor. As he always said, if a good hit man sets his sights on you, you might as well bring it on; he'll get you one day. Like many young crims, Benji had grown up on the stories of Victor's dash – how, when the jacks had killed his friend Graeme Jensen, Victor had said he would knock two cops for every one of his crew that fell. At least if Victor clipped him, his killer would be a pro and a childhood hero to boot.

Victor was too clever to show his hand in a park. There would be plenty of time to square up with Benji. Instead, he was cool and conciliatory. Yes, it was true that he had lost his boss and a good friend too, but he bore no grudge against Benji. He respected the fact that Benji had had a job to do, and that was that. They shook hands and walked away, but in his mind Victor swore that he would clip the little dog the first chance he got.

Victor now had a problem. Without Frank, he had no regular form of income. He was moving some drugs for an interstate syndicate, but that was an irregular earner and he had a family to look after. He wanted them to do better than he had in life, to avoid the killing that had followed him. He took a job down at the docks, driving cars off the container ships that brought them in from overseas. It wasn't hard work, but the endless night shifts were boring for a bloke used to the excitement of robbing banks. He had never been into drugs, though he had earned his living from the trade in recent years. Some of his younger workmates told him that an ecstasy pill or two would help the hours fly past, so one night, against his better judgement, he tried one. Suddenly the docks took on a different look altogether. The lights of the car terminal were beautiful. He loved his workmates and his family. One pill became two, which quickly became five and then ten. Soon he was throwing the little pills down like lollies. The only way he could come down when he got home from work at 6 a.m. was to drop a Valium or two. On the pills, Victor felt like he was eighteen again. He started to hang out with kids half his age who introduced him to the club scene and techno music. He began to go to dance parties and raves where the rest of the ecstasy crew gathered. Over two years his appearance changed dramatically. He lost weight and had his wavy, grey-flecked hair cut short into a fashionable crew cut. He told his mother that he had met a new girl and it was getting serious.

Victor and Wendy had been sweethearts since their teens. They had not always been faithful to each other – Wendy admits now that she was having an affair with Victor's best mate, Graeme Jensen, when police killed him – but there was a deeper loyalty between them. Victor was a conservative force in the family, kept his business very separate. The kids never saw a gun in the household, and there was no talk of stick-ups or killing while they were around. Victor didn't even like to see the now-teenage Katie getting around in crop tops that revealed her midriff. 'There'll be no boyfriends till she's twenty-one,' Victor declared to Wendy. 'And if I catch any young blokes trying to con onto her, I'll bloody knock the father.'

Of course, the small matter of Walsh Street had come between them for a while. Under pressure from the police Wendy had decided to testify against Victor and his brother Trevor Pettingill, putting them in the frame for the murders with mates Anthony Farrell, Peter McEvoy and Jedd Houghton. In more than a dozen raids, the police had literally demolished Wendy and Victor's home in Chestnut Street, Richmond looking for clues. As the jacks blew off the front door, excavated the garden with bobcats, cut off the gas and electricity, Wendy continued to run the family as best she could, because that's what Victor wanted. She'd had a thing about keeping the place tidy ever since.

But the pressure told on Wendy. Two days before Christmas in 1988, she slashed a woman in a pub with a broken beer glass and was charged with attempted murder. It wasn't until the police told her that they had love letters Victor had supposedly written to other women that she finally cracked and agreed to finger her husband and the others for the Walsh Street killings. Later she sensationally withdrew her statement and any cooperation, and all the accused were acquitted. She was sorry that she ever thought of lagging Victor, but the love letters had hurt her 'just a little bit'.

When Victor got home after Walsh Street, he and Wendy agreed there would be no more affairs; they needed each other too much. The agreement lasted a while at least.

The presence of firearms in the Peirce household could turn an ordinary situation into something potentially fatal. One day in early 1988 Victor and his mate Graeme Jensen were sitting in the lounge room with Wendy and another woman when Victor decided he wanted to liven things up. So he went to the bedroom and got his .357 magnum. As Wendy tells it, 'He pointed it at me and said, "Do the Mexican hat dance." I said, "Piss off – I'm not doing no Mexican hat dance. If you're going to shoot me, go ahead – but I'm going to die with dignity, not jumping around like a goose." So, BOOM! He puts one straight into the sofa, right between my legs. It went into the wall and took out the telephone. My ears rang for a week. Then he pointed the bizzo at my girlfriend's head and pulled the trigger. It just went CLICK! She shit herself and ran out. Victor knew there was only one bullet in the gun.' There was never a dull moment in the Peirce household.

In this line of work you needed a solid base, a woman to keep the house and the kids in good order when you were off in prison. Victor had taught Wendy how to shoot a handgun, how to strip it down and reassemble it. She had taken the rap for him on firearms charges, because with his record he would go straight back into prison if convicted. But now Victor was in a world Wendy couldn't understand. He had taken up with a new girlfriend, Desiree, and she had had a child, a boy the image of his father. Victor had told his mother, Kath Pettingill, the matriarch of the crime family, that he was trying to change his life.

Pettingill told me, 'He met a girl and this is what he said: "Mum, she doesn't talk gangster talk, she doesn't pop pills, she doesn't do this and she doesn't do that, and I intend to marry her".'

Wendy always believed this was the ecstasy talking. Victor's mind was scrambled from all the pills he was flipping up. After years of vigilance he was dropping his guard, and Wendy could see that it was going to cost him dearly. 'It was the pills. Ever since Walsh Street, Victor had his guard up like the Commonwealth Bank, but with all the pills he was just not the man I knew, not the real Victor,' she said.

I met Wendy by the bay at Station Pier in Port Melbourne, just a few blocks from where Victor lost his life in Bay Street. She had arrived in his old Commodore, the car in which he'd been shot dead in 2002. 'Me and Katie tried to tell him, but he wouldn't listen to reason. He thought he was a young man again and that he was indestructible,' she said, looking sadly out to sea.

For a while Katie had found her father's new image appealing. Suddenly, he was familiar with her music and could get her and friends into nightclubs and raves. For her sixteenth birthday, he organised a double-decker bus and entry to an exclusive nightspot though all the kids were under age. That night, through the hazy glow of alcohol, Victor's violent life of crime had seemed remote to Katie, almost mythical. There was a new lightness about him. Her father was opening up to her and they were closer than ever. Maybe this time he wouldn't leave her for another stint in jail, she thought. In the club, he smiled at her and motioned her over, then whispered into her ear, 'Hey Pooh-bum, you wanna see Daddy's gun?' As she looked on in horror, Victor pulled out his .45 and waved it around as it if it were a water pistol and they were at a kiddies' party. Katie felt hot tears of shame welling up and soon she was sobbing uncontrollably. It wasn't that her friends had seen her father's gun or that he had ruined her birthday party – she was crying because as soon as she saw the gun, she knew it was over. Her dad would be going away again soon, maybe this time forever. As if to reassure her, Victor handed her an ecstasy pill.

Ecstasy's reputation as the 'hug drug' is well-earned. Any regular user will tell you it's hard to hate someone while under its influence. Suspicion melts away and the world is suffused with a warm, fuzzy glow. The most trivial of emotions become the grist for aimless, saccharine-sweet conversations. Petty jealousies and rivalries seem irrelevant in this new, enlightened space, and your enemies become your friends. This is all very well if you are a middle-class kid running around dance parties and rave clubs, but if you are a middle-aged villain with a list of enemies as long as your heavily tattooed arm, an outbreak of mercy is a dangerous thing indeed. It's bound to get you killed sooner or later.

Wendy had been astounded at the new, compassionate Victor Peirce she was seeing. 'It was unbelievable. He was hanging around with people he had declared as dogs years ago. He was ringing them up to forgive them stuff he never would have forgiven them for in years past. He'd tell me, "So and so's not so bad" and I'd say, "But Victor, that dog's been lagging people for years." He would just laugh it off.'

More dangerous for Victor, he was becoming soft about collecting money owed to him, money for drugs he had taken on consignment – and credit gets more people killed in the underworld than anything else.

He may have been a happy hit man but Victor was still taking care of business. One of the friendships he rekindled was with Sharon Mercieca, the elder sister of Roberta, then the fiancée of one Carl Williams. Sharon had been girlfriend to Victor's great mate Graeme Jensen, breaking up with him six weeks before Jensen was killed. Victor had fallen out with her years ago, but now they were getting on famously again. When Sharon went along to Carl and Roberta's wedding on 14 January 2001, Victor accompanied her. It was hardly his scene but there was method in his madness, he told Wendy: apparently, one of Williams' many enemies had offered Victor a substantial sum to knock the bridegroom in retaliation for the murder of Mark Moran six months earlier.

Victor wasn't going to carry out the hit at the wedding, but it was a chance to get close to Carl and his cohorts, a valuable opportunity to research the assignment. He watched as the bride and groom entered the reception centre to the strains of Shania Twain's 'You're Still the One'. One hundred and ten guests, a roll call of the western suburbs criminal elite, were on hand for the celebration and clapped loudly as the couple, with Roberta seven months pregnant, made their stately progress to their table.

They said, 'I bet they'll never make it'
But just look at us holding on
We're still together, still going strong

Peirce might have thought to himself, *Not for too much longer, sport, not for too much longer*. The couple retired to the bridal suite at Crown Towers that night, oblivious to the fact that at least one of their guests had gone home wishing them a short and miserable life.

It was a contract Victor never got to fulfil. On the evening of 1 May 2002, he was preparing to meet up with some associates to transact business in Bay Street, Port Melbourne. He was a little early so he killed time with Wendy and Vinnie, kicking a footy back and forth with his son. He told Wendy to go home and put on the coffee machine; he'd be there very soon. After they left, Victor strolled to his car, which was parked across the street in front of a Telstra shop, and sat inside it to wait. He was unarmed, expecting a close family friend.

Minutes later another vehicle drove alongside and a gunman fired three .45 slugs in rapid succession through the driver's door window of Victor's car. In a shower of glass, one round crashed through his right elbow as he raised it in a defensive posture, and continued on into his chest, sending him sprawling sideways onto the passenger seat. Another ripped into his chest, passing through both lungs and his liver and finally exiting through his left shoulder. A third shot missed altogether and lodged in the pillar of the driver's door.

It wasn't exactly a textbook hit. There was no head shot: the killers had not delivered the coup de grace that would have settled the issue.

One night in mid-2003, Carl's two favourite hit men were exchanging notes over a drink at the Limerick Arms hotel in South

Melbourne. The Raptor had recently shot Jason Moran and had hardly been aware that he had also killed Moran's companion, Pasquale Barbaro, sitting next to him. The Raptor said Benji asked why he had shot Barbaro. It was because Moran, in the driver's seat of the van, had ducked down, he explained. 'Have you ever tried to shoot someone through a car window and somehow got the feeling you have missed the target?' asked the Raptor.

'Yeah, with Victor Peirce. I had to lean out of a car to shoot Victor Peirce,' Benji said.

'Bullshit!' came the reply.

'Yeah, but I got him,' said Benji. For Carl, he said.

By this time, however, another theory was doing the rounds on the identity of Benji's paymaster in the shooting of Peirce. Carl's mate the Gunsmith told police that Benvenuto had fallen out with Gatto. Benji and Victor Peirce had been contracted to kill Mick, but he had found out and confronted Benji. The Gunsmith told police that when Benji confessed, he was given an ultimatum: kill Frank Benvenuto or face death himself. It was the easiest hit of them all. Benji, smiling and friendly, had climbed into Benvenuto's car and shot Melbourne's most powerful don from the passenger seat. Now all Benji and his employer Gatto had to worry about was the vengeance of Victor Peirce. And that's why, in this version, Victor had to die. This theory came to light in the press and Gatto strenuously denied any involvement.

Certainly both stories are hearsay, but the Raptor's version has one big hole in it: Carl only met Andrew in late 2002 – after Peirce's murder. However, it wouldn't have been the first time that a shooter had worked for someone he was yet to meet.

Victor didn't die at the scene and might have survived but for his massive internal bleeding. He was taken to the Alfred Hospital, where he underwent emergency surgery, but there was little the surgeons could do. Another relic of Melbourne had passed into history.

The hard man that Wendy had grown up with would never have fallen into a trap like this one. It was the drugs that had killed him, made him drop his guard, she said. An official autopsy showed the presence of Victor's cocktail of choice in his system: some speed, ecstasy and a little Valium to take the edge off.

Wendy and the four kids posted tributes. 'My darling Victor, you were the love of my life. Now we can no longer grow old together,' Wendy put in a death notice. 'I can't explain the devastation I feel of losing you. I will never ever forget you Victor, Your broken-hearted wife Wendy (Witch).' Katie called him a 'soldier in life, an angel in death. Whenever I was lonely, whenever I was in strife, it only took one phone call and you would be there morning, noon and night.'

After Victor's death, Kath Pettingill told the media that she would have her revenge. She seemed to have a fair idea of who had pulled the trigger on her favourite son. 'All I can say to the two people involved is: they can run, but they can't hide.' Benji wasn't hiding, though.

The killing of Victor Peirce brought to a close the last tawdry chapter in the story of Melbourne's best-known crime family, the Pettingill/Allen/Peirce faction. Kath had raised the cream of Melbourne's armed robbers, drug dealers and murderers, but now their power base was gone. Victor was the third son she had lost to drugs and misadventure in the underworld. There was no one left to seek revenge. Three sons remained alive, but Peter was in jail, Lex had distanced himself from the family, and Trevor was trying to go straight, having taken a job laying asphalt with a road crew. He was doing it tough, but swore he would never return to crime. Kath was still a beloved figure among the older heads and knock-about coppers who remembered her days as one of Melbourne's most colourful brothel keepers.

When I met her in December 2003, it was clear that the fire was going out in the matriarch known to a generation as 'Granny Evil'. In the eighteen months since Victor's death, her desire for revenge had cooled. She was resigned to his murderers going free, believing the police would let the villains in this gangland war catch and kill their own, as they always had. Meanwhile, Kath was sitting this one out and living a quiet retirement in Venus Bay, a seaside hamlet in Victoria's East Gippsland.

I was at the Spencer Street bus terminal when she arrived from Venus Bay. She had come to Melbourne for a meeting with producers who intended to turn the story of her life, which she had written with Adrian Tame, into a movie. She looked like the rest of the nice old grannies who got off the bus and headed off to the casino to play the pokies or to shop in the city. She wore a floral dress and a cardigan, and she was carrying Christmas presents for her grand-children. Her shock of peroxide blonde hair, now turned grey, had been neatly set for the journey. I walked with her and Tame to a nearby coffee shop to discuss the ground rules for a television inter-view on the murders, finding it hard to equate this old lady with armed robbery, murder and mayhem.

As we walked, she talked about her deep admiration for Steve Waugh and her passion for watching the cricket on television. I broke in with a question and she craned her head to fix me with her left eye. (She'd lost her right eye in 1978 when she was shot through a door while trying to repay a $300 debt on behalf of her daughter. The .22 slug took her eye out but, having already passed through the door, lacked the momentum to kill her.) With her working eye on me she didn't see the fire hydrant in her way and crashed into it at groin level with a sickening sound: CLANG! She shrugged off the collision and kept talking cricket as if nothing had happened.

Huh? Clang? She just crashed into a metal fire hydrant. That's metal on flesh, and it comes up with CLANG? Is Granny Evil packing some heat down there? I speculated. This was one tough granny. *Be nice, very nice*, I thought, offering to carry Kath's parcels for her. She agreed to do an interview and we parted, arranging to meet at her home in Venus Bay later that week.

At sixty-eight, Kath was trying to put her past life in the underworld behind her. When I visited her, it was bingo day for the local ladies. The only concession to the past was a sign on her front door saying, 'This house is protected by shotgun three days of the week. Guess which three?' She greeted me with coffee and biscuits and talked about a tradesman who had tried to rip her off recently. She had taken him out the back, shown him a freshly dug pit the size of a grave and suggested he would find himself in the hole if he didn't act right.

Kath had moved to Venus Bay after the death of the eldest of her ten children, the notorious mass murderer Dennis Allen. She had lived next door to Allen in Stephenson Street, Richmond at the height of his reign as a drug lord, when he was known as 'Mr D' (Death) for his penchant for dispatching his rivals. While he was formally connected with just two murders, it's thought that Allen had a hand in more than a dozen. Some of the killings took place inside his nondescript little cottage in Stephenson Street during drug binges. He would stay awake for two weeks at a time, injecting himself with speed whenever he felt sleep coming on.

It seems that Dennis took special pleasure in killing. He used a chainsaw to chop up one of his victims, a Hell's Angel named Anton Kenny. The legend goes that he casually shot another man, Wayne Stanhope, after asking him to play his favourite song on Allen's stereo. Dennis suspected Stanhope of being a police informer sent to infiltrate his gang, or maybe it was just a whim. Of course, this aversion to police informers hadn't stopped Dennis buying insurance from his crimes by dobbing to the police himself. In one year alone in the 1980s, information supplied by Dennis helped Brian 'Skull' Murphy to collar thirty-three armed robbers.

Even Kath knew things were getting out of control in May 1985, when Dennis ordered his brother Jamie to blow up the Coroner's Court with a homemade bomb to disrupt an inquest into the death of a thirty-year-old heroin-addicted prostitute named Helga Wagnegg. By all accounts Dennis had at least been involved in the disposal of her body, which had turned up floating in the Yarra four days after she visited the Pettingills' empire of brothels and drug houses in Stephenson Street.

Kath told me that Dennis had been so out of control in this period she had contemplated shooting him herself, so she could 'save the others'. 'At the end, when all the guns were supposedly gone, Dennis used to walk around with a big drum of petrol and a lighter because if they [police] came near him he was going to set 'em on fire,' she said.

When Allen died in 1987 of heart failure, his trustee in bankruptcy sold the house and a group of young people moved in. For Kath, the sound of their parties next door brought all the ghosts back to haunt her: 'It was like Dennis had never left. So I had to come down here for me own sanity.' The locals were wary when Kath first moved to Venus Bay, but now they were fiercely protective of her. If a stranger came asking for her address, they got short shrift, she said.

She spoke of her sadness that Victor hadn't managed to get away, too. On one of the last occasions he had visited Kath, he had brought Desiree and their baby girl. Kath said her son had finally escaped the malevolent influence of Wendy. In passing, he had told his mother he had a minor problem: a debt of $29 000. He seemed unconcerned, so she let it go. If he had asked, she would have mortgaged her house to pay Victor's debts.

In the fourteen years since Walsh Street there hadn't been a day that Kath hadn't worried about Victor, wrote Adrian Tame in *The Matriarch*, his biography of Pettingill. Victor had found it hard to stay out of trouble, drug trafficking and even shoplifting a jar of coffee from a supermarket. She was still haunted by regret that as Dennis had descended into criminal madness, he had taken the others with him. She had watched her own flesh and blood infect the entire family. Victor's death was just another chapter in this dismal legacy.

She sat in her lounge room surrounded by memories of

Dennis: his oriental sculptures, replica samurai swords, daggers and assorted other trinkets the bankruptcy trustee had left behind. 'My one regret was having Dennis. If I didn't have Dennis, I don't think any of this would have happened,' she said sadly. 'Look at how the police reacted when Victor died.' Detective Inspector John Noonan had spoken for many in the force when he suggested that perhaps this was Peirce's comeuppance for his role in the shooting of the two young police constables in Walsh Street. Noonan had led the investigation into the police shootings, for which Peirce and his brother Trevor Pettingill were ultimately acquitted. 'It's just nice that people pay for their sins. Certainly, I don't view it [Peirce's death] with any sadness,' Noonan had told the press.

Kath still rankled at the message in Noonan's comments that there was no escape from the ganglands: 'You saw how Inspector Noonan carried on. "You live by the gun, you die by the gun." He wants to think about that himself.' The sad reality that her family had reaped what it sowed weighed heavily on Kath. She expected no favours from the homicide squad, 'because of what Dennis got away with. I had them ring here a few years ago and say, "Don't you think it's time to tell us where the bodies are buried, so we can let the families have them back to bury them?".' She predicted there would be no justice for the families in the present war. It was only the mothers of crims who mourned heads like Victor. 'Why would the police want to solve them? It's only going to bugger up the courts . . . And they'll be there forever and they'll [the killers] probably be found not guilty!' she said, jabbing a bony finger at me. 'I just want it go away. I don't want anything done about it.'

Then she reminded me that the tradition of 'catch and kill your own' was perhaps alive and well. She said that a year after Victor's death she had received a telephone call from a homicide detective with a tantalising opportunity. She claimed the detective had told her the names of four men police were planning to arrest on suspicion of Peirce's murder.

Later, police did arrest five suspects in a series of raids in country Victoria, but they were all released without charge. To Kath, the detective's message was clear: 'They wanted us to shoot 'em dead, to catch and kill our own. But I'm sorry – it's not going to happen.' A flash of anger rippled across her face, so strong it seemed to light up even her dead eye. (It was terrifying how much expression she could put into a glass eye. You had to remind yourself which was the live one.) Perhaps it was anger that police would try to pitch her back into the old ways. She had gone to the extent of banning her son Peter Allen from visiting her down here because 'he would fuck things up for me, going around nicking stuff and so on'. And now here were the police giving her the opportunity to slip straight back into the days of gore and vengeance. 'Why else would they have told me? And make sure that I took the spellings right? What does that say to you? That we were supposed to clean 'em up.' Benji's name was not among the suspects.

I suggested that there was a time when she would gladly have sent more sons after the suspects. She was quiet and I could hear the roar of the sea behind her. 'No, no . . . It's not on any more.' So there was no one in the clan prepared to take revenge? Even when they gave you the names of the suspects? 'I don't know. None in my family will,' she said coyly. That wasn't to say the

Pettingills had lost their dash. 'Chopper Read said I'm running out of sons . . . Well, let me tell you, there's forty-nine of us left in my family, and that's a lotta people.'

Even if Kath and the boys had acted on the detective's tip, they would have been chasing the wrong men. In September 2004, homicide detective Sergeant Steve White travelled from Melbourne to Goulburn Jail in New South Wales to visit a prisoner serving a sentence for two unrelated charges of manslaughter in Albury. White had taken more than an educated guess that Warren Alan 'Peter' Forbes could help him close another murder docket: that of Victor George Peirce.

In the early hours of 6 January 2002, 31-year-old Forbes had stabbed a Wodonga man, Ross Kimball, to death after a confrontation in an Albury street. Forbes had moved to Albury in late 2001 immediately after his release from jail in Victoria, where he had convictions for four armed robberies. While on bail for the Kimball killing, Forbes killed again. On 3 May he went to visit his then best friend, 41-year-old Andy Hullick, a former member of the Albury-based Black Uhlan motorcycle gang. They had met in jail in the late 1990s when Hullick was on remand charged with murder (a charge he ultimately beat) and Forbes was serving time for attempted armed robbery and assault. On that May morning, Forbes was visiting Hullick in his caravan when an argument broke out. Forbes claimed in evidence that Hullick had come at him with a weapon and they had wrestled. During the struggle, Forbes had wrenched a .357 revolver from Hullick's hands and shot him once in the abdomen. Two days into his murder trial, Forbes pleaded guilty to the manslaughter of his best friend.

In visiting Forbes, Detective White was acting on information that the bone of contention between Forbes and Hullick had been the proceeds of the contract killing of Victor Peirce. But evil as he was, Forbes was not the man who killed Victor Peirce. He must have enjoyed playing with the heads of the homicide squad as they earnestly tried to extract a confession month after month. Finally in March 2007, the homicide squad officially transferred the murder to the Purana Taskforce.

No matter how the end comes for the villains, it's always the women who pick up the pieces. There is no such thing as liberation in this world. Only in death is there freedom for the wives of crime. At 5.30 on the morning I interviewed Wendy, her youngest-born, twelve-year-old Vinnie, had suffered a seizure and been rushed to hospital. Katie, then nineteen, had been drifting in and out of depression since Victor's death, and the anger in young Victor, now twenty-six, was turning inward. There was only worse to come for this family accursed by their own actions.

On Remembrance Day, their father's birthday, the kids had gone down to Bay Street to attach flowers and birthday wishes to the light pole where Victor had parked the car for the last time. It was only now that Wendy understood the meaning of death. 'Beforehand, I thought it was quite funny – nothing at all. I would have probably shot somebody if I could. I would have. It wouldn't have worried me. But as soon as Victor was shot, my whole life turned around. I couldn't wish anybody in life to go through this. I lost the love of my life. I felt so sick in the stomach, an emptiness I couldn't explain. And I thought, death isn't the solution.'

I asked if she could remember when she saw her first dead body. 'Hmmm, no – it wasn't Sissy in the boot, she wasn't dead. Dennis only cut her throat, she wasn't dead. Let's see – I guess it must have been Anton.' Victor and Wendy had walked into the house in Stephenson Street to be confronted by the sight of Allen chopping the legs off a Hells Angel named Anton Kenny with a chainsaw so he could fit the body into a 44-gallon drum for dumping in the river. 'Victor picked up a toe with a bit of leg still attached and chased me round the house with it. I'm dry-retching trying to get out of there and Victor's just laughing, and I'm saying, "Please, Victor, that's sick." I had nightmares over that for ages.

'I didn't really feel no sympathy for nobody. That's what I don't understand. It's taken Victor's murder to change me – and it's too late in life.'

I left Wendy with her sorrow and regret. She was waiting for the sheriff to turn up with a court order to repossess her car, the Commodore that Victor had died in. Even Victor Peirce, stick-up man, accused cop-killer, drug dealer and criminal legend, had to pay his traffic fines. He and Wendy had racked up $45 000 worth of speeding tickets and parking fines. Now the sheriff was at the door. It was time to count the cost of loving her villainous Victor.

Perhaps she wasn't finished with underworld beaux after all, though. Later a card landed in her letterbox from none other than the Gunsmith, now hidden away in a jail interstate. He wrote that though he had never met Wendy, he thought about her 24/7 and perhaps one day his dream could come true. He finished the card with kisses and hugs. Wendy didn't know what to think.

Perhaps the Gunsmith was demonstrating his love by helping police to nab the three other men suspected of involvement in Victor's murder. Only one had been convicted at the time of writing. But the misery goes on for the Peirce family. On December 15 2009, Katie Peirce, now twenty-four, was found dead of pneumonia and drug toxicity after ingesting methadone with a man, just out of jail, she had met three days earlier. Her two-year-old daughter was on the scene when police attended. Katie and her mother were awaiting trial for attempted murder at the time. It was alleged they had paid a heroin addict to attack the father of a man whose son had been in a relationship with Katie. It seems the attacker got the wrong man, but still sliced his face open with a meat cleaver. So much for lessons learnt.

13 | A GOOD FRIEND IS EVERYONE'S ENEMY

Very early on in our relationship, Carl Williams and I established some ground rules. It was as much for my self-preservation as for anything else that I brought up the matter.

Whenever I discussed the conflict with outsiders, the same question always came up eventually: 'Aren't you concerned for your own safety when you are having so much contact with these kinds of people?' I would answer that covering this story was less scary, in a relative sense, than the couple of minor civil wars I had encountered as a reporter in Africa. Unlike those conflicts, the killing in Melbourne was targeted to individuals and generally neat. Bystanders had no need to fear random attacks, and the generals, including Carl, were approachable, negotiable and surprisingly media-savvy.

However, I did have the welfare of my two young children and ex-wife to worry about. To feel completely safe, I needed Carl to understand that I meant him no harm, that speaking to a reporter might actually help him in his various legal manoeuvres.

'The way I see it, we have something in common,' I began. 'I am trying to write stories that will sell magazines and put bums on seats on Sunday morning. You are trying to get off your drugs trial on the basis of pre-trial publicity, that the media won't leave you alone. Correct?' He nodded. 'So it occurs to me that you and I are in something of a partnership, as unusual as it might seem. Every time I write something nasty about you, it actually helps you. And the worse the publicity, the better for you.'

Carl was a businessman and that was how he saw the world. 'Good as gold,' he said.

Over a coffee one day with Carl and his father, George, I asked straight out whether as a journalist I had anything to fear. Carl looked shocked and slapped a meaty hand on my shoulder. 'Oh no, this is not your fight, buddy. Don't worry. People actually like you. Not everyone, of course . . . But you're sweet.' He was laughing with his eyes.

So nothing I could write would move a sinister hand against me? 'No, no way,' Carl and George chimed, almost in unison.

Carl took a long, loud draw on his low-fat fruit shake, turning the straw to get all the pink chewy bits at the bottom. 'No, they wouldn't hurt you,' said George soothingly. 'Not unless you really took, like, a *vendetta* out on someone – you know what I mean.' He had one blind eye that seemed to wander at moments like these.

I found his words less than reassuring. *No, George, I don't know*. The idea of taking a vendetta out on these types was indeed suicidal, but the problem was who defined the term 'vendetta'. I told Carl, 'As Bob Marley said, "The truth may be an offence but not a sin".' He smiled and looked down sheepishly. 'Therefore, you have no reason to have me dealt with for anything I might write. We're involved in the first gangster war of the information age, whether we like it or not.' Carl and George liked this line, sounding as it did like they were involved in something historic, not just a messy bloodletting in the less civilised end of town. With this idea in mind Carl and I could have a dialogue, even though in reality our interests were utterly opposed. Yet it wasn't my role to judge him, so I could take him at his word.

As our relationship progressed, I found that rather than tell a lie, Carl would simply not answer a question. He would tune out into silence or, more occasionally, tell me, 'You're off your head' and drift onto something else. We stayed away from the obvious no-go areas. Carl would give me his version of life in the under-world, explaining the language and customs, how one group fitted with another, what it was like to get shot, character analyses of his enemies, and so on. When I produced stories on the police's efforts to pin the latest murder, he would critique them for me. If he was displeased, he might say, 'There wasn't much punch in that one, was there?' Or if he had enjoyed the story, he would chuckle and say, 'You know what? You're learning fast, buddy. You're learning fast. You had better put me on a wage soon.'

'Sure, Carl, when you solve all the murders and prove your innocence, mate,' I would say.

'Nah, reckon we'll let Purana do that, eh?'

Carl saved the Nine Network a considerable sum in 2004. I had produced a forty-minute documentary detailing the state of the war, due to screen in Victoria on Monday 31 May. Over a cup of coffee on the Thursday before, Carl casually mentioned that the Office of Public Prosecutions was going to seek a suppression order the following day on further reporting of his cases, and his counsel, Peter Faris QC, would be supporting the OPP's application. This tip-off was typical of Carl's ambivalence towards the press. Here he was, paying his legal counsel thousands of dollars a day to shut the media down, yet at the same time leaking to the enemy.

The next day, Nine and the other media outlets opposed the OPP application in court but failed. The judge imposed an interim injunction until the Monday morning, which meant he would make a final ruling just hours before our doco was due to air. On the Monday afternoon, I sat next to Carl in the Supreme Court fully expecting the injunction to be upheld, torpedoing our doco and any further reporting of the war. Much to my amazement, Justice Cummins lifted the suppression order, effectively ruling that the widespread media comment then appearing did not mean that Carl could not get a fair trial on his drug-trafficking and threat-to-kill charges. Justice Cummins said that 'juries are robust and responsible . . . time and again, [they] come to court in cases of great notoriety and publicity and demonstrate by their evident application of mind that they act according to their oath or affirmation to give a true verdict according to the evidence led before them in Court. Juries see the effort which all counsel put into cases, they see the attention to evidence, they see the testing of evidence and often the destruction of apparently persuasive evidence by cross-examination, they hear the directions of the trial judge and they are in law bound by them. Juries by direction, observation and osmosis assume a proper and responsible role as the judges of the facts, judging the case solely on the evidence led in court.'

Carl had been in an ebullient mood when he arrived at court an hour before, resplendent in a long, black leather overcoat, his hands thrust into the pockets. 'What have you got in the pockets, Carl?' I asked him as we walked to court.

'Two .44s [pistols],' came the reply.

He listened carefully to the judge's ruling, a frown developing on his face. 'Does that mean youse can write what you like about me, mate?' he whispered.

'Yeah, that's right, mate,' I said, before racing back to the station to resurrect our documentary. It screened at 10.50 that night and attracted a primetime-sized audience despite the late hour.

Rightly or wrongly, I began to see Carl as a man caught up in circumstances. He had not provoked those circumstances: Jason had shot him. But by not reporting the shooting he had made the war inevitable. Once you put yourself outside the square of civil society, there is no right or wrong, only trust – and Carl could trust very few. He now had to play out the drama he had created before he was swept away by it.

He believed he was involved in a struggle with the criminal establishment – mobsters with friends high in the police and government, who were protecting them. Every time he was arrested between 1999 and 2004, he expected to be killed by police. Yet he had survived, and now it could be said that he was winning the war. He told me that ordinary citizens approached him in the street to encourage him to keep plugging away. 'Good on you for taking on the biggest bullies in town,' they had said to him. He knew his ability to manipulate the emotions of an entire city wouldn't last, but he was going to enjoy it while he could.

He was a character riven with contradictions: an alleged gangland killer who was completely terrified of spiders, a man who could take a bullet in the guts but would never subject himself to a tattooist's needle. He was the head of an empire that depended on utmost secrecy, yet he was happy to befriend a journalist, get on the grog and the coke and shoot his mouth off.

Carl loved to trade gossip and learn what the cops were up to. I was aware that at times he wanted to use me to send messages to the Purana Taskforce. He knew that the Dog Squad were probably listening in on our telephone conversations – most areas of his life had been under electronic surveillance since the late 1990s. So after a few drinks, he liked to test the boundaries, often coming tantalisingly close to giving me a confession. In particular, he liked to report what others had said to him about his team. 'Someone said to me that even if we had been doing anything, it would be just like we were cleaning up the waste of the underworld anyway. No one's going to miss these villains, that bloke said.'

'What do *you* think, Carl?

'I dunno . . . they're all off their heads really.' (By 'they', he meant the media, the cops and other crims.)

I had another, more personal interest that drew me to Carl. During Easter 1995, I had been filming with a television crew in the squalid townships of Johannesburg, South Africa. One cold, drizzly morning, six drunken local street thieves had held us at gunpoint to rob us of our rental car. As an afterthought, one of them decided that it would be good business to kill me and the cameraman, lest we could later identify them to police. The two ringleaders slowly levelled their 9mms centimetres from our faces and prepared to shoot. It's an indescribable feeling to look down the barrel of a gun held by a man who obviously thinks nothing more of shooting you than putting down a dog.

For half a minute, our destiny was in the balance as our sound recordist, a local Zulu man who happened to hail from that township, desperately bargained for our lives, using his own as a chip. He stepped between us and the guns. As he was with us, he said, they would have to shoot him too; otherwise, he would bear witness against them. However, his family was well-known in the area, and if they shot him there would be repercussions. There were people peering at the scene through the ragged curtains of the surrounding shanties, so word would spread in the neighbourhood of who had done the deed, and others would seek to revenge him. No one would lag the men for killing two white guys, but to kill a brother from their own township would take the matter into a whole new realm. He stood firm, the upraised palms of his hands almost covering the muzzles of the guns. Better they take the car and leave quietly before a simple robbery became something much messier, he said. Reluctantly, they took his advice and drove away.

It was all over in less than five minutes, but that memory of feeling utterly helpless has never left me – the pounding of blood at my temples, the sphincter in my rectum threatening to give way. I didn't shit myself from fear, but I went close. Carl had been in the same position on his twenty-ninth birthday, at the hands of the Morans – but Jason had actually pulled the trigger. I hadn't been shot, but for more than a year after, the anger and fear had spilled over into the rest of my life. I became impatient and argumentative, impossible to live with, and increasingly remote from my wife and child. We were living in Harare, Zimbabwe, but I contrived to spend most of my time away, somewhere else on the continent, taking ever more bizarre risks. I was happy only when I'd had a skinful of beer and had an African girl under my arm. Even then,

I couldn't bear anyone coming up behind me, especially at night. I would have done anything to avoid looking down the barrel of a gun again, even if it meant shooting someone – yet I kept putting myself in harm's way. I felt in control and self-righteous. Looking back now, I think I was totally deranged.

Billy Longley told me that in the underworld a man changes once he's been shot: he has an aura about him that sets him apart. 'It's like an animal that has the memory of being wounded. They will come at you hard if they believe you are a threat to them,' he said. Carl had that aura, and I wanted to know what it was like to feel the way he did.

Though we began speaking by telephone most evenings and sharing more and more of the personal details of our lives, Carl and I still observed an unspoken protocol. If I called him on his mobile, he would rarely, if ever, answer it. Instead, he would use it like a pager, noting that I had rung and returning my call, presumably on someone else's phone. That way, I reasoned, he could dodge the surveillance teams he believed (with some justification) were listening in on his phone calls. Later, word filtered through from police sources that I should be careful what I said on my phone, as I was being picked up on surveillance tapes. As far as I was concerned, I was doing nothing wrong in talking to Carl, and I sent a message back to the police that I would continue talking to him regardless. I wondered then whether they were tapping my phone, too. If their main suspect was calling someone at all hours of the day from 'safe' phones, it would be a simple matter to put my phone 'off' too. The word of caution from police about my conversations with Carl seemed to confirm this suspicion.

Carl was always careful not to give away where he was when he called me. He would usually just say he was 'out and about' or 'on the move'. Likewise, I decided that keeping my precise location a secret wasn't a bad idea. I had taken my phone number and that of my ex-wife out of the telephone book, and made sure the gas and power bills weren't in my name. All my correspondence went through a post-office box or my office address. Whenever I wasn't producing work that indicated I was in Melbourne, I would tell contacts I was away in Sydney. Carl would call and ask, 'Where are you, buddy? Up there [Sydney] or down here [Melbourne]?'

On more than one occasion when I was actually in Melbourne, I replied, 'Down there. No – I mean up . . . Up here!' Carl never pulled me up on these petty deceptions. I think we both understood that it was in our respective interests. We needed a little mystery in our relationship.

By February 2004, Carl and Benji had moved into a splendid two-bedroom apartment, Unit 3004, on the thirtieth floor of Regency Towers, the residential wing of the Marriott Hotel. Carl's life had become an endless schedule of court appearances. There was a string of committal mentions on his two sets of drugs charges, and yet more trips to court for his threat-to-kill charges. He didn't take much interest in the fine detail of his legal defence. As long as his lawyers kept him out on bail for as long as possible, he would happily pay their bills. Peter Faris QC, the leader of his team, was one of the city's most senior silks and one of the most combative advocates going around. A man with a towering intellect and a temper to match, and a former chief of the National Crime Authority, Faris regularly acted as a Crown Prosecutor. He knew the system inside and out. Better still for Carl, Faris was his neighbour in Regency Towers. On their way to court, client and silk sometimes bumped into each other in the foyer, Carl in his beach fashions and Faris in his robes ready for another day of combat.

In Regency Towers Carl and Benji felt on top of things, at the centre of their own universe. The law courts were a short drive downtown, Crown Casino was just across the river beyond the strip of lap-dancing clubs and girlie bars on King Street, there was a KFC on the corner and a plush lobby bar where the waiters ran around for them as if they were celebrities. And there was always Barb's place in Essendon for home-cooked meals. A plate of eggs, baked beans and chips was just a phone call away. Entering and leaving the underground car park presented the only security risk. Routines had to be followed.

While Benji would be in and out, spending his evenings with his various girlfriends, Carl went to Barb's almost every night for her cooking. Very few meals were ever cooked in the apartment's splendid kitchen. Carl was happiest lying on his mother's couch with his mobile phone in hand. He spoke to a number of journalists regularly. His mother told me she would hear him laughing while he was on the phone flat on his back, the remains of his KFC Meal Deal on the side. She'd ask who it was and he'd say, 'It's just Adam, that journo.'

For Benji, a secure location in the city had obvious benefits. His home in Sunshine was well-known to friend and foe, and there he was an easy target no matter how many guns he had stooked around. If someone wanted to get him, it would be as easy as waiting for him to pull up in the driveway. He had seen how vulnerable a tough man could be, the look of terrified surprise when he realises it's his turn. Benji knew that his own death was now inevitable – he was way past due already – but he wouldn't make it easy for them. They would have to earn the pleasure of popping him. It would have to be well-planned to get him on the thirtieth floor. Only when he and Carl went to court did he leave his toy behind – he knew his foes in the Carlton Crew would never try to clip him while they walked to court. They were more likely to try to run him over. The old trick was to get a squarehead to hire a car, set up a theft and then use it to turn the enemy into roadkill.

In the last two years of his life, Benji was increasingly haunted by the prospect of his own death. He stayed at his sister Helen's house one night in late 2003 and told her of the recurring dreams that assailed him. In one, he saw a man in a big long coat walking slowly and purposefully after him. No matter how fast he ran the figure kept pace, and Benji would stumble and trip until finally he turned to face the spectre. PK's words kept coming back to him: 'We've done so many bad things to so many bad people, something has to come back to us eventually.'

In late 2003 he told Johnny of another recurring nightmare. 'Benji said in his dream he was standing in the garden of his house in Sunshine,' Johnny told me, 'and he could hear a big group of guys on motorcycles – you know, Harley Davidson choppers – rolling down Glengala Road towards his place. He couldn't see them but he knew they were coming for him, and the sound was getting louder and louder all the time. He said there was nothing he could do but just stand there all by himself and wait for them to get there. He said he was calm, prepared to take them, but before they came into view he would always wake up.'

As Benji contemplated his own death with a growing sense of occasion, the silliest thing happened: he realised he had something to live for. Perhaps he should hang around after all. It was inconvenient – he hadn't planned to stay around, much less leave anything for others to take care of. His brother crims always wondered why Benji used condoms when he slept with his women. Why bother – you wouldn't be around long to enough to suffer the rigours of HIV, and unwanted pregnancies would be someone else's problem. To Benji, that was the point: 'I'm not having some other dog raising my kid.' But in late 2003 one of his girlfriends, a Maltese girl named Natalie, gave birth to a daughter, Jessy.

Benji hadn't planned on having Jessy, but he clearly enjoyed the idea of fatherhood. 'Come on, babe,' he would say when Natalie was breastfeeding. 'Hurry up with the milk, will ya? I wanna take my darling girl for a cruise!' And off he'd go into the streets of Sunshine with Jessy in a baby capsule in the back seat of his Mercedes.

Benji told Natalie that he would never be an ordinary suburban dad to Jessy, and that she had to know he wouldn't be around forever – but she would always be welcome in the Veniamin family. He asked Helen to make sure Natalie and the kid had everything they needed.

Across town in Carlton, Mick Gatto was becoming ever more concerned at the precarious state of affairs in his city. He didn't know what to think any more, and there were some around him doubting his honour and integrity, too. When the Munster was knocked in December, there was suspicion among the boys that Mick's little mate Benji was involved. The press also made the connection. Carl denied any involvement, saying he had never met the Munster. 'The only things I have heard about Kinniburgh are good things,' he blithely told the press. Privately, the Morans believed the Savage had been the shooter that night. But in the autumn of 2004 the public consensus was that Benji was most likely to cop it for the Munster.

Yet police were quietly saying they couldn't put Benji in Belmont Avenue the night the Munster was hit. They had tracked his mobile phone and had placed him in the western suburbs, more than twenty kilometres from the scene.

Some of the city's worst gigs – idle gossips – began to weigh up what Mick had gained from the Munster's untimely demise. They began to speculate that Mick or somebody else might have used the cover of Carl's publicity to change the pecking order.

Then there was that silly business with the Chief Executive. Mick now regretted ever agreeing to mediate at the meeting between John Kizon and the other West Australians back in late 2002. There had been a follow-up meeting between Mick and the Chief Executive in October 2003 – one last chance at mediation as the bodies began to pile up – but that too had ended in bad blood.

Since Christmas 2003, Gatto had been aware that someone had a contract to kill him. And in February 2004, he found out who it was. A former policeman came to see him at La Porcella with some rather urgent news. The ex-jack had been in a pub on Royal

Parade, Carlton, with a man we'll call 'The Rat', who in his mid-fifties now fancied himself as a born-again hit man. The Rat loved a beer and a chat and this late-summer evening he'd been in fine form, talking loudly of a great little earner he'd picked up from the Chief Executive. It was a contract to knock Mick Gatto and it was worth $400 000, the biggest payday anyone had enjoyed in six years of contract killing. Many doubted that the Rat had the dash to kill Mick. He had killed three people in his career and came from a three-generation crime family, but had never sneaked a man of the standing and power of Gatto.

Not surprisingly, Mick was straight on to the Rat, asking for an explanation as to why he would consider such a heinous act. The Rat quickly denied he had any intention of offing Mick: he had just been shooting his mouth off in the pub. The Rat was loyal only to his own continued existence, but he pledged whatever fidelity he had left over to Mick, and the big man who liked to take people at their word, was content. The Rat went back to his drinking buddy, the former jack, and waved a large gun under his nose, warning him that contract killing was one business where it didn't pay to advertise.

Then Skull Murphy heard that Benji was also hot on Mick's trail. When Murphy told Mick, he had refused to believe it. 'He's my little mate – I have squared him away. It's sweet,' said Gatto, but Murphy was far from convinced.

There was also the matter of the contract still outstanding on Lewis Moran. With the Munster gone and Mick in the big chair in Carlton, it was his duty to protect Lewis – even if Lewis hadn't done much to protect himself since Jason's death. By six o'clock every evening you could find him and his mate Bertie Wrout in the front bar of the Brunswick Club enjoying a beer and a punt. Wrout would be perceived as a potential threat to anyone who planned to knock Lewis. They all knew the old saying from Ilario 'Larry' Zannino, one of the bosses of the Boston Mafia in the 1980s: 'If you're clipping people, I always say make sure you clip the people around him first. Get them together, 'cause everyone's got a friend. He could be the dirtiest sonofabitch in the world, but there's someone that likes that guy, and that's the guy that sneaks you.'

To make matters worse, men who were once loyal soldiers to Carlton were now sitting on the fence, reluctant to involve themselves in other people's fights. They'd been happy to show up at the Munster's funeral, but since December had made themselves scarce. The fence-sitters had their own connections to Williams and the Chief Executive and Benji; they had done drug business with Paul Kallipolitis and Dino Dibra. This is what happened when you allowed non-Calabrians into their little thing. The Calabrians had shared the love – Greeks, Albanians, Croatians . . . anyone with enough dash was welcome at Mick's table. The lines of respect that had always bound Mick and the boys to the deepest elements of the Calabrian leadership had been destroyed. People did what they thought they could get away with. Everyone was a big shot.

From the bleachers, the media were asking why, four months after the Munster's death, there had been no retaliation from the Carlton Crew. Were they a spent force? Chopper Read had called them 'the plastic godfathers' in his first book. Perhaps they had no stomach for the fight.

Gatto met Carl and Benji one night at Crown Casino in late December 2003. It was a brief and wary exchange, the tension between the parties clear. People kept reminding Mick that Benji had a contract on him and maybe a little part of him started to believe it. But Mick still looked upon Benji as a son. All would be well if he would just deny that he had killed the Munster. So Benji did, and it was enough. 'I've done my homework, and yes, Andrew, I believe you didn't kill Graham,' Mick said. Then he turned to Carl and stared at him hard for a moment. 'But you, buddy, I'm not sure about. Not sure at all.'

Carl denied any involvement with the Munster's murder, putting forward a theory about Asian gangs and even the police being the culprits. Mick was far from convinced, but all he wanted was to be left alone. 'You walk away from this and mind your own business,' he warned Carl. 'Anything with you, that's your problem. But if anything comes my way then I'll send somebody to you. I'll be careful with you, [and you] be careful with me. I believe you, you believe me – now we're even.

'That's a warning,' he declared. 'It's not my war.'

Assistant Commissioner Simon Overland was watching the play with increasing bemusement. He had locked up just two men, the Raptor and Goggles, for the murder of Michael Marshall. Nobody was talking. In his heart he knew it was only a matter of time.

Right now he could tell the story on his own, but stories are not evidence and there was not a jury that could convict on the cases Purana had. Victoria Police had dropped the ball on organised crime long before; now it was playing a desperate game of catch-up. For the present the wise guys were talking more with the press than with his investigators, but Purana was close to cracking Goggles – and if he sang, the rest of the criminal chorus would be close behind.

The underworld was buzzing with rumour and assumption parading as fact. Overland worried about what effect all this media pressure would have on the levels of paranoia already rising. There were police officers entangled in this: if backed into a corner they could strike out too.

'Be careful,' Overland warned me, not for the first time. 'You may say you are merely an observer, but what's that theory – even in the act of observation, one may change the nature of the thing one is observing.' His message was that everyone, from the murderers to the media, had become a player.

14 | BENJI'S BLUES

A soft wind was blowing in my face as I watched the waves break on the shore, the water glistening in the dying summer sun of 2004. It was hard to believe it was all over, that as the autumn shadows lengthened in Melbourne there had been an outbreak of good sense. It had been four months since the last hit.

The media were still feverishly speculating as to who might cop it next, but the underworld had retreated to the darkness again. Some said a peace was being negotiated, others said the guns of Carlton were being readied for a big hit on the upstarts of the western suburbs. The media, myself included, had absolutely no idea. Soon the newspapers front and back would be full of AFL footy, the gang war dismissed as a colourful aside, and I would be looking for another story.

As an afterthought, in a story for the *Sunday* program, I had posed the question: 'Will Benji take a bullet for his boss?' Not for a moment did I believe this might actually come true. I had sat back and admired the line, a parody of something I remembered from an old gangster movie. Until now those sort of clichéd gangster moments had only happened in movies.

Now, on 24 March, I thought I had put the whole subject of the war away for good, and was sitting enjoying the last rays of summer at a favourite camping spot on the south coast of New South Wales. My Nine colleague Brendan was off walking in the scrub with my sister, while two friends from New York were buying supplies in town. I was half asleep in my deckchair when Joe and Phil drove back into camp. Joe dropped the *Herald Sun* at my feet, saying something I didn't catch as he passed.

'Uh? What did you say?'

'I said, Benji's been whacked.' I looked down and saw the front page. The huge, bold print swam in front of my eyes: VENIAMIN SLAIN. For the past twenty-four hours, while I had been sunning myself, the underworld had been ablaze.

I spent the next twenty minutes running in ever-decreasing circles. Should I drive back to Melbourne and get straight into the fray? Should I go north to Sydney, as I had planned, to cover the nice, staid business story that awaited me? Or should I just throw the *Herald Sun* in the fire and pretend this hadn't happened?

Driving to a spot where I could get mobile reception, I found twenty-seven messages waiting for me. Roberta was one of the first to have called, just an hour after the shooting. Her voice was hoarse with grief and anguish: 'I suppose you have heard the tragic news about Andrew. Ring me. The fucking gangsters have killed him.'

I called Carl. He was cool and collected. 'They've got Andrew,' he said, then, recalling his 1999 birthday present from Jason, 'It was just like me. He was summoned to a meeting and then shot. You've got to tell them the truth about Andrew – he died an innocent man. There were no charges pending.'

I guess Carl was technically right. Except for forty-four unpaid traffic fines and a charge of driving while disqualified, Benji had a clean sheet – which of course didn't make him innocent. Far from it. Benji had gone into the lair of the enemy.

Earlier, Benji and Carl had gone to support the Raptor at a hearing. Television pictures showed them leaving the court, laughing as they ran the media gauntlet together one last time, stepping off the kerb and heading downtown. They walked out onto the road without looking for traffic and Carl put an arm out to stop Benji. 'Now who's the bodyguard, buddy?' he said. They got to their car and then Carl dropped Benji off in the city. Even one day after the incident Carl couldn't remember where he had gone next, but that was nothing unusual. He dimly recalled meeting up with his father, then coming back into the city. He had missed Benji by minutes, maybe less, at Regency Towers; he thought he smelled Benji's aftershave in the lift as he rode to the thirtieth floor.

It was Roberta's birthday, and at 1 p.m. Benji had called her, cheeky and bold as always. He had wished her happy birthday and told her he loved her. In Benji, Roberta thought she had found a friend who understood her. Maybe he wouldn't let her down like the others had, the dogs she had called friends over the years. Maybe she could trust him.

Then he had rushed to an appointment with Roberta's most feared enemy. At 2.01 p.m. Mick Gatto had called his little buddy. A police bug in Benji's Merc had recorded the short and cordial exchange: 'Hello . . . Hey, buddy, what's doing? Yeah . . . What? . . . Where's that? . . . The same place? I'll see you soon . . . See you soon, buddy . . . Affirmative, bye . . .'

Benji wove through the afternoon traffic, heading for La Por-cella, on the corner of Rathdowne and Faraday streets in Carlton. The days of 2002, when he had been at Mick's elbow down there at the big fella's office, must have seemed a thousand years ago. They had been close then, close like father and son.

Benji took another call two minutes later from an unknown party. 'Yeah, mate . . . Yep . . . Nah, nah, I'm not . . . I've just got to catch up with someone, just rang me, the big bloke. I'm just going to catch up with him . . . I'll ring you when I'm done . . . All right . . . See ya.'

There was nowhere to leave the car, but a double park outside Mick's place would do. He would only be a minute, and if he got a ticket, what did it matter? The car wasn't in his name anyway.

There was no mystery about who shot Benji, but whether it was murder was another matter. Witnesses heard a volley of shots fired in a back passageway just metres from Mick's table. Gatto came back into the restaurant tucking the alleged murder weapon – a .38 Smith and Wesson revolver – into the front of his trousers. He claimed that Benji had tried to kill him, saying Benji had fired on him and the bullet had just missed his ear. Then he called his friend Mattie Tomas, who was working with Gatto's two sons that after-noon on a building project. Fearing reprisals, he told Mattie to send his sons home for the day without telling them why. From the tone of Mick's voice Mattie knew not to argue or even ask ques-tions. After making the call to Mattie, Mick sat calmly and waited for the police to come and take him away, along with the body of his 'little mate'.

When he heard that Benji had been hit, Carl went straight to

La Porcella to see for himself, though he knew the place would be swarming with media. He stood behind the line of cameras and reporters outside the restaurant for a few seconds before somebody noticed him there in his stone-washed jeans and red Polo top, a sheen of cold sweat on his face. Then they turned their lenses and microphones on him, and for the first time he felt real fear. Alone and confused, Carl began to run. Where he was going he didn't quite know – he just wanted to get away from everything, from the ambulances, the jacks swarming everywhere, the media and their stupid questions. Gone was the cool, cocksure gangster from the morning's matinee session at court. Now he was a target, and the media were not about to miss.

Carl's mind was racing as the phalanx of media caught up. *What of the rest of the Carlton Crew? Is someone lurking in the street waiting for their chance to put me off, too? If they can kill Andrew in a cafe, then why not me?* Anything was possible right now. He decided to flag down a car. The Mazda 323 had to stop or it would have hit him. Carl jumped in and, to his great surprise, found he knew the driver – he was the cousin of a friend. Unfortunately he wasn't going far, just to the BP service station 150 metres up Rathdowne Street, and when they saw Carl getting out the media resumed their pursuit, chasing him around the petrol pumps, firing questions at him. Finally, he reacted and gave them the quote they needed for the 6 p.m. bulletin. 'You fucking vultures! Don't you know someone's just died?' he shouted, and then locked himself in the staff toilet to ring Roberta and ask her to bring up the car.

That night Carl lay awake thinking about Andrew. Who was

that 'someone' lying in the morgue? The same thought kept turning over in his mind: why had Benji gone to La Porcella to meet Mick without telling him or Roberta? Had he been a friend to the end, or had he been in the act of betrayal when he went to La Porcella that day? If Benji had been in the act of somersaulting Carl, well, he had got what was coming to him. What did that say about their friendship? Maybe it was just like Philly hit man Nick Caramandi had said: 'You heard of the double cross? In this business you gotta watch for the triple cross. You gotta always be alert. There's so much jealousy. Guys always trying to set you, put you in traps. Trying to get ya killed. There [is] so much viciousness in this thing.' It had all got too much for Caramandi, who lagged his boss Nicodemo Scarfo in 1989, bringing to a close Nicky's bloody 10-year reign over Philadelphia, the city of brotherly love.

In Cairns and on the Gold Coast that summer, feelings had stirred in Carl that he had thought lost and forgotten. Ever since Jason had shot him, there had been a numbness in his soul he couldn't explain. Not even the birth of his daughter had managed to soften the hardness in his heart. When his mate Dino Dibra had been shot in 2000, probably by Benji, Carl's heart had hardly flickered. Though he still had a picture of himself and Dino by his bed, he hadn't even gone to the funeral. The thought that Benji would sell him out after all they had been through, all they had said to each other, seemed impossible. But why would he go to La Porcella without him? Carl would never get to ask him now, so he tried to block it out of his mind. The death notices he wrote for Andrew spoke of the void in his heart:

We mourn the loss of a soul whose life was taken in the blackness of deceit. Only in good faith did you attend but were wounded by the Judas you thought a friend – Your friend Carl Williams

To ANDREW MY FRIEND It has taken me years to finally experience a broken heart. You were a sensation. This great loss is only God's gain. You put a roof over my head when I most needed one. Your generosity could not be matched by anyone. If I was not convinced before I am now that only the very special are taken before their time. Till we meet again. Thanks for being such a special friend. All my love to my friend. – Carl Williams

Back on the coast, I finally got down to the last of my messages. It was from Skull Murphy and was short and sweet. 'About time you did some work . . . See ya,' he said.

When Benji was laid to rest at St Andrew's Greek Orthodox Church in Sunshine, a week after his death, I was in Sydney. I had decided that the funeral was the last place I wanted to be. There would be too many cameras, too many reporters and too many mourning hoods ready to vent a little aggro on the media. Every angle would be covered by the press in exhaustive, intrusive detail. I had decided that out of respect for the family I would stay away. One less reporter would not be missed. So I remained in Sydney, keeping in touch with the players by phone.

The mobile had rung every five minutes since Benji's death, with radio stations from all over the country wanting to know the inside story. Basically, anyone who could reel off the names of the players had been transformed into an instant expert. For the first few days I had taken every call, but then I began to read my own words in stories by reporters from Queensland and Western Australia – they had taken my words from interviews I had done. I realised the media was feeding on itself. A TV crew flew in from New Zealand to cover the drama and in the absence of anyone else to interview spoke to me. The reporter asked whether it was safe to drive into town from the airport – it was getting that silly.

The night before Benji's funeral there was talk that Carl would be hit on his way from the city to the church in Sunshine. I called him and he confirmed that he had heard the same thing. Looking out at the lights of Melbourne from his high-rise apartment, Carl might have been forgiven for feeling alone, or even a little scared. The next day he would bury his friend, and now he was apparently marked for death in the morning. Yet he was calm and cool as we discussed how he might spend his last night on earth.

'Oh, not doin' much, buddy. I'm just having a quiet night at home,' he said absently. 'I'm certainly not goin' out for pizza, not even home delivery.' It was an absurd thought: Carl going to La Porcella, the restaurant where Gatto had allegedly shot his friend. He wouldn't have to wait for a table – maybe he could even take Gatto's, now that 'The Don' wasn't using it, making do as he was with prison food on 23-hour-a-day lockdown. I laughed along with Williams' gallows humour until it occurred to me that his best friend was lying cold in a funeral parlour across town, dressed for his date with eternity. Carl and Roberta had been to see Andrew at the morgue. The bullet wounds in his head and throat were neatly stitched, but the mortician's make-up couldn't conceal the powder burns from the muzzle flashes. Carl was oblivious to my discomfort. And here he was, making jokes about Italian restaurants.

From his window, he could look westwards to the endless expanse of suburbia he had left behind. I asked him if it had all been worth it. He replied that the story was not over yet. Even if they threw him in jail for all the murders, it wouldn't bother him. You did time easy when you were among friends, he said. 'I'm very popular in jail – I've got mates from Broadmeadows right through the system.' He warned that Gatto might do it tough considering how many associates Carl and Benji had in the nick. 'He might have a few problems inside,' said Williams, adding that of course he would never wish any harm to the Carlton boss.

In the days after Benji's death Carl had had time to think about his friend's last appointment with Gatto. Andrew (Carl never called him 'Benji') had been stupid to go to La Porcella by himself, he said. To go alone to see Gatto had broken every rule they had ever shared. From there, Benji's fate had been a simple matter of cause and effect. 'Of course it affects you. He was a good, loyal friend to me,' he began, but then stopped himself, remembering he had an image to maintain, 'but you should remember the good times you had with people, rather than sooking about losing them.'

Carl had turned the heat back on the media. It was one way of quelling the doubts in himself. He blamed the media for failing to understand that Benji had not shot Graham Kinniburgh. The constant pressure of media innuendo had made everyone nervous, he said. 'Andrew was tried by the media and sentenced to a public execution,' said Carl.

How then did he explain Gatto's words to police when they arrived at La Porcella, I asked. Mick had said, 'There's a man out back who said he shot Graham and he was going to do me. I took the gun off him and he came off worse.' Carl told me he had never seen Benji with a gun, but he must have been the only person in the western suburbs who hadn't. Stories were leaking out that Benji hadn't gone to the bathroom without a trusty toy or two in hand, but in his grief and confusion, Carl obviously needed to cling to his version of the truth. Otherwise, the implied disloyalty of Benji's meeting with Mick would not have allowed him to continue in calm control of his boys. What of the rest of the team? Where did their loyalty ultimately reside? Bonds forged in the best of times would now be tested in the very worst. They all wanted to be next to Carl as he moved around the nightclubs like a celebrity, but what if the money ran out? Everyone had their price; Carl knew that much for sure. He had given Andrew a 400-gram gold chain worth about $20 000 a few months earlier as a token of his genuine affection and a material sign of the renewed trust between them. The chain was now sitting on the dresser in Andrew's room. Just where the trust had gone was difficult to say.

Together Carl and Benji had made quite a team. They had let it be widely known in the underworld that they would take on anyone. Carl had always surrounded himself with guys more violent than he was, but Benji had had more dash than anyone he had ever seen. The two of them had been like Tony Montana and his sidekick, Manolo, in *Scarface* when they paraded for the media at court – Benji all loose and casual in his track pants and T-shirt, like he was off to the shops for a souvlaki, and Carl walking tall and tough, arms swinging, like he was off to a gunfight.

I could almost hear Pacino's Montana taunting the onlookers at a restaurant midway through the movie. 'What are you lookin' at?' he screeched. 'You're all a bunch of fuckin' assholes. You know why? You don't have the guts to be what you wanna be. You need people like me. You need people like me so you can point your fuckin' fingers, and say "That's the bad guy". So, what'll that make you? Good? You're not good. You just know how to hide, how to lie. Me, I don't have that problem. Me, I always tell the truth . . . even when I lie. So say goodnight to the bad guy. Come on. The last time you gonna see a bad guy like this again, let me tell you.'

When I told Carl about that *Scarface* scene, he said he had never seen the movie. I described how it ended, with the boss, Montana, wired to the gills on coke and taking on a whole army of guys who stormed the house with machine guns. They shot up the house and then turned their attention to Tony, who ended up face down in the fishpond. And what happened to Manolo? Well, Montana had shot him for sleeping with his sister.

Carl didn't seem very impressed. He said he preferred action movies. *How much more action would a guy need in a movie?* I thought. But, of course, Carl lived in Melbourne. Montana's Miami simply couldn't compete.

We talked for half an hour and it struck me just how alone Carl sounded that night. He was going to his first underworld funeral in the morning – he wasn't like the rest of them, who would turn up to every send-off just to be seen. The last time Carl had been to a funeral was for his brother, Shane, seven years before. He had cried hard that day and sworn he would never go through it again.

I wished him luck at the funeral. I knew this could be our last conversation, so I made a point of saying that I really did hope he survived the day.

As bad as he was, I was getting to like him. I had put on a mask in order to get close to him and Roberta so they would tell their stories, but I couldn't be sure I was still wearing it.

'I know you want me to survive. I know that, and I do appreciate it, buddy,' he said, then, changing the mood with some more black humour, 'Hey, I know what — why don't you come down one night soon and sleep over? Be my bodyguard for the night. There's a spare room here now, ya know.'

Was this a serious invitation? 'Sure, Carl,' I said.

'Yeah, no, come over and stay here. Okay, you don't have to stay in Andrew's room — you can come and share my bed. I'm not gay or nothing, you know. We'll sleep top to toe,' he said, laughing hard now. In the past few months I had been toe to toe with some of the city's biggest crims, but top to toe was an angle I had never contemplated. I nearly said yes, but even my editor at *The Bulletin*, Garry Linnell, who was usually in favour of a calculated risk or two, advised against it when I rang him later that night.

If my objectivity in this story had been in doubt before, entertaining the idea of a sleepover at Carl Williams' house settled the issue. To have any kind of relationship with the players in this story required a person to choose sides, and I had done so, quite against my better judgement. Earlier in the piece a Purana Taskforce investigator had asked me which of the warring parties I was backing and I had rather grandly replied that I was on the side of civil society and therefore the police, no question and no doubt. Now, with allegations of shadowy police involvement in the murders and talk of historic links between the coppers and the Carlton Crew, it was getting harder to pick black from white. A dozen or more officers were awaiting trial on a wide range of offences, from drug trafficking to selling information to villains – but why was no one who was in the dock above the rank of senior sergeant? Did corruption begin and end in the lower ranks, or was there a much deeper status quo being challenged here?

Carl saw the Carlton Crew as a privileged clique who, with their cop mates, had run the underworld like a parallel government, dishing out opportunities only to those who paid tribute to them and shutting down anyone who didn't. Carl had revelled in his outsider status and had drawn soldiers away from the bosses of Carlton and poked fun at their old-fashioned ways. If he was taking on the power, then there was a dread certainty that he must eventually fail. Someone would get around to the job that Jason Moran hadn't had the bottle to finish back in 1999. In the meantime, Carl was going to rewrite the script, pull down the scenery and steal the best lines in the play for himself. He fully expected to be killed, so he had no fear. To be the underdog seemed a more honourable position.

Here was a man offering a qualified look into his underworld, not to mention a sleepover. I just had to hang around to see how this thing played out. He said not to worry about him – he had asked an associate to scope out the venue for Benji's funeral. He described to me in detail the layout of the grounds, then said cryptically, 'You've got to be on the ball to fall off it.'

Almost as an afterthought, he added that the media should be careful about getting too close to the mourners the next day. This wasn't the kind of funeral where people came to be seen by reporters and camera crews, who would run the risk of 'a clip over the ear' if they got too close. Maybe they should stay across the road, he suggested.

More than 800 people turned up to farewell Benji at St Andrew's in Sunshine, where, a lifetime ago, he had been an altar boy. As Carl had predicted, the media were not well received: a group of young boys pelted them with eggs and golf balls and a large and menacing bikie stood watch, giving threatening looks towards any who strayed too close. It was clear that, in death, Benji had become a folk hero to the young people of Sunshine, and everyone wanted to get near him. The tales of his big heart were already growing and reputations were at stake. A good performance here could set you up for a while.

During the service the Chief Executive hovered close to the front of the church, just a few metres from Benji's open casket. Roberta sat in the front row, comforting Benji's mother, Marianna. Carl was one row back alongside Terrence Chimirri, who had quickly elected himself Carl's new shadow. The service was conducted in Greek, and one of the three priests gave a prophetic warning, admonishing the mourners not to point 'the finger of blame' because the finger could also be 'pointed at you'.

As the service concluded the Chief Executive stepped boldly forward before Benji's family and friends could rise, and planted a tender kiss on the dead man's bandaged face. Benji had seen the

Chief Executive betrayed and beaten in the Carlton lair and had sworn he was through with Mick and the boys. For him to go back to La Porcella, even for money, made no sense. The Chief Executive could buy and sell those guys a hundred times over. He had shown Benji a new vista of opportunity, and still Benji had gone back to Mick.

One thing you could rule out for certain: Benji had not gone to La Porcella to make peace. If someone had wanted peace, Benji was the last person they would have sent.

15 | CHOPPER'S BLOCK

Mark Brandon 'Chopper' Read couldn't understand it. After eleven books of crime fiction, the words had just stopped coming. The early books, written while he was still in jail, had literally flown from his fingers. But he couldn't get started on number twelve.

We were in a cocktail lounge in Sydney, eight days after Benji's death and thirty hours after he had been buried in the biggest and flashest black granite grave the cemetery had ever seen, one that towered over the others like the Rialto dwarfed the rest of the Melbourne city skyline. Chopper was in Sydney for the opening of his latest exhibition of paintings, and a queue of young people was lining up to shake his hand and ask his opinion on the latest gang news. They were mostly uni students, polite young kids. This was as close as most would ever come to the underworld. 'HELLO, CHOPPER . . . I mean MARK . . . MY NAME IS JUSTIN,' yelled one. The artist might have no ears, but he isn't deaf.

Read just couldn't come to grips with what was happening out in the ganglands. He felt as clueless as the rest of us in Melbourne. Williams' crew was something new and different. Chopper had lost count of how many times he had heard of so-called new generations in the ganglands. It was a theme that had run through villains' heads ever since 1931, when Lucky Luciano had taken his famous leak, the signal for Bugsy and the boys to run into that Coney Island Italian restaurant and put a couple into Joe 'The Boss' Masseria.

Most of the crew who had inspired Chopper's stories were now dead. Jason and Mark Moran, Alphonse Gangitano, Frank Benvenuto and 'Mad Charlie' Hegyalji had all gone the same way. He missed them in a kind of sentimental way – even Alphonse, whom he had sworn to kill back in the 1980s. He thought of their feud now with fondness. It had all been a simple personality clash with Alphonse, exaggerated and inflamed by the media. 'He was born and bred from upper-class Italians. He was an educated Italian who went to a private school, and I was an uneducated sort of peasant in his mind,' Chopper said. 'He used to call me dumb. [I'm] dumb enough to live longer than him.'

For all his swagger and fine clothes, Alphonse had made a very unstylish corpse. He had been shot in the back as he fled his killer, who had delivered a coup de grace to his forehead, and his wife, Virginia, had found him in his underpants bleeding to death on the laundry floor, another victim of 'friendly fire'. Alphonse's life had been a triumph of style over substance. The self-styled 'Robert De Niro' of Lygon Street had died with barely $5000 in the bank, a $220000 mortgage on his Templestowe home and another $200000 owing on a half-share of a Lygon Street property his mother had bequeathed him.

Not that all the fallen hoods had been Chopper's enemies, he was quick to tell me. Victim number two, Charles 'Mad Charlie'

Hegyalji, who died on 23 November 1998, had been a close friend and a villain Chopper regarded as 'probably the most glorious in Melbourne's criminal history'. A Hungarian immigrant, he had thought his mother was bringing him to America rather than Australia. He told Chopper he had thought Melbourne was New York and asked his mother what had happened to the Statue of Liberty. Getting over the initial disappointment, he set about learning every-thing he could about the New York mob. 'All he wanted to do was to grow up to be a gangster,' Chopper said.

In the early 1970s, Charlie and his family actually went to New York to visit relatives, and for a week he waited outside the Hotsy-Totsy nightclub for a glimpse of the boss of all bosses, Carlo Gambino. Finally Gambino pulled up in his Rolls Royce and got out and there was a teenaged Charlie standing freezing his arse off in the snow. He went over and jumped in front of Gambino, jumbling out a well-rehearsed spiel in Italian. Gambino gave Charlie a pinch on the cheek and patted him on the head affectionately. It was a crowning moment for Charlie, who felt like he was well on the way to becoming a 'made guy', or an initiated member of the Sicilian Mafia. He finished up one of the wealthiest middlemen in Australia's amphetamine trade, controlling just about all of the distributors of the precursor drug ketone.

Charlie began his criminal career calling himself 'The Don' after his hero Gambino, but later decided that 'Machine-Gun Charlie' was a more suitably fearsome moniker for a man on the rise. That nickname was already taken: Dragan 'Charlie' Arnautovic, a heroin dealer, had been using the handle 'Machine Gun' for years. Hegyalji objected loudly whenever he got the chance – Arnautovic didn't even use weapons and had got the name from the way he spoke: he jabbered away like a machine gun. His real name wasn't even Charles. It was a terrible waste of a great nickname, argued Charlie, and *he* should have it. But it never stuck. Popular consensus was that because Arnautovic used 'Machine Gun' as his fighting name in the ring, the honour was rightfully his.

Hegyalji was stuck with 'Mad Charlie'. It was unfair, but everyone agreed that the name pretty much summed up the man and his approach to life and business. In 1989 he was shot in the stomach over a drug deal gone bad, and a few months later he shot and wounded a man in a St Kilda car park as payback. He was charged with attempted murder after a blazing gunfight in Prahran in 1997, but all the witnesses developed spontaneous amnesia and refused to testify, so the case was dropped. In his last years Charlie was working both sides of the fence, selling precursor chemicals to his associates on behalf of the Victorian drug squad, who would then follow Charlie's customers back to the speed labs and bust them. It worked well for him, providing a nice little insurance policy for his own activities. At the time of his death he was said to have been owed up to $100 000 for various outstanding bits of business. If that's right, it was Mad Charlie who had the problem. Back then, when the demand for shooters was weak, a contract hit could cost you only $50 000, or less. Do the maths.

It's also said that it was Dino Dibra, a long-time customer of Charlie's, who led the hit squad on 23 November 1998 when Charlie was shot to death at 1 a.m. outside his home after a night out with friends. Despite the elaborate security system he had installed, his body lay by the shrubbery in his front garden until eight o'clock the next morning. 'Poor old Charlie,' said Chopper. 'He was a good bloke.'

This rich crop of characters had been grist to Chopper's mill for years. Now they were all gone, and he didn't know where his next characters would come from. At forty-nine, he had become an artefact of another era, a piece of living, breathing tattooed history. 'You know, if the definition of being a successful crim is living well and never having to work for it, I reckon I've been a bloody huge success. I've done all right, I have,' he said.

Chopper did not owe his survival to the exercise of good judgement. In January 1978 he had attacked Judge Martin of the County Court in a plan to force the screws to let Chopper's friend Jimmy Loughnan out of Ararat Prison. Chopper got seventeen and a half years for that one. It was a scheme doomed to failure, but he might have expected a little respect from Jimmy – gratitude, even. Not so. 'I got stabbed by him a year later,' he said. '[By] the age of forty-five, I realised I could no longer tell my enemies from my friends, which had resulted in various attempts to kill and injure me. I kept trying to convince myself that I could tell my friends from my enemies, but my friends kept turning into my enemies all my life.'

And just because they turned up to your funeral didn't make them your friends, I suggested. 'No, no. I'll be very suspicious of anyone who turns up to my funeral,' he said, without a hint of a laugh.

He wondered how Mick Gatto had got himself involved in this mess. He had known Gatto since the 1970s. One summer night at the Myer Music Bowl someone had smashed Chopper over the head with a claw hammer. The assailant had been preparing to stove Chopper's head in when Big Mick had stepped in and saved him. Chopper was backing Gatto to get off on self-defence for the murder of Veniamin: 'When I shot Sammy the Turk [outside Bojangles nightclub in 1987], I had on my person a sawn-off shot-gun, a Beretta and a stick of gelignite . . . and I was wearing a bulletproof vest [which Skull Murphy later told me had mysteriously disappeared from his locker at Russell Street police station]. Mean-while, Sammy was unarmed.' Chopper claimed in court that Sammy had grabbed the Beretta, so he, Chopper, had opened up with the sawn-off, the Turk taking the full force of the blast in his throat. 'It was a fanciful story, really,' said Chopper, smiling with satisfaction as the art dealer put a red 'sold' sticker on another of his creations. I suggested that perhaps it was time for him to put away the 'fac-tion' and simply tell his own story – maybe that would unlock the words again. He said it was a rather novel idea and that he would think about it. (Finally, in late 2010, the twelfth Chopper title did emerge, but only after his wife Margaret got involved as co-writer.)

'But there is one fact I'm sure of,' said Chopper. 'Mick will get off this [the killing of Veniamin].' Police were very confident that Gatto would go down for the murder. A body bag had been found in the boot of Gatto's car, plus ammunition for a hand gun. It looked bad for Gatto but forensics were already going his way. If the Crown were to prove that Gatto had murdered Veniamin, they had to prove that Benji had come to the meeting unarmed. The defence alleged that Benji had a pistol down inside his track pants, the weapon that Gatto finally killed him with. If the gun had been in Benji's track pants or briefs there would be oil, dust and gunshot residue on the inside of the fabric. The state of the drawstring in Benji's pants was also crucial. If it wasn't tied, the elastic waistband of his trackies could not have supported the heavy firearm. The clothes needed to be separated, bagged and tagged individually. However, experienced forensic officers inexplicably placed all of Veniamin's clothes in the same bag, contaminating the evidence and meaning gunshot residue from the exterior of the clothes could be spread to the inside fabric. At that moment Gatto's acquittal was more or less assured. With the forensic evidence silent, the only voice the jury would hear from that back room at La Porcella would be Mick's.

'The living man controls the crime scene,' said Chopper. It's how he himself had beaten the murder rap for Sammy the Turk. 'The living man gets to tell the coroner what happened.'

In the end, defence counsel Robert Richter QC did much more than he had to in getting Mick off. He constructed an elaborate forensic case that showed the struggle between Gatto and Veniamin had continued until the last of five shots. He presented photographs of the revolver showing the second-last shot had been a misfire. The gun's hammer was slight faulty, never striking dead centre. Under pressure from both Gatto and Veniamin's hands during the struggle, it didn't fire. At this point Veniamin was already wounded once in the neck and once in the head, but he could, in theory, still have been fighting. After the misfire, the fifth shot severed Benji's spinal cord, immediately paralysing him.

Richter even broke with tradition and put the accused murderer in the witness box. He could have sat back and done nothing, because without the gunshot residue evidence, the Crown could never prove its case beyond reasonable doubt. The living man told the coroner what had happened.

'Thank God for the jury system,' shouted Mick in triumph as he was swamped by family and friends on the steps of the Victorian Supreme Court after his acquittal. I noticed that among the well-wishers hugging Mick was the proprietor of La Porcella. The shooting had destroyed his business – the only diners since then had been journalists and sightseers – yet here he was blessing and cuddling Mick in joy. Go figure.

It had been the most extraordinary few days Melbourne had seen since the homicidal merriment of the Painters and Dockers era. Chopper and I agreed that the best place to be in Melbourne at a time like this was Sydney. He said he expected the Williams team would respond to Benji's death, and there were no prizes for guessing who might be the target: Lewis Moran.

In *The Bulletin* that day I had broken the news that Veniamin had once been a loyal soldier for Gatto, the man who had killed him. Details had begun to tumble out about Veniamin's double life, with lurid tales of his involvement in earlier murders. Girlfriends were coming out of the woodwork to declare their undying love for their gangland beau. The *Herald Sun* quoted one as saying she had spent the night with Benji in Apartment 3004 in Regency Towers the night before he died. A second suggested she and Benji had been becoming a serious item. 'I wouldn't say we were boyfriend and girlfriend, but we were heading in that direction,' she had coyly told police, according to the newspaper.

Chopper listened intently as I passed on the latest intel. Just five months before, I had gone to him to interpret the goings-on in the underworld, and now the roles were reversed. It was somewhere past seven when, out of habit, I went to check my mobile for any new messages and remembered I had left it behind the bar. When I retrieved it, the screen showed that I had missed seven calls. Ominously, the first had come from Billy Longley, always the quickest off the mark with scoops from the ganglands. His message was simple: someone had shot Lewis Moran in the Brunswick Club.

It was on again. In a daze I went back to Chopper, who was now fielding questions from a doe-eyed French exchange student. I whispered the news in his ear, beginning with, 'You are not going to believe this . . .'

'Now *this* is getting exciting,' he said. I spent the next hour running to and from the men's toilet, away from the noise of the bar, to take calls and make them, trying to find out as many details as I could. Listening in must have provided some cheap entertainment for the kids coming in to chop up lines of speed in the grimy cubicles. 'They got him with a shotgun *and* a hand gun? Is that right? Two blokes in balaclavas . . . How many shots did they fire? Four?' When I took Roberta's call I noticed one bloke just standing there at the trough, listening with his fly open, not doing anything, just looking at me. She had heard the news on her car radio driving home to Moonee Ponds. 'What's happening? What have you heard?' she screeched down the phone. I told her all I knew, while the man at the trough edged ever closer.

'When is this all going to end? This has gotten right out of control. I feel like I'm goin' crazy,' she moaned, over and over again. I could hear children shrieking and arguing in the background. 'Do you think someone's going to come and get me and Carl?' It was a distinct possibility, I replied. 'No one deserves to die like this,' she said.

By the time of his death, Lewis Moran was a spent force. His counsel had told a court that Moran, assailed by arthritis and gout, was now physically incapable of firing a pistol. Everyone from the police down to the lowest cadet on the *Herald Sun* knew where to find him if they wanted him: propping up the bar of the Brunswick Club with his old china Bertie Wrout. Since he had lost Jason, Lewis had also lost whatever remained of his dash. He blamed himself for everything that had happened. If only he and Jason and Mark had dealt with Williams early on, his sons would have been alive today. And then Graham Kinniburgh had died, too – first his sons and then his best friend in the world. At the funeral he had hardly been able to look Graham's widow in the eye. His life now was nothing more than a daily routine of reporting to the police to satisfy his bail conditions and then going to the Brunswick Club.

At six o'clock, when he was killed, Lewis would have been at the club for a couple of hours. Usually, after a half-dozen seven-ounce beers and a few flutters on the dogs or the trots, he would be in his cups and off home. He might slide past the video store to pick up a movie, and then it would be onto the sofa for an evening in front of the box. Certainly neither he nor Wrout was carrying a weapon when they went to the Brunswick Club that Wednesday night.

Moran had apparently had quite a last day. According to Skull Murphy's sources, he had been seen enjoying a long lunch at a Middle Park restaurant with a number of his underworld mates.

He had told associates that he had nothing to live for after the deaths of Jason and Mark, and the murder of Kinniburgh was just a dismal epilogue to his wasted life. At fifty-eight, it was as if he was waiting for death. He had even refused police protection.

As the two hit men in balaclavas strode in the door of the Brunswick Club, Lewis was heard to say, 'Looks like we're off here,' but when it came, he apparently wasn't ready. He didn't take his bullets stoically, like the movie gangsters he loved so much: he ran for dear life. One shooter stayed by the door on guard as the other pursued Lewis with a shotgun and a handgun. Lewis ran toward the gaming area, his killer in hot pursuit. There was no escape, but when the shotgun failed to fire Lewis doubled back towards the bar. His killer caught up with him and fired into his head almost from contact range as a horrified female employee looked on. Bertie Wrout made a break for the door and the second shooter opened fire. Lewis Moran lay dead by the pool table, leaving a half-full beer and a betting slip on the bar – two items that neatly encapsulated his life in recent years.

A getaway car picked up the killers and screamed away into the night. A couple of men were seen arguing with police for the right to play pool as Moran's body lay inconveniently by. Bertie was grievously wounded but would recover, and had seen nothing that could help the police. Despite the jamming shotgun, it had been a textbook hit. Even the rush-hour traffic on Sydney Road had been compliant. Anyone who has ever sat behind a tram headed north on Sydney Road knows there is no quick escape, but this team had been blessed.

An hour after I heard the news I was back at my hotel when Carl called, opening with his now-familiar greeting, 'What's happening, buddy?'

'Not much, Carl,' I said, slipping into his tone of understatement. 'What about you, mate?'

'Nah, not much. A quiet one, buddy,' he said.

'I suppose you have heard about Lewis then?'

'Yeah, I heard it on the radio. It was pretty brazen, wasn't it. They just walked in off the street and give it to him, eh?'

'No ideas who might have done it, mate?'

'No, not a clue, mate,' he said.

Carl said he was at his mother's house in Essendon. He had hardly spent any time at Regency Towers since Andrew's death. At the time Lewis was getting shot, Carl had been getting his dinner from the local KFC. 'What did you have, Carl?' I asked quickly, trying to pick some little hole in his nonchalance.

'Zinger burger, chips and a Coke,' he replied, without missing a beat. 'Poor old Lewis.'

With Moran quickly forgotten, the conversation drifted to the dangers of fast food and cholesterol. Carl said he was trying to lose weight but it was difficult. The fast food had probably saved his life the night Jason had shot him, he said. He had KFC founder Colonel Harlan Sanders to thank for his survival, because his ample belly had taken most of the force and the bullet had been slowing dramatically when it struck a layer of muscle. It had deflected downwards and missed everything.

'No side effects, mate?' I asked.

'No mate, no worries. It come up good as gold. Anyway, gettin' shot didn't hurt that much,' he said, as if discussing a trip to the dentist. 'It didn't even bleed that much.' He said he'd heard the shot so he knew he was all right: 'If you don't hear the shot, you're in trouble . . . It means you're dead.'

If Carl was elated at the death of Lewis Moran, he didn't show it. In fact, he didn't betray anything at all. The death of Lewis seemingly meant nothing to him, except for the fact that it had proved the police wrong. All along, newspapers had carried comments from unnamed investigators suggesting that Carl would be next.

It was the end of a five-year feud, the last shots of a war that Jason had sworn would last forever. It was over for the Moran family. Only Lewis's brother Desmond 'Tuppence' Moran remained, and the next day it was reported that he had cleared out of the city just in case the killers came after him, too. *The Age*'s crime writer, John Silvester, came up with one of the best quotes of the war when I asked him whether anyone with the surname Moran should be feeling nervous. 'I wouldn't have a Moran couch,' he said.

Three generations of Moran crooks had now passed into history. Lewis was buried a few days later at St Therese's Church in Essendon. Only a small crowd of associates turned up to farewell him, mostly drinking buddies and mates from the racing industry. Saddest of all, when it came time to carry the coffin into the hearse for its final journey, there was no one close enough to him left to act as pallbearer. The undertakers put him on a gurney and wheeled him out of the church.

It had been easily the worst week of Purana's year-long existence. Taskforce chief Assistant Commissioner Simon Overland had raced to the scene of Moran's murder and held an impromptu press conference there. For the first time, it appeared that the strain was telling on him. When he spoke it was not the voice of a dispassionate science-led officer following the evidentiary trail, but a man shocked at the depravity taking place in his city. 'I think it's reached new depths of stupidity, to be quite frank. It is just stupid, wanton killing. And we are committed to doing everything that we can to stop it and to bring this to an end.'

For the best part of a year Overland had kept his cool while the body count continued to rise, fronting the media to assure the public that Purana would eventually bring the killers to justice. But his first duty was always to prevent the loss of life, and the murders of Veniamin and Lewis Moran hit the squad hard. Months of surveillance and forensic work now seemed to have gone to waste. The entire credibility of his operation was on the line. The newspapers began to speculate that this was just another investigation – a perfunctory effort and nothing more. One cartoon depicted Overland's squad as a toothless piranha swimming helplessly through an underwater field of dead gangsters in concrete boots.

Brian Murphy had been watching knockabouts bowl each other over since 1954. He'd seen forty-odd die in the Painters and Dockers war; he'd been there on the day in 1979 when Brian Kane had knocked Ray 'Chuck' Bennett inside the Magistrates' Court, setting off a struggle that claimed the lives of both Kane brothers; he'd watched on for two generations as the Carlton Crew settled its squabbles in blood. But he had never seen anything like this. The death of Andrew Veniamin had again prompted talk on the streets and in the media that this was a struggle between two generations of villains – the old school of Carlton versus the new of the untamed west – but Murphy wasn't convinced. 'That's what people would like to believe. I don't think there's any age barrier to being a villain. I think a lot of the young villains haven't done their time, haven't finished their apprenticeships. And with the greatest of respect to all those involved, this is just a matter of villains falling out,' he said.

It was a job for the most skilled of mediators, not that Skull was putting his own neck on the line. He said that if you called a meeting now, everyone would front tooled up to the eyeballs, even the mediator. Eventually, he said, sense would prevail. 'It has to, because if they keep going the way they are going, there's no end to it. There'll be retribution time after time.'

Men like the Raptor and his co-accused, on remand in Barwon Prison for the murder of Mick Marshall, were probably lucky to have been arrested, said Murphy. 'Some people say it's better to be tried by twelve than carried out by six. And from time to time that [being carried out by six] happens.'

A few months later I was invited to Chopper's fiftieth birthday party, held at the Leinster Arms in Collingwood. I was amazed to learn that this was his first-ever birthday celebration and his first birthday cake. Such was his concentration when he blew out the candles that I thought he must have been counting them, perhaps still doubting that he could have ever reached such a ripe old age.

Later, an old mate from Pentridge came up to shake his hand. 'C'mon, Chop, old son,' he said, with a wicked grin. 'One more murder – let's go. Just one more. We get manslaughter, we'll be out before we're sixty.'

'Nah,' said Chopper. With two little kids under his feet and a loving squarehead wife, he finally had something to live for.

I thought of a conversation I'd had with Carl on the night Lewis Moran was murdered. During his last phone call, well after midnight, I had suggested that he owed it to his daughter to survive this war. When he was old and grey he would be able to sit back and tell his story, just like Billy Longley was doing these days.

'You think so, Adam?' he said. 'I have never really thought about getting old.'

I suggested that when I returned home I would set up a tutorial for him with Billy on the delicate art of staying alive through the gang war. 'Thanks, buddy. You really do care,' he said.

16 | TIGER FOR A DAY

It was a bright autumn day, but Roberta was lighting candles and placing them all around her rented bungalow. Each had its own little memorial card bearing a picture of her beloved Benji, showing him looking out with an expression of faint amusement.

It was nine days after his death and Roberta was wearing a silver heart-shaped locket around her neck with a picture of him inside. She had arranged every photograph she could find of Benji on the shelves and counters of her home. There he was outside court, on the Gold Coast, standing close by her side. She had turned the house into a shrine to her fallen hit man. There was no trace of recent habitation by Carl, but there was a large photograph on the wall of him cradling their newborn daughter in his arms.

I had caught an early flight from Sydney and come straight to Roberta's place in Moonee Ponds. The traffic rushed past a few metres from the front of the house, and I was grateful when Danielle ran to open the door – this was not the kind of doorstep where one wanted to linger on a day like this. I stepped inside the house and was immediately enveloped in the smell of incense and candle wax. Roberta said she had been expecting something to happen that morning, maybe a drive-by shooting or perhaps even a bomb, so she had kept the kids inside. Someone might think it would be cute to get on the news by putting a couple into the house just to scare her. But no one had come, not even the media. Just the jacks from Purana and then me.

Roberta's sister Michelle was there, cooking food for the kids, while a very large, heavily tattooed young man named Beau was sitting on the couch watching the big-screen television. Roberta's sorrow had hardened to anger, and she talked of her deep hatred for the Morans, the fake displays of grief they'd put on at Jason's funeral. She had no doubt that they had been involved in Benji's death somehow. Her eleven-year-old daughter, Danielle showed me a picture that she had taken on her mobile phone of a sleeping Benji. She had put a sticker on his forehead and he had played along. *This man had so many faces*, I thought, *and nobody, except perhaps some of the dead, saw them all.*

'I think we should just go get 'em,' the child said, with quiet menace. She had loved Benji with all the force of a schoolgirl crush. He had tormented her mercilessly at the beginning, but in the end became her favourite babysitter.

Roberta had compiled a video of tender moments of Benji – portraits and footage shot during their Gold Coast holiday, set to the theme from *Titanic* by the kids. The video had been played at Benji's wake, where, police believed, the plot to hit Lewis Moran had been hatched. I imagined Benji's cohorts from Sunshine listening to Celine Dion warbling away, promising that the heart would indeed go on and on. Roberta had previously accused the police of orchestrating a campaign to kill Carl, but now she said she had changed her mind about them. They had told her Veniamin's murder would be investigated just like any other killing. It seemed to surprise her, this change of heart.

Roberta had been through all the mayhem and conflict, but until now she had never really been touched. Killing was something that happened to other people in the dead of night, a threat or problem solved by remote control. Killing was a death notice in the *Herald Sun*, the media seeking interviews, long sleek limos at funerals, floral tributes and cards with reams of pretty words. Killing meant a guilty sense of relief: *there but for the grace of God go I*. But then she had seen Benji on the slab, the wounds the morticians' make-up had not been able to cover, the livid powder burns, the coldness of his skin when she kissed him. Now killing was personal. For years they had been winning, but in one afternoon in Carlton she had lost everything. And Lewis Moran's death had not eased the pain – not even a bit.

I looked around the living room of the modest suburban home, at the little trinkets and furnishings, the family photographs (Carl and his groomsmen, all in sunglasses, striking gangster poses), the framed bouquet with tiny handcuffs attached from her wedding. On one wall was a movie poster of Marlon Brando as Don Corleone in *The Godfather*, his cheeks stuffed with tissue paper to get the puffed-out look. On the floor in the hall was another picture, its face turned to the wall. I couldn't resist taking a look: it was Tony Montana from *Scarface*, gun in hand, primed and ready for his final scene.

It was now only a question of time before someone got Carl, or so the press believed. *The Daily Telegraph* ran a picture of him running from La Porcella, with a target sight superimposed over his red Polo top. The headline read: THE NEXT DEAD THING.

'Fair dinkum,' Carl said, outraged, when I told him. 'How would people like it if I did the same thing to them?' He wasn't afraid of his enemies, but he was concerned that someone else might knock him, a nutter who wanted to make a name for himself by shooting the mobster of the moment. For the first time I could sense that he was feeling fear. But he wasn't going to hide himself away. 'If they want to kill me they're going to have work for it. You know what I mean, Adam. They're going to have to put in the hard yards. I'm not going to fall for any set-ups. Not going for no pizzas, no meetings, nothing,' he said. 'I don't go nowhere for no one.'

Even some police were in awe of the front that Williams was putting up. 'He's got a tiger by the tail and there's nothing else but to hang on,' one of them told me.

Carl had a different view: 'I reckon it's better to be a tiger for a day than a sheep for a thousand years.' He had borrowed the line from Italy's wartime fascist leader, Benito Mussolini, but it seemed appropriate. There was no point hiding and running anyway. As Benji had said, if someone's out to ambush you, then he'll get you – there's nothing surer.

The etiquette of a gangland execution was important to Carl. How you died determined how you would be remembered. He scoffed at talk that Lewis Moran had been waiting for death, fronting up to the same place every night. From his jail cell, Mick Gatto put an obituary in the *Herald Sun* for his friend Moran, suggesting that the crime patriarch had known it was coming and 'just didn't care'. A Gatto obituary was a must-have endorsement for fallen wise guys. It was said by crims that until Gatto rhapsodised you, you couldn't call yourself a gangland casualty. 'Gatto must have the *Herald Sun* classifieds on speed dial, he's so fast with them death notices,' said Carl, pointing out that when the two gunmen in balaclavas had confronted Moran and Wrout in the Brunswick Club, Moran had shown by running that he did care after all. When Carl's killers came for him, there would be no running away: 'He should have just charged at them. If they are going to mow you down anyway, then you might as well run at them.'

They knew where to find Carl: either at his mum's place or at his apartment. He was regularly seen in the lobby bar of the Marriott Hotel with an entourage around him. One night I joined the clan there. Carl appeared from the lifts and sauntered over to the group, flanked by three likely lads from Sunshine just a pace behind. The boys sat quietly on a couch at first, watching all the goings-on, but soon one of them got bored and decided he would gatecrash a twenty-first birthday party that was going on in the ballroom. The boys were young friends of Benji's whom Carl had recruited into the team. With Benji gone, they were still hanging with Carl. For these boys from the badlands, this uptown life was novel indeed. International media had become fascinated by the story now and when Carl and the team fronted court, pictures were beamed around the world. If you were with Carl, you were somebody. Even I felt it, sitting there with the family.

'You're on television, are ya?' one of the lads asked me, then, to the amusement of all. 'Can you make me famous?'

'I want to get on *The Footy Show*. Can you get me on?' another said. 'What about *Who Wants to be a Millionaire*? I wanna meet [host] Eddie McGuire.'

'Yeah, sure,' I said. 'But what are going to *do* on telly?'

'I dunno. I just wanna be famous,' came the reply. 'I just gotta get famous, mate, as soon as I can.'

Carl listened to all of this with a crooked smile, cradling his ouzo and coke. At thirty-three he was a veteran compared to his young cohorts. He had survived six years of bloody conflict and was still at the head of the city's most powerful team. He said that despite his friendship with the Chief Executive, he was a follower to no one. Carl would never be seen at Mafia funerals with the rest of the rent-a-crowd. He despised the Carlton mob with their Mafia affectations, the cheek-kissing, diamond pinkie rings and sorrowful play-acting at the graveside. He objected to their life-style: 'One minute they're kissing you on the cheek and the next they're planning to kill you . . . No cheek-kissing and arse-licking for me.' The old school relied on standover and protection rackets for its living, activities frowned upon by the new generation. 'It's a process of "problem, reaction and solution". But it's them that create the problem, then they come along and say "We can fix the problem for you". It's a disgraceful way to do business,' said Carl. By comparison, drugs were a more acceptable form of underworld business. At least willing sellers met willing buyers there.

Carl said he didn't touch drugs himself. I allowed him the little white lie – he was telling the story. I later heard that he was partial to the powders, cocaine either up the snout or by pipa (crack pipe). He was strictly a spirits drinker – whisky, vodka or ouzo. But the hangover could be a killer: 'You wake up and think "What did I do last night?"'

Life for Carl had become a three-dimensional chess game. He was dealing with plots, intrigues and opportunities on several different levels. On one plane he was on a collision course with his enemies, some of whom still professed to be his friends. The Carlton Crew were not all set against him; Benji had almost won a couple over to Carl. These were boys with their roots deep in the western suburbs, who had got their start with Paul Kallipolitis and Benji in the Sunshine drug scene and then gone uptown with Benji to Mick's table. These up-and-comers greeted Carl warmly at the nightclubs; they bought him drinks and slapped him on the back, then later listened to their mates plotting against him. It was part of the macho culture that prevailed in Melbourne. To be a follower was unfashionable. With a drink in hand and a toy down the strides, everyone was his own man.

Every media outlet in the country had visions of an exclusive interview with Carl and was trying to get close to him. The Purana Taskforce had identified one of his circle, David McCullough, who was acting as an informal public relations consultant to Carl, advising on strategies for maximising the effect of the daily coverage he was receiving. Carl had met them all for coffee, lunch or dinner, knowing that media exposure would help him in his pretrial pleadings. He didn't care if the journalists thought of him as simple. Even as they bagged him he was using them to fight his battles, sending little messages to the police and even to the politicians on Spring Street. He had information that could potentially bring down a government, that would expose the rot at the heart of the police force. Everyone else was either dead or in jail, and he was living large in a five-star hotel complex – so how dumb *was* he?

Carl didn't mind a joust with the media as long as they kept the story going. That night at the Marriott he told me that *The Age*'s John Silvester could expect a can of dog food to hit his desk that week, and he was sending a slab of beer to radio shock jock Derryn Hinch, who had been off the drink while he tried to resurrect his career. 'He really should go back on the drink with all the stupid things he's saying about me,' said Carl. And what was Hinch's heinous crime? Williams could cope with all the allegations of being a gangster and drug dealer, but just don't call him a dickhead.

This week's agenda included fighting the edict of Victorian Police Commissioner Christine Nixon barring him and Mick Gatto from Crown Casino. Carl was a roulette fan who played the percentage game: odds or evens, red or black. 'I don't understand it. One minute they're saying that they fear for my safety and then they bar me from one of the safest places in Melbourne,' he said.

Soon, along with the Chief Executive, Carl would be banned from all pubs and clubs in two municipal areas in the eastern and western suburbs. But for now he still had the run of the city. After chatting in the bar for an hour, it was time to leave for his next appointment, though it was now well after midnight. He excused himself, suggesting I keep drinking and eating on his tab with Roberta and their friends, and motioned to his three young retainers. As they disappeared into the night, Carl turned back and gave me a mischievous wink, as if to say to the reporter, 'If only you knew where I was going now . . .'

In the last week of April, gunsmoke was again in the autumn air. Late one night, one of Murphy's fizzes – let's call him 'The Dentist' – called me to say that two more villains had gone down. They were two older hands said to be running with Carl's team, armed robbers turned hit men. One was Steve Asling and the other Phillip Collins, a former cellmate of the Savage, Williams' mentor. They were hard, old-school men, the best of a dying breed. Asling had been with Normie Lee when he was shot dead by police as they they robbed an Armaguard van at Tullamarine Airport. Collins was a fierce and respected crook. The story of their demise was making its way around town, and if it was right, it would go down as the strangest of them all.

Eight hours earlier, so the story went, the two men were in a car on their way to do a job in inner Melbourne. In their possession was a machine gun, fully loaded and ready to go. When driving in city traffic it's always advisable to stow loose items, especially automatic weapons, as this story seems to demonstrate. There was an incident in the traffic and, the next thing, said machine gun was spraying rounds inside the car at full bore, like a garden hose let loose. Collins was apparently killed outright in the car, while Asling was wounded in the shoulder.

I made some frantic calls to police and villain contacts, but no one had heard anything – or, at least, anything they would share with me. It was now after 10 p.m. and my weekly deadline for *The Bulletin* had just ticked over. I went to bed resigned to reading all about it in tomorrow's *Herald Sun*. To my surprise there was no mention of it in the newspaper the next day, and nothing on the radio either. Now with another week to land the story, I began researching in earnest. One of the MIAs, Collins, was a regular every weekend at a bayside hotel in Chelsea, so I arranged for a cockatoo to stake it out on the next Saturday. The missing gunnie didn't show that day, or the following Saturday either. Further intel suggested that Asling had buried Collins' body upcountry and it would never be found. Then, late in the week, another snippet: Asling was alive but grievously wounded in the right shoulder and was hiding on a property in central Victoria. The weekly deadline loomed and I prepared a story that seemed a little outlandish, even to me. Editor Garry Linnell's only query was succinct: what happens if the first bloke turns up alive tomorrow and we have buried him on page three of the magazine? *Good point*, I thought. We concluded that if the men were still MIA in another week, their time would be up, dead or alive.

I had been speaking with Carl almost every night through this period. If he had lost a soldier, he was giving away nothing; he wanted to talk footy. It was looking like a long year for the beleaguered Richmond coach, he said. 'What about that Danny Frawley, eh? They've got the knives out for him, buddy, haven't they? I wouldn't like to be him, wouldja?' he said. *Sure, Carl, but at least they don't have machine guns out for Frawley*, I thought.

With a third deadline looming I couldn't stay coy any longer. I asked Carl if he happened to know Asling, the wounded gunnie. 'Yeah, he's a top bloke. Knew him in jail. One of nature's gentlemen,' he said, matter-of-factly.

'You wouldn't happen to have seen him lately, would you?' I asked.

'I can't think of when exactly, but yeah, he's around,' said Carl.

'Listen – I heard he may have had . . . a little accident,' I said, not mentioning the machine-gun affair. 'You couldn't get him to call me, could you?'

'I know – you just want me to do your work for you again, don't ya, buddy?' he said, laughing. 'Yeah, good as gold. I'll get back to you.' He never mentioned the issue again.

The urge to publish was now overwhelming. The police were also hearing the same grisly story and apparently 'looking into it'. Here was an opportunity for a neat set play. The reporter goes around the underworld asking for details of a story, and before long he's joined the dots of a very small circle. A fizz passes the details onto the cops and they begin investigating a story that may not exist. But the intrepid newshound is able to report that police are 'looking into reports of a bizarre double shooting'. As I was writing, I had the strange feeling that the police were quoting my own words back to me. Like a perfect echo from the underworld, the words had come back without alteration and further explanation. Perhaps I was being set up to write this yarn. Was I unwittingly part of someone's PR agenda?

The third deadline passed and I abandoned the story, fearful of the consequences of getting it wrong. Two days later, the 'dead' gunnie, Collins, walked into his favourite watering hole. A month later, the 'wounded' Asling was arrested on another matter. In mid-December 2004, officers from Purana intercepted him driving into the car park of a suburban hotel. 'You're supposed to have been shot,' one of the officers reputedly said. Police investigating the pair's whereabouts discovered that Collins had not accessed his bank account for nearly a month while he was believed to have been dead.

It took me another year or so to find out what had actually happened. The Rat had taken a contract from Mario Condello to hit Asling and Collins, receiving a down payment thought to be around $100000. Condello had understood that Asling was about to kill him or Lewis Moran, so he wanted to get in first. But the Rat had a soft spot for Asling and Collins and decided to pull a scam. He went to them and told them of his cunning plan: they would disappear for a month or two and the Rat would tell everyone that he had killed Collins and wounded Asling. They would be paid $40000 to play dead and wounded for a little while. Others in the team would blather on about the shooting while in earshot of Purana's surveillance team, giving the story more currency. What a bonus if the yarn could then appear in the media – which it very nearly did.

The Dentist was with Mario Condello the day that news of the pair's amazing recovery began to circulate. Mario was yet to find out.

'It's sad about those two fellas who got shot the other week,' ventured Mario. 'I wonder who hit them?'

'They're not dead,' came the reply.

'Yes, they are. What are you telling me?' asked Mario, his eyes widening.

'They've turned up breathing,' said the Dentist. Condello flew into a murderous rage, furious that he had been double-crossed. He had been had by the Rat.

A strange lull settled over the ganglands. The death of Lewis Moran had shaken the foundations of Carlton, yet still the Crew's guns remained silent. Williams was parading his freedom around town in the certainty that no one would knock him while police and the public watched his every move.

Billy Longley wasn't so sure. 'Listen, son, a good hit man will get you even when you're talking to the Pope. All the careless people are in the cemetery,' he said. There was an art to staying alive, and as the survivor of more than twenty attempts on his life during the Painters and Dockers War of the 1970s, Billy believed he was uniquely qualified to advise Carl. He suggested that Carl might like to employ his services as a 'staying alive consultant'. For a fee, Billy would share the tricks of the trade: how, for instance, he had avoided being shot when a bloke with a machine pistol had opened up from close range in a city street, or how to 'go in smoke' or disappear, to evade enemies and the jacks. The fact that Billy had survived without so much as a scratch was a powerful endorsement for his skills. 'Tell the young bloke [Carl] that I have had more shoot-outs than he's had Christmas dinners,' said Billy.

The best advice he could impart to Carl was to choose his friends wisely. 'I have one criterion for friendship,' he said. 'A friend is someone who will stand by you no matter what, even if it means standing back to back and shooting it out with your enemies.' And there were only two blokes left in Melbourne like that: Skull Murphy and James 'Jimmy' Bazley, one of the all-time greats of the Melbourne ganglands. Bazley had been convicted of the 1977 murder of Griffith anti-drugs campaigner Donald Mackay and served a long sentence. Even now Bazley's was a name to be reckoned with. Members of the Carlton Crew would take Jimmy along with them to the kickboxing just to strike fear into the hearts of their rivals.

Yet Jimmy, now in his eighties, only wanted the quiet life these days. You could usually find him at the local pool four mornings a week doing water aerobics with Billy.

Billy said Carl needed friends he could count on, like Jimmy, if he was going to survive. Running with a big team would bring him undone. Sooner or later one of his mates, with ambitions of his own, would be prevailed upon to position Carl for a hit, or they would just lag him out when they wound up inside a police station. I arranged for Carl to speak to Billy on the telephone and they apparently chatted for more than half an hour. However, Carl decided he didn't want a 'staying alive consultant' after all. 'I do all right on my own,' he said. 'But hey, buddy, thanks for thinking of me.'

Meanwhile, Purana wasn't wasting its time. In the first week of May, officers raided Roberta's house and charged her with multiple counts of fraud after allegedly finding signed credit card applications filled out with false information. On a visit to Purana headquarters for questioning on the matter, Roberta was observed receiving a ticket for parking her four-wheel drive in a disabled space. The dragnet was closing in. Soon they would have their greatest windfall of the entire investigation. Goggles was about to crack.

17 | BELLIES AND BULLETS

At the heart of every great gangster story there's a woman. Depending on how much dash a bloke has, there might be several. In fact, it could be argued that a lot of the dumb things that happen in the underworld go on because dopey villains try to impress women. That's one of the few similarities between squarehead men and their villain counterparts: once the weapons are cocked, all rational thought ceases.

In this story there are several women with enough balls and brains to give the men a run for their money. After the deaths of Andrew Veniamin and Lewis Moran, the battle lines were drawn between the two grandest dames of Melbourne's underworld, Roberta Williams and Judy Moran. Both had lost the men closest to them. Judy's two sons, Jason and Mark, were gone and now her ex-old man had followed. She'd already lost another gangland beau in Les 'Johnny' Cole (Mark's father), slain in 1982, and had nothing left to give. 'Poor old Judy. She's lost two sons and two husbands,' observed Chopper Read. 'Now that's just bloody careless.'

Judy had begun life as a lady – a ballroom-dancing champion, no less. The bright young men of Melbourne had competed for the hand of Judith Brooks, but she'd chosen to run with villains.

Now, by late afternoon you could often find her in the public bars of a couple of West Melbourne's old dockie pubs, whiling away the hours in the company of an old pug named Frankie Flannery. Frankie was a legend in Australian lightweight boxing ranks, the first Australian to fight for an Empire title in Australia after World War II. Judy had refused all requests for interviews, but Billy Longley suggested that an approach from a trusted mate like Frankie might just do the trick for me. I called him to ask if Judy would consider a request for an interview – maybe we could have a couple of drinks one afternoon to discuss the possibility? Frankie came back to me the following day with her considered reply: 'Mr Shand, with all due respect, get fucked.' *She's all class, our Judy*, I thought.

I should have realised that money was the only way to this dame's heart. A few weeks later, Judy was pictured in the newspapers taking tea with her new publicity agent, the inestimable Harry M. Miller. She'd signed an exclusive deal with Miller for him to hawk her story to the highest bidder, in print, on television and perhaps even on the big screen. Miller was reportedly asking up to $100 000 for Judy to share her secrets and the story of how she had lost two sons and two husbands in two gangland wars. There's a nice symmetry to the numbers – $100 000 was also the going rate for a contract hit in Melbourne. With Lewis's grave barely cold, Miller was promising 'an extraordinary story' that made him 'sick in his stomach', he told the press, without specifying whether the sick feeling was from revulsion or excitement.

I couldn't blame Judy for wanting to turn a dollar for her story. Apparently Mark and Jason hadn't given their mother a brass razoo from their villainous activities over the years. (There was also a widely circulated story that Jason, her little angel, had once bashed her in the bar of a hotel.) Just how she was surviving without resorting to crime was a source of some curiosity in police circles. She certainly wasn't cut out for regular employment.

The Purana Taskforce wanted to know what Harry had put in Judy's tea. In several police interviews she had copped it sweet. As the bodies piled high in 2003 she had remained an 'uncooperative witness' in interviews, said one investigator. 'We are trying to keep good relations with Judy so that we can get her to the stage of cooperating with us willingly. I sometimes think that in the year 2050, to interview a witness I will have to make an appointment with their literary agent.'

The pre-publicity for Judy Moran's story began that day outside court in December 2003 when Moran had bumped into Carl in full view of the press and warbled, 'Why don't you admit you murdered both my sons?' It was a coup that only good luck or Harry M. Miller could have dreamt up.

Roberta was also planning to write a book on the gangland murders and promised to donate all the proceeds to the Starlight Foundation. At Easter Mick Gatto had donated $5000 to the Royal Children's Hospital's 2004 Good Friday Appeal from his prison cell. All this charity was going to give the underworld a bad name. Roberta summed up Moran succinctly: 'She's a nasty, manipulative, vindictive cow. If you looked up the word "evil" in the dictionary, there would be the name "Judy Moran". And you can write this too, mate. If I see that fat bitch on the street I am going to fucking flog her, punch her fucking head in. She thinks she's fucking royalty.'

'I'm not going to write that, Roberta. Let's keep the violence out of it, shall we?' I said.

'Sorry, sorry – I just get a bit carried away when I think of that—' What was worse was that Moran's funeral dress sense was appalling, according to Roberta. 'How does a grieving mother turn up to the funerals of her children with perfectly done nails and hair like she came straight from the beauty salon? There she is with brand-new matching dress, handbag and shoes, but still it looks like she's trapped in the 1980s. Come on, Judy – get with the times.' Then she went straight for the jugular and accused Judy of having had all manner of cosmetic surgery, from facelifts to boob jobs. 'I'd be suing the plastic surgeon for all the fuck-ups,' she laughed.

'But hang on, Roberta,' I said. 'Haven't you had a bit of body work yourself? A boob job? Some implants, maybe?'

'No way, mate. I only had a reduction. Went down from a double-D to a C.' That settled that, then.

While Judy had lost two sons and two de factos, Roberta had lost Andrew Veniamin and was mourning him as if he'd been her beloved husband. The fact that her actual husband, Carl, was still standing around, conspicuously breathing, didn't seem to impact on Roberta – she was living in a shrine to her cocky hit man.

The fact that there were probably another half-dozen women around Melbourne with their own little shrines to Benji mattered not to Roberta. On the day Mick Gatto first appeared in court after Benji's death, it was Roberta who fronted the media to protest Veniamin's innocence. Dressed in a smart, black fitted dress, she told the media she had never seen Benji carrying a gun. She confronted a group of the Carlton Crew who were there to support Big Mick, telling me later that she'd been so angry she wanted to flog them all, spit on them, 'kick their fuckin' heads in'. For once, she chose restraint, simply yelling at the bemused Mafiosi: 'Fucking gangsters – killing people on the fucking corner!' It wasn't her best media performance, but she got her message across.

In all the time I've known her, Roberta has been fighting with someone – gangsters' widows, police officers, lawyers and even the tradesmen renovating her house. It is her nature, and it has got her into trouble since her earliest days. When Roberta was growing up she had struggled for any kind of identity. One of seven children born to a Maltese immigrant truck driver named Emmanuel and his Australian wife, Dorothy Hughes, she grew up in Frankston, at the time one of the most down-at-heel suburbs in bayside Melbourne. The kids looked after each other even if their parents couldn't, but it all fell apart after Manny's death. He was involved in a collision in his truck near Wagga Wagga in southern New South Wales and was trapped in the cabin as the rig went up in flames. Manny was virtually incinerated, but survived for another six days.

Dorothy drifted from one abusive relationship to the next, and at eleven Roberta was made a ward of the state and packed off to foster homes and orphanages. There she learned to fight for whatever she had and drifted into the juvenile justice system. It was always her fists that got her into trouble. Hard and wiry, she was a ball of fury when she went off. Anything to hand became fair play. She once chased her elder sister, Sharon, with a shovel over a money dispute. When Sharon locked her out of the house, she took to Sharon's BMW with the shovel to vent her displeasure, totally destroying the car.

Everything written about Carl's team was subject to scrutiny and instant comment by Roberta. Any reporter who crossed her could expect a personal telephone call and perhaps the threat of a flogging. If her mobile wasn't on you would get an answering-machine message, set to Lou Bega's 'Mambo No. 5':

> *A little bit of Gucci for tonight,*
> *A little of Armani for my man*
> *I'm out shopping for my man*
> *I'm out shopping cos I can*
> *Leave a message and Roberta will get right back to you*
> *When she's found the lippie that matches her dress . . .*

Roberta hadn't written the message – it was an off-the-rack version – but it seemed to sum up her attitude to her situation. While friends and foes were dying in the streets, she was going to step over them and go shopping. She was later charged with going on a $20 000 spending spree using a credit card she had obtained by giving false details. However, there was a creative, romantic streak to Roberta. She told me she had written a song for Benji and was preparing to record it at a friend's studio.

She threatened me with a flogging so many times that it became a standing joke between us. One night in the lobby bar of the Marriott Hotel, she suggested that if I wrote a certain line again, I would catch it from her big time. Looking around for a suitably violent metaphor, she lit on the swizzle stick in her drink. 'You do that again and I'll jam this up your fucking nose,' she said, with a broad and dangerous smile.

'Well, you can do that, Roberta, but you are going to spoil a perfectly good drink,' I replied.

Melbourne quickly became in thrall to Roberta, in whom they could see a bizarre mix of domesticity and danger. Until now, mass murderers had been strange reptilian creatures in the public's imagination – lonely nutters like Julian Knight who had killed seven people on Hoddle Street, or crazed office workers like Frank Vitkovic who had shot up the Australia Post building in Queen Street, or the speed-ravaged Dennis Allen who had killed for the sheer pleasure of it.

Here was a family that seemed relatively normal, at least on the surface. The kids went to private schools. The couple was renovating a house together, even if they were currently living apart.

By April, Roberta had moved her kids into a two-bedroom apartment in the Regency Towers block, about ten floors below Carl's place. Lawyer Peter Faris's apartment was five floors above Roberta's. Though Mr and Mrs Williams were officially separated, they kept in close contact.

With her thick, curly hair straightened and highlighted and a wardrobe of expensive leisure wear, Roberta had acquired the image of a middle-class housewife. When I interviewed her at her home for the *Sunday* program, she delivered a line that became a catchcry. I asked her whether the Williams clan was involved in murder and drug dealing, or the police just had the wrong family. She composed herself, looking for the right words to describe her life: 'We are just a normal, everyday family. We get up in the morning, take the kids to school and come and cook dinner of a night . . .' She even offered to hang some washing out on the line for the camera to prove her point, then moved into the kitchen to demonstrate her dishwashing skills while her three daughters watched daytime soaps on the big-screen television. Roberta said Carl was an everyday, average suburban guy and a fun-loving dad, and Benji was no desperado with a one-way ticket to hell – he was 'a good friend' and, most incongruously, a very reliable babysitter. There were few others Roberta would happily leave the kids with. She said she hadn't been authorised to give me the interview – Carl had specifically forbade it – but had done it anyway to make her point.

There was nothing in it for Roberta, really, to be grilled on national television, but I think she wanted to believe what she was saying. If she said it loud enough, it might somehow come true. She inhabited a world where celebrities used the media to create their own images, and I guess she reasoned there was nothing stopping her from doing the same thing.

That April night in the Marriott, at the height of the drama following the murders of Veniamin and Moran, she put the whole thing into perspective for me. In death Benji had achieved the fame he'd always craved: he and Carl were now among the top ten most-mentioned people in the Australian media. It was eleven o'clock and Roberta was surrounded by her sisters, friends and a posse of children running riot. The table was piled high with all kinds of food and drink, most of it untouched, but Roberta made great play of ordering still more. Her own personal waiter was summoned, club sandwiches and drinks were brought and a space was found on the table for the new supplies. I might die in the crossfire, or from a fatal flogging from Roberta, but I wasn't going to die of hunger. It was pure chaos – kids running here and there, chasing a small white dog named Simba around the foyer. The other guests smiled politely as the kids bumped into their tables and Simba ran under their legs. Everyone in the place knew exactly who the team in the corner was.

We talked about the media coverage and the endless speculation that Carl would be the next to die. Roberta looked at me and smiled broadly, exposing her expensive, gleaming dental work. 'You know, I always wanted to be famous. As a child I always dreamed of being a celebrity, but not like this.' She laughed uproariously.

'You're *in*famous, not famous,' said her sister Sharon, rolling her eyes. (Sharon had had her own brush with fame in the 1980s, when she was girlfriend to Graeme Jensen, the man whose death at the hands of police had sparked off the Walsh Street killings. Unfortunately she had broken up with Jensen just six weeks before his death, which spoiled the moment for her somewhat. History would record that the Rat had lagged Graeme for the Armaguard robbery that led to his killing by police, because at the time of his death Graeme had been sleeping with the Rat's ex-wife.) 'I'm always trying to get her [Roberta] to come out and stay with me out in the bush where I live now, but she never wants to come. I think she enjoys the spotlight.'

'Famous, infamous – it's all the same,' said Roberta. 'Ever since I was a kid I always wanted my name to be up in lights. But not like this.'

One afternoon that April, Roberta was watching television and saw one of the networks advertising for contestants for a local version of *Wife Swap*, a reality show where disgruntled spouses get to change places for a week or so to taste another version of domestic bliss. She was straight onto the phone to me. 'Hey, Adam, I want to go on *Wife Swap*. You're s'posed to have some pull over there, mate. Can you get me on?' I began to regret my flippant promise to provide tickets to Roberta in return for her cooperation in giving me the *Sunday* interview. *The Footy Show* was one thing, but *Wife Swap* had truly surreal possibilities. Not content with saturation media coverage and constant surveillance from the Dog Squad, she now wanted to go on air 24/7 with somebody's else's husband.

'Surely you are kidding,' I said.

'Nah, nah, I want to try someone else's life for a while. I'm serious. All I have ever wanted is to be married to a bloke who goes out to work while I stay home and cook dinner for him and the kids. And I fix him a drink when he gets home and he tells me all about his day at the office,' she said.

'Uh-huh, but aren't there already enough cameras and microphones pointing at you?' And, I asked, what about some other woman having to put up with Carl's unique lifestyle – the surveillance, the police raids, the media crowd every time he stepped out?

'I just want people to understand what it's like to be Mrs Carl Williams,' she said. 'It's a circus. No one can understand what I am going through.'

Roberta was certainly the most media-friendly madam of the mob that Melbourne had ever seen, but she was a beginner compared with some of the city's all-time favourite broads. In early May, Billy Longley called me to complain about the undeserved publicity the Williams pair were getting. If I wanted to learn about a real gunnie's moll I should be writing about the 'Angel of Death', he said. 'Pretty Dulcie had more gunnies than I've had shoot-outs. Well, maybe not that many, but a lot, let me assure you.'

I'd never heard of Pretty Dulcie, but that was all he would say. When I asked for more details, he said, 'Hey, hey, hey – steady on, son. You expect me to do all the work. I just set 'em for you, son. You've got to knock 'em down.'

It turned out he was talking about Dulcie Markham. In the 1940s and '50s Dulcie had lost eight lovers and two husbands to assassins' bullets, while many more men were maimed in the gangland wars that followed her fragrant fatal path around the country. Over her career, she herself was shot, bashed, slashed and thrown off the top of a block of flats. Through it all she always copped it sweet. She never talked. When the gunsmoke cleared and the wounds healed, she was on the arm of her next gangland 'gunnie'. There would be no book deals for the Angel of Death, but Pretty Dulcie might have forgiven Judy Moran's decision to sing for cash. She once told a policeman, 'There are ways of getting money without working for it, and what does it matter so long as you get the money?'

If Dulcie were around today, Harry Miller wouldn't be bothering with Judy Moran. By the time she was fifteen the gunnies of Sydney's Kings Cross were killing each other for the flaxen-haired, doe-eyed temptress they called the 'Blonde Bombshell'. Here was a woman who inspired a famous machine-gun battle near the Melbourne Cricket Ground in the early 1950s. Even *People* magazine fell under her spell in June 1952, observing that, 'Experts on the subject declare that the guileless expression of her eyes, more than the slightly rounded beauty of her face, makes her so bewitching to men. This look of artless lovely frailty . . . could be matched only by a Mary Pickford or a Jean Simmons.'

'Markham' was in fact an alias Dulcie had apparently plucked from a 1930 Alfred Hitchcock film called *Murder!* Her criminal history was unimpressive – convictions dating back to 1931 for consorting, vagrancy, soliciting, using indecent language, stealing, assaulting the police and destroying a cell bucket – but she was the acme of gangland style in her day. She arrived at one court appearance in the mid-1930s dressed to the nines with fifteen 'shiny-faced retainers' in 'brand new double-breasted suits, with silk shirts, striped socks, broad-brimmed hats and flaring multicoloured ties', according to one press report.

One by one Markham's menfolk died in the predictable hail of lead that followed a dalliance with her. As one suitor was led away to the cells charged with murdering another of Dulcie's beaus, it was reported that Pretty Dulcie called out, the tears welling in her eyes, 'Goodbye, sweetheart!'

With typical panache Markham had married legendary Collingwood gunnie Leonard 'Redda' Lewis in 1951 even though she was still laid up from a gunshot wound sustained three months earlier. The press were invited to Dulcie's home to witness the touching bedside nuptials. Redda was later shot a couple of times himself, but remarkably he was the only one of Dulcie's gangland guys to die of natural causes: a heart attack in 1965.

Certainly Markham could have told Judy and Roberta that gangland fables never end well. Pretty Dulcie, no longer pretty, died in 1976 after falling asleep with a lit cigarette. Her third husband, a merchant seaman, provided perhaps the worst indignity, telling the press she had been a marvellous housewife.

Judy was only married once, to Johnny Cole. Lewis Moran never took her down the aisle. Roberta, on the other hand, would not let her beaus get away without marrying her. She wed a Flemington man first: Dean Stephens, an associate of the Morans who had met the boys through football. They did not welcome her into the family; the Moran men liked their women a little more submissive than Roberta could manage. She took their coolness towards her as snobbery, thinking that they believed she was beneath them.

The Moran women were worse. 'We'd go to a party and those girls would all be sitting together and I'd be on the outer,' she told *The Australian* newspaper. 'I didn't mix with them – I don't . . . I can't get into their fake boobs and their fake teeth and their whole fake everything about them. They think they are better than everyone else, but they get their money from drugs.'

Roberta told the reporter that, by contrast, her family had survived on social security payments. She worked on the theory that once the public read it in the newspaper it had to be true. She said she had broken up with Dean before taking up with Carl. 'One day we were just sitting on the couch mucking around and then we kissed – and that was it. Carl was fun. I could be myself around him and he would never criticise me. He's not one to judge people,' she said. In reality, Carl took up with Roberta in 1998, while she was still with Dean. Once the affair became public, she moved out of their home in West Footscray.

With the death of Mark Moran in 2000, relations between the

Moran and Williams families understandably sank to an all-time low. Because they both had children attending Penleigh and Essendon Grammar School, there were plenty of opportunities to carry on the feud. Roberta claimed that Jason tried to run her over three times while she was dropping the kids at school, and spat at her on other occasions. She also claimed that she once gave Jason's wife, Trisha, a solid flogging outside the school after Trisha, under her breath, had called her a 'thing'.

Trisha packed up her twin boys and headed for Perth after Jason's death. No one would have blamed her for getting out of Melbourne. On the evening of 21 June 2003, after she returned from Cross Keys Reserve in Essendon, the scene of Jason's murder hours earlier, Judy Moran took a chilling telephone call. The caller warned that the killing was far from over. Jason's father, Lewis, would be next, then Graham 'The Munster' Kinniburgh, and after that the shooters would be coming for Judy and others close to Jason.

The freshly painted sign on the frosted glass proclaimed the location of Melbourne's newest criminal law partnership: 'Garde-Wilson and Caine – Barristers and Solicitors'.

The door swung open to reveal a large, airy suite overlooking the old sandstone walls of the Victorian Supreme Court. A tall, angular young woman looked up from the fax and smiled warmly in greeting. No, she was decidedly not the receptionist. She was the managing partner, Zarah Garde-Wilson. Her partner, the Mr Caine on the door, could not be with us today. Lewis Caine had been shot in the face on 8 May 2004 and his body dumped in a Brunswick lane – victim number twenty-five in the war. The Rat and his associate, who we'll call 'The Pug', had been charged with the murder of Caine. The Rat told anyone who would listen that he was innocent, but his background of murder and mayhem, stretching back thirty years, would not assist him in persuading a jury.

His alleged victim was no high-tone gangster, either. Caine was a bar-room brawler who had become a murderer in a moment of inspired misjudgement. One night in 1989, in Lazars nightclub, it all went wrong. A fight became a killing and Caine suddenly moved up the criminal pecking order. In Melbourne a murderer is worth more than an armed robber, but Caine was a squarehead who fantasised he was a gangster.

At first detectives weren't even sure that Caine's killing should be included in the gangland killings, so tenuous were his links with the main action. In prison he had been close to Rocco Arico and Terrence Chimirri, who in turn were close mates of Carl Williams. Carl and Roberta had seen Caine the night before his murder when he'd walked past the restaurant the pair were dining in. 'He wasn't no gangster. He was just a squarehead,' said Carl, when he rang me the night of Caine's murder. 'Just a squarehead – a bit like you, actually.'

The only other official tenant at Garde-Wilson and Caine was a goldfish in a bowl perched on a window sill, from where it could observe the wigs and gowns floating to and from court in the street below. Mr Caine's presence was all around the new office. From the layout and the office furniture to the smart pantsuit with the plunging neckline his partner was wearing, Lewie's touch was everywhere. He had designed everything, said Garde-Wilson, and was an angel looking over her shoulder 24/7. If this 26-year-old had her way, the partnership would be more than just symbolic or spectral. Zarah was fighting for the right to bear Caine's child using frozen sperm taken from his corpse and presently stored on the authority of the Coroner's Court.

Zarah had met Lewie three years before, when she was a junior solicitor with Pryles & Defteros, the partnership that had been the city's top crime firm. Lewie had come in charged with drink-driving. Working with Defteros, Zarah had seen all kinds of criminal heads come through the door, but none quite like Lewie. He had done a twelve-year stretch for the nightclub murder, but was no career criminal. He was clean-cut and handsome, with a solid 'Chesty Bond' kind of jaw and piercing blue eyes. She had been saving her virginity for the right man, and this was him, she told me.

Zarah reviewed his old murder case minutely. The jury had been allowed to believe that David Templeton died after a 'frenzied' attack, but in fact, she claimed, Lewie had thrown just three punches, even if he *had* pursued his fleeing victim in a taxi to administer the beating. Had she been his counsel, his life might have turned out quite differently. Another legal strategy may have been the difference between a verdict of murder and one of accidental death, she said.

Zarah's parents, conservative rural types, had given up on her a long time ago, she said. They had wanted her to forget about law school and marry the farmer next door, not take up with some knockabout at the centre of a gang war. But Lewie was the first man Zarah had ever loved and she vowed he would be the last.

Lewie had started out as Adrian Bligh, a middle-class boy who had done a stint in the army. By the time he got out of jail in 2000, he was a different person. He had tasted life outside the square, and Adrian Bligh was left far behind. A stubborn disregard for authority led him into trouble time after time.

When she rose in the Supreme Court, Zarah would think of the story Lewie told her about the day in 1989 when he escaped from custody in that august building. A deft martial arts exponent, he had knocked out four guards with Hollywood haymakers and then burst out into the sunlight on Lonsdale Street with a huge smile on his face. He got halfway down the street, en route to who knows where, before they collared him. There was press comment about the level of fitness among police officers after one fell down in the pursuit and broke his leg.

In Barwon Prison, Lewie tried to tunnel his way out of an exercise yard, *Great Escape*–style, while he was digging a vegetable garden. They concreted the yard after that. He became a popular man in jail, a physical powerhouse who would take on all comers in the boxing gym. Carl Williams' deadly foe Jason Moran introduced himself, hoping to get Lewie on side, but Lewie just turned his back and walked away.

He was thirty-nine when his killers, the Rat and the Pug, caught up with him. (Lewie had been approached by enemies of Williams to see if he would position Carl for a hit and had refused, which in turn made him into a target.) When he turned up dead that night, Zarah swore she would not give up their dreams. Press comment that she was so devastated by Lewie's death that she had collapsed and returned to her family in northern New South Wales only made her more determined. She hadn't collapsed, and she was staying in Victoria. In reality, she had nothing left to lose, except, of course her legal career.

She was fighting to build her practice in a profession dominated by grey-haired, middle-aged men. She had already made legal history by becoming the first solicitor in Victoria to be strip-searched by prison staff while trying to visit her client Carl Williams in Barwon Prison the week before our meeting. (Zarah was initially Roberta Williams' solicitor, but over time she took on Carl's work too. In press interviews she fondly called Carl and his associates 'the boys'.) She claimed that prison staff had ordered her to strip after a sniffer dog picked her out as carrying contraband. She denied the dog had shown any interest in her whatsoever. She could have refused the search but would then have faced a twelve-month ban on visiting her client at the time when he needed her most. She considered mounting a civil claim over the incident, but she would have much bigger issues to worry about.

Meanwhile, she was struggling to make good on Lewie's bequest to her. Zarah said that Lewie had foreseen his death and they had discussed the issue of freezing his sperm. A precedent for the removal of semen from a dead man was set in 1998 after the Victorian Supreme Court ruled it permissible for a woman whose husband had died in a road accident to remove his sperm. However, in a catch-22 it was still illegal to be impregnated with sperm from a dead man. Victorian law also prevented Zarah from taking the sperm to another state for the purposes of insemination. She intended to fight on, but preferred to keep her tactics to herself rather than share them with me.

She said she was unafraid of dealing with clients with a capacity for violence and intimidation. 'I know it sounds a bit corny, but I became a lawyer to help people. Lewie always believed in standing up for the underdog, and that's what I want to do in this practice.'

18 | THE SUNSHINE BOYS

Forty days after Benji's send-off, the mourners were gathering again at St Andrew's Church in Sunshine. When Carl and Roberta, officially separated but united in mourning, suggested I come with them to meet the Veniamin family that Sunday I was sceptical, to say the least. I thought of the huge, menacing bikie who had stood watch over the media at Benji's funeral. The idea of meeting him, this time as the sole representative of the media, was deeply unappealing. I didn't even want to meet the mini-mobsters who had bombarded the TV crews with eggs and golf balls.

Roberta assured me that there was nothing to fear. This would be a different occasion, with just family and close friends gathering for an intimate ritual. None of the bosses or their boys would be turning up and jostling to the front to be seen. Benji's mother, Marianna, was cooking traditional Greek-Cypriot dishes for a turn at home after the service, and all were welcome. 'Don't worry. You'll be with us, anyway. We'll introduce you to everyone,' Roberta said.

That Sunday, as Carl had suggested, I drove to meet them at Regency Towers in the city, calling them on approach. Carl's phone rang out, but there was nothing unusual there. He often let his calls go to message bank and then would call back from another phone, hoping to evade the electronic ears of the Purana Taskforce.

I was early, so I sat in my car outside the hotel and waited, watching the icy clouds that were rolling over the city swallow up the weak morning sunshine. I phoned again a few minutes later, but there was still no call back from Carl. A third try got the same result.

I took stock of the situation. My first thought was, *Go home, throw the suit in a corner and crawl back into bed*. I should have listened to that one, and not the next: *Well, you are all dressed up in a nice dark Zegna suit with a black silk tie and cashmere over-coat. You're looking sharp. It's a shame to waste it. And besides, Carl and Roberta will be there sooner or later.*

So, looking like a refugee from the Carlton Mafia – or worse, an undercover cop – I pressed on. The slightest sense of foreboding stirred in me as I took the hard right-hander off the Westgate Free-way that leads out to Sunshine. The outer suburbs of Melbourne sit on an ancient flood plain that stretches out to the Great Dividing Range, which at its southern extreme is just a ripple of weathered hillocks. The fringe of the city seems to go on forever. Amid clumps of stunted gums, mottled clusters of houses huddle together.

A stiff south-easter was blowing huge, dramatic clouds across the plains, and towering shapes of horses and dragon's heads clashed and melted as they raced ahead of me. In the rear-view mirror I caught a glimpse of the city, momentarily bathed in white shafts of sunlight against the dark background of heavy rain clouds. It seemed very far away.

St Andrew's Greek Orthodox Church marks the back edge of a

small, triangular precinct known as the Glengala shops. It's just a motley strip with a tattoo shop, a couple of milk bars and a video rental store, but it's one of the most important pieces of turf in the Melbourne underworld. In the recent past at least four men have died over disputes emanating out of this place. In August 2003 a chunk of the burned and battered Mark Mallia was recovered from a drain not far from here; he was only able to be identified by a tattoo on his shoulder. The mail in Sunshine was that Mallia had posed a threat to his old school chum Benji. Mallia had also made himself unpopular by standing over some of the local shopkeepers, forcing at least one to sign over the lease to his shop at gunpoint.

The air in the church was heavy with the acrid scent of incense. A priest with a wild grey beard and a greasy yellow ponytail was swinging the burner and chanting in Greek. Two laypeople in the choir stalls answered his mournful calls, creating an eerie, sorrowful three-part chorus. The occasional burst of light through the amber-coloured glass of the church windows gave everything a hazy, orange glow. Dozens of little electric flames flickered and danced in a huge fake candelabra. The church was only half full and I took a seat midway to the front. No one seemed to register my presence, and I scanned the room looking for familiar faces. Three rows ahead I could see Benji's sister, Helen, and her husband, Andy. Two weeks earlier I had gone to their home with a TV crew to interview her for a special on her brother's role in the war. When we'd got there we'd found that Helen was too overcome with grief to meet us, so Andy had made us a cup of coffee and we had chatted for half an hour about his job as a mechanic. Today, he walked right past me as if I wasn't there – and I was hard to miss.

After forty-five minutes the church had filled up. Old women, ancient widows in black and young children filled the pews, while prominent-looking families sat in stalls ranged around the walls. People had started noticing me. From the corner of my eye I caught a hawk-faced old woman as she tapped another and motioned towards me. From across the church, a big fat man with a luxuriant moustache locked his gaze onto me. I made matters worse by glancing back every few minutes expecting to see Carl's happy, smiling face. Instead, each time I saw more young Sunshine boys staring back at me with unconcealed hostility. It was now clear that Carl and Roberta were not coming and that I was on my own here. It was time to go, but I would have to pass through the growing throng of lads at the door. Girding my loins, I offered my seat to an old lady, who took it suspiciously, and walked purposefully to the rear, planning to stand among the crowd until the right moment came to make a discreet exit.

The vestibule was full of young men with hard faces and impassive eyes. This was Benji's peer group, a melange of European faces of many nationalities. The man standing next to me threw me a glance and stepped closer. Through his crew cut I could see a livid scar on his head that seemed to catch fire under the lighting. An older, more distinguished man with wavy, swept-back hair came to greet the lads but stopped and stared hard at me. The fear was rising in me fast now. A church attendant extinguished handfuls of fifty-cent candles in a dish of water and smiled at me. Crossing myself one last time, I turned and moved to the door. A large, half-smiling man blocked my way, but I pushed past him and hit the street.

Outside, the wind was howling and the temperature had dropped. I was relieved to be out, but knew I was still far from safe. I threw a glance over my shoulder as I made for the car and saw that a lean figure dressed in a silver parka was following me. His face seemed familiar and I looked back at him twice, trying to place him. I decided that going to my car parked right outside might be a mistake, so I walked across the road and into a newsagent. I figured that if I spent a few minutes reading a magazine, my pursuer would lose interest and I could escape. But it just made me look even more suss.

I should have been in bed now, the doona pulled over my head, but instead I was alone on foot in Sunshine at the mercy of a large crowd of hostile hoods. My telephone was in the car and I had put my last five dollars in the collection plate. As I read the magazine, I began to sort through the catalogue of dismal possibilities that now confronted me. *Just go straight for the car – they must have gone back into the church by now,* I thought.

When I came out, far from dispersing, the posse was now seven guys fanned out along the opposite footpath waiting for me. I had an urge to run, but where to? In fifty metres, I would be out of the shopping centre and beyond the view of witnesses. I was odds-on for the biggest kicking of my life. I thought of Mallia's charred, battered body in the wheelie bin and decided that if it was going to happen, then it had to be in full view on Glengala Road.

I turned at a pedestrian crossing and the man in the silver parka stopped and leaned against a fence, staring hard at me. The single-lane strip of road was deserted, but I stood there watching the red don't-walk signal for a full cycle. *Plik . . . plik . . . plik . . .* I looked over at the man, who had his hands shoved deep into the pockets of his parka. He could have been carrying anything. The rest of them were sauntering over.

The crossing signal counted down . . . *plik* . . . *plik* . . . *plik* . . . before changing to green with a startling '*tatta-tatta-tatta*'. My heart leapt into my mouth and I crossed on rubbery legs as if in slow motion.

He cut me off before both feet had touched the pavement.

'Excuse me, mate,' he said, with a seething hiss. 'What the fuck are you doing here?'

'I'm a friend of Carl's,' I said. It wasn't the answer he'd been expecting – if what I said was true, then something straight-forward was now complicated. Perhaps I had some standing in this situation after all. 'And I knew Andrew, too,' I added. 'I'm here to pay my respects.'

'I'm Andrew's brother,' the man said quietly. 'And I am telling you that he didn't know you.'

'I knew him through Carl. I'm a friend of Carl,' I repeated.

'I don't believe you,' he said, with the hint of a smile.

'Ring him, then,' I said. 'I'll give you the number.' He said he already had it. I knew this was only a momentary stay, as Carl was probably still snoring on the thirtieth floor of the Marriott.

Steve Veniamin started to dial Carl's number, but by now the other boys had caught up and he had an audience, so he had to give it to me. I didn't look like Carl's friend, and certainly wasn't acting like it. Everything about me screamed 'cop'. 'Who are the fuck are you to come here, you fucking jack dog? Motherfucker!' shouted one, his face so close to mine I could smell the coffee and cigarettes on his breath.

It was the time to reveal I wasn't a cop, but being a journalist seemed to make things much worse. All seven of them went at me then. 'Fucking jacks and journalists. It's the same thing. You—' said one, stepping up to jab a finger into my chest. Steve finished his sentence for him: '. . . you killed my brother, you fucking dog, you fucking rat,' he spat with utter contempt. Not *youse*, but *you* killed my brother.

His words sent a shiver of fear right through me, but at the same time I had to agree he was probably right. There was no escaping it – the media had been there unseen at Gatto's table at La Porcella that afternoon. Whatever had happened out the back in the final struggle, the media coverage had led Gatto to invite Benji down there. Reporters like me had built up Carl, Benji and Roberta. They were a new generation coming to sweep away the old mob that Mick had ruled for a decade. The whispers had come back to Carlton from the pubs and clubs frequented by Carl and his crew. The media, in thrall to Carl and Benji, believed the Carlton Crew were finished.

This was intolerable for a man of honour like Mick. A bogan drug boss like Carl could never command the respect that Mick had earned in Melbourne. Mick had loved Benji but finally he was persuaded that his protégé was in fact his executioner.

Now, in the cold bleakness of Sunshine, the media were being called to account. Every mistake, every slight and insult, was standing there wrapped like Christmas in front of them. 'I should bitch-slap your stupid face,' said Steve, sending a tremor through my sphincter. I had killed his brother, and all I could do was mumble that I was sorry and had come to pay my respects, not to try to file a story.

I looked into Steve's face, so similar to his brother's, and saw a totally different man. In life he had copped it sweet for Andrew and never questioned him. When Andrew was in his heyday, the jacks had never left Steve or the family alone. Many times they had harassed and battered him to get him to somersault his brother. But he stayed staunch, even when he was sentenced to two years' jail after being caught 'sitting' a crop of hydroponic dope for Benji in a house in Sunshine. Andrew warned him that he had to align himself with the strength in jail – even a popular man like Benji had enemies in there and Steve would meet them. Yet Steve was a quiet, reflective sort of man. He didn't make friends easily, and in jail he went his own way. One day he was working out in the prison gym when a group of Benji's enemies jumped him. They iron-barred him, breaking his nose and one arm, and left warning there was more to come. Through all the trouble, Benji had loved him. No matter how big he had become in the underworld, he hadn't forgotten Steve.

Yes, Steve had suffered for Benji and he was suffering now. While he had that name and that face, there would be no escaping his brother's legacy. I looked into his sad brown eyes and saw his broken nose and his scars. He was filled with sorrow and anger, but perhaps he knew that kicking me wouldn't take it away. Besides, he couldn't tell what ramifications would lie ahead if he hurt me. What if I really was Carl's friend?

With no one willing to throw the first punch, the mob's outrage threatened to spill over. 'Benji was my best friend in the world. What have I got left now?' said one man. Journos like me had put Benji in the ruck and got him killed and I would do the same thing to Carl. What sort of friend was I?

None of the other reporters had ever come out to Sunshine to find Benji's story, I told them. They didn't know about the shop-keepers who had loved him here on Glengala Road. You didn't read about Benji's loyalty to the underdog, but he had always been there to help. Even when he had become a big man in the underworld, they had still seen him walking out in his trackies and moccasins to get a souvlaki, just like anyone else. That was why I had come there that morning, I said. The media hadn't been there to find out, but here I was. 'Don't batter me for fronting up,' I said.

Steve Veniamin backed off a step, having made his point, but now a wild-eyed man came running from the church towards me. I just stood there, waiting for the beating that still seemed inevitable, but as he approached, another man ran from the church and held him back. It was Andy, Benji's brother-in-law. In the church he had ignored me but now he was saving my arse. 'Adam!' he exclaimed warmly, clasping my hand and throwing an arm over my shoulder. I could have hugged and kissed him. 'Don't worry, guys – he's okay, he's okay. Just come back into the church.'

'But he's from the newspapers. He killed Andrew,' said one.

'No, he's different. He's from the magazines. *The Bulletin*, you know?' said Andy, standing between me and certain disfigurement. As they debated the difference between the two forms of media, I didn't wait for a second chance to escape. I turned and walked as fast as I could without running to get out of Glengala Road. Once into the back streets, I ran as hard as I could. I wanted to put as much distance between myself and the mob as I could. I walked for an hour. The fear was receding but it was replaced by a growing sense of alienation. Every car that passed seemed to slow down to check me out. Old women in black like the ones from the church glared out at me from behind chintz curtains. Even small dogs barked at me. I kept walking through bleak, windswept reserves under towering power lines as flurries of icy rain came off the western plains. *This is another country*, I thought, *for which I have no visa*. I had fallen off the edge of the map. Here in the wetlands, in the maze of courts and closes, there was stuff going on that the police could not fathom, much less control. There were legends being made.

Finally, in the distance, I saw a drive-through McDonald's by the highway and made for it. By now I didn't care whether the hoods had retired from the church to Macca's for brunch. The golden arches were going to be my sanctuary. I called my brother-in-law, who lived nearby, and he came to pick me up and drove me back to my car outside the now-empty church. Ignoring the speed signs, I drove out of Sunshine with unseemly haste.

Fortunately, someone else far more deserving got the kicking that had been marked for me that morning. The congregation moved on to the Veniamins' home and a great crowd of the boys gathered in the front yard. Carl and Roberta finally turned up, bringing an old friend, Greg Domaszewicz, with them. Domaszewicz's notoriety was fading since he had beaten the rap for the disappearance and murder of Moe toddler Jaidyn Leskie in 1997. He had been baby-sitting Jaidyn, the son of his girlfriend, Bilynda Williams (no relation to Carl), on the night the two-year-old disappeared. Domaszewicz could not explain what had happened to Jaidyn, nor how it was that a few weeks later the boy's body, weighted down with a crowbar, had been found in Blue Rock Dam. Carl and Roberta had lived next door to Greg's cousin for a short while and became friendly with Greg. They believed his heartfelt pleas of innocence and felt sorry that he would never be able to clear his name. Roberta occasionally cooked meals for him and let him tag along when they went out drinking. Domaszewicz attended their daughter's christening in late 2003 and believed he was a part of the crew. Eventually he fell in love with Roberta and begged her to leave Carl, saying he would help raise the baby and the other three children, but this was an offer Roberta found easy to refuse.

Benji had enjoyed having the creepy Domaszewicz around for a laugh, and he was useful for running errands. In any case, Domaszewicz felt he was welcome to turn up at the Veniamins that Sunday. Someone apparently objected and gave Greg what Carl later described as 'a clip over the ear' (I understand he suffered a broken cheekbone). He came in to Roberta and Carl with blood streaming down his face, complaining that they hadn't looked after him. (*Well, at least they turned up*, I thought.)

Roberta later claimed that Domaszewicz had demanded she pay him $20 000 or he would go to the newspapers with an embarrassing story about their short-lived friendship. You know a bloke's hard up when all he can threaten you with is his own unpopularity. She claims she refused and the story duly appeared in the *Herald Sun*. But that day in Sunshine left me feeling that Steve Veniamin and his mates were not a bunch of low-lifes seeking revenge. If they were, they would have given me the flogging instead. I got Steve's mobile number from Helen and called him, much to his surprise. He listened as I thanked him for showing restraint that day. I had been in a place where I was not welcome and he'd had every right to hold me to account.

Steve was still grieving hard for his brother. He would have given up his own life to bring Andrew back. However, not even resurrection could have changed Andrew. Two or three years later, he would have been dead again and Steve's sacrifice would have been for nothing.

The Sunshine boys were lost now. Men like Benji, PK and Dino had provided some glamour in their otherwise ordinary suburban lives, and in death the boys would protect their friends' memory. A week after the memorial at St Andrew's, another of PK's boys passed away. Though he had run with the Carlton Crew as a young man, 'Bulldog' was no big shot – just a bumbling, lovable bloke who had come along for the ride with the team. The words 'I LOVE PK' were tattooed on the palm of one of his hands. An old, battle-scarred man though he was only in his early forties, Bulldog went to bed one night and never woke up.

Early in May Carl called to tell me, with some outrage, that he had uncovered a plot to kill him. I remarked that this was hardly surprising for a person in his present circumstances, and tried to move onto something else. News of a contract on Carl's life was nothing remarkable any more. He wasn't an easy target, if you wanted to get away with it. Police were watching him twenty-four hours a day, tailing him as he went about his business, while listening in via telephone intercepts. It must have been tedious to listen as Williams meandered through the city and the suburbs, making pit stops in fast-food joints, the TAB, or pubs and clubs in Moonee Valley. This was punctuated with visits to Mum for dinner or sleepovers. He might disappear for a while and cop a firestorm from Roberta when he returned. It was like listening to *The Jerry Springer Show* on a loop, according to one of the Dog Squad. The cops had warned my editor that I was being picked up in telephone intercepts talking to Carl and that I should be careful. We were all together in a bizarre reality show. It was like *Bad-ass Big Brother*, and any hit man brave enough to sneak-go Carl would land a cameo.

Carl was more interested in the two-year-old contract he'd called to tell me about. It was an insult, he said. 'Lewis Moran was going to have me knocked for $50 000. That's pathetic. That works out to just 400 bucks a kilo. Only *400 bucks*. I've got to be worth at least double that. It's going to be bad for my reputation, when everybody else is fetching $100 000 and up.' I agreed it hardly seemed fair when the price of high-value targets like Mick Gatto had risen to nearly $400 000. I could see his point – a contract was probably the only time a villain could truly assess his self-worth. Carl was indignant. Williams had paid Lewis's killers $140 000 for the hit in the Brunswick Club a few weeks earlier. And it wasn't danger money either: anyone could have capped Lewis standing there in the bar every night in full view of the street. It was a back-handed compliment to pay such money for a killing. Lewis's stinginess had probably saved Williams. Of course, Carl and the Chief Executive had failed to cough up the last $10 000 on Lewis's murder.

How had he come up with this information, I asked. 'Someone gave me a copy of this document. Been passed around through lots of blokes, apparently,' he said. 'It's a police report. The copper's written that [police informer] Terry Hodson was talking about the contract to hit me with another bloke, Mark Moran's mate – you know, the bloke who carried his coffin at the funeral.'

Oh yes, now I remembered. The same man had agreed to lag the Chief Executive in return for an immunity from prosecution.

He had been a major cocaine dealer, one of the Chief Executive's boys, who had distributed gear through the clubs and dinner parties of Melbourne's A-list. He had been linked to celebrities such as the host of Seven's *Today Tonight* show, Naomi Robson. He knew where every celebrity skeleton was buried, not to mention a few real ones. I wondered who would be brave enough to be seen carrying that bloke's casket, if the Chief Executive ever caught up with him. The papers said there was a $1 million contract on his head. 'Now that's a contract,' said Carl.

He was still alive, for only a fool would take a $1 million contract unless at least half was paid up front. Think about it: you're owed a million for the hit you've just done when the going rate's only $100 000 or even $200 000. The bloke who has issued the contract now has an incentive to have you knocked for $100 000, thereby saving himself a cool $900 000.

I had never heard of Terry Hodson, so Carl gave me a quick rundown. He was a drug-dealing dog informer, but other than that a perfectly nice bloke, explained Carl, saying he had never met him. Hodson had allegedly been tied up with a drug-squad detective, Senior Sergeant David Miechel, who was interested in doing a bit of business on the side. In September 2003 Miechel and Hodson had allegedly tried to burgle a house that was to be raided by the police in search of $1.3 million worth of drugs. They had been spotted by neighbours and the Dog Squad had been called in. Miechel had been savaged as he tried to get away from the hounds, while Hodson wisely gave himself up – at fifty-seven, this career drug dealer had learned a thing or two about self-preservation. He told police that another drug-squad member, Paul Dale, had been in on the burglary, but had not been there on the night. Bizarrely, Dale had pulled out at the last minute, citing a dinner party.

Carl reckoned Dale had been his best mate in the force, having apparently saving Carl's arse on more than one occasion, tipping him off when other officers planned to raid him.

Staying alive being an ever-present issue for Hodson now, he scarcely had time for plots against Carl. Still, Carl believed he should have been informed by the police at the time Lewis Moran's plot was discovered. It was a matter of public safety, he said. I suggested perhaps they hadn't told him because they feared he might order a pre-emptive hit. 'Hmm,' said Carl. 'They're off their heads, really.' I made a mental note to do some research on Terry Hodson.

Less than two weeks later, on 16 May, Hodson and his wife, Christine, were found murdered in their East Kew home. They had been ordered to lie face down on the floor of the living room while their executioner dispatched them with shots to the back of the head. There were no signs of forced entry, and the Hodsons' two German shepherds had been locked up in the garage. The murder had been carried out just 200 metres from a police station.

When I called Carl, he professed shock at yet more deaths while making the point that the life of a police informer was often short and exciting. I asked him if he had done it, knowing that he had already established an alibi. He reminded me of our phone call two weeks earlier. Why would he tell me about the police report if he was planning to hit the Hodsons? The jacks were listening to every phone call. He might as well take himself down to St Kilda Road headquarters and give himself up if he was that stupid. Carl had an alibi, but what of Paul Dale, whose career had been hanging by the thread of Terry Hodson's story to the Ethical Standards Department.

Days after the murder, ABC radio broadcast details from the police report Carl had spoken about, which turned out to have been compiled by David Miechel. Carl had offered it to me but said it was incomplete, with some details blacked out. I declined the opportunity, thinking there would be little interest in a two-year-old contract. But with Hodson's death, the police report took on a whole new meaning. Later it was revealed that Miechel had been sleeping with Hodson's daughter. After he was busted, he had sent Hodson a card with a picture of Tony Montana. Still on bail on the drugs charges, Miechel had unwittingly made himself a murder suspect. But Miechel was already sunk on the charges – Paul Dale had a lot more to gain from the Hodsons' demise.

Having been offered Miechel's intelligence report by Carl before the Hodsons' murder, I wondered just how long it had been circulating. Why had it surfaced days after the murder? The whole thing smelled like a big set-up. The initial ABC report had not indicated the 2002 date stamp on the document: it had been presented as if it were a document from 2004, a clue to a very contemporary murder conspiracy. Through his lawyer, Miechel was forced to deny he had murdered the Hodsons. Later, the ABC journalists who had compiled the radio report, Rafael Epstein and Nick McKenzie, won a major journalism prize for it. Certainly, the report changed the entire tone of the conflict, even if the underlying facts were not quite what they seemed. Hinting at much greater links between police and organised-crime figures than had hitherto been thought, it turned a gangland squabble into a serious systemic issue. If Carl's team had orchestrated this public relations coup, then police were dealing with crime organised as never before.

In the public uproar that followed the suggestion of police involvement in the gangland murders, the war moved from the suburbs to the seat of power in Spring Street. If the affair had been orchestrated – from the leaking of the police report to the murder of the Hodsons – it was a stunning piece of political theatre. The state Opposition leader, Robert Doyle, had been searching for a link between the gangland murders and the corruption of Victoria Police's drug squad, and this had provided it. He joined with the Victorian Bar Association in calling for a judicial inquiry into corruption in the police service – either a royal commission or a standing crime commission. (A royal commission is a temporary body set up to investigate specific incidents or allegations and report back to parliament. A standing crime commission is a permanent body, such as New South Wales's Independent Commission Against Corruption or Queensland's Criminal Justice Commission, set up to investigate and prosecute organised crime. Both confer special investigative powers on police and investigators.)

And who knows how high it went. A judicial inquiry could topple a government once the dominoes began to fall. Certain senior state Labor politicians were known to have mixed with underworld figures; they had been seen greeting each other at the kickboxing like old friends. There were electoral records that showed that companies associated with Mick Gatto had contributed to Labor's election campaigns. One Labor MP had apparently been copping free head jobs from Lebanese hookers for years: it had been suggested to me that if ever I wanted to unsettle this minister in an interview, I had only to utter the phrase: 'Fatima says hi.'

The Bracks Government had stoutly resisted the calls for a judicial inquiry, but now Assistant Commissioner Simon Overland's handling of the crisis was being called into question. At a press conference on the Hodsons' death, Overland called for a public debate into the establishment of a crime commission – even the cops were putting pressure on Spring Street. Instead, Premier Bracks announced that he would invest the police ombudsman with the powers of a royal commission, while the police commissioner would get the powers of a standing crime commission. Under the new powers, the ombudsman could subpoena witnesses and jail them if they refused to answer his questions. The police commissioner could seize the assets of suspected mobsters and freeze their bank accounts, even if they had not been charged with offences. Suspicion was enough now to shut down men like Carl Williams and the Chief Executive. In the background, Purana's team of forensic accountants, lawyers and other experts was following the money trail, slowly tracing the ownership of various properties and assets to their real owners. Purana chief Simon Overland knew that locking up the killers would not be enough to stop the killing. Leave the assets untouched and the bosses could go on knocking their enemies and running their affairs from behind bars. Choke off the money supply to the army and the soldiers would desert the cause.

Though he was facing a lengthy jail sentence on his cocaine drug charges, the Chief Executive was still living the high life. In mid-May, a contact rang me to say he had seen the Chief Executive the night before having dinner with a leading bookmaker, Frank Hudson, in a Chinese restaurant in the city. The contact said the Chief Executive had been negotiating the purchase of the bookmaker's luxury penthouse apartment in one of Southbank's ritziest buildings. When the pair finally settled on a sale price of over $3 million, the Chief Executive handed it over in cash from his briefcase right there in the restaurant.

Former Queensland corruption investigator and royal commissioner

Tony Fitzgerald QC was appointed to investigate links between the murder of the Hodsons and the leaking of police intelligence revealing their status as police informers.

There were many assumptions dressed up as facts in Melbourne after Terry and Christine Hodson's deaths. The town was abuzz with talk that someone had mailed two 'police issue' .38 calibre bullets to a police internal investigator, and the media interpreted this as further evidence of deep links between police and the underworld. Virtually every story highlighted the dozen or so police officers facing charges, suggesting that they might soon be roped into the main action of the underworld war. What most reporters failed to realise was that there is no such thing as 'police issue' rounds – a .38 slug is a .38 slug (as Murphy said, it was two less rounds that the cop's enemy could fire at him) – but in the hands of a hysterical media, the bullets were ammunition for an official inquiry.

Peter Faris QC, who was coincidentally acting for Carl Williams, went on the attack in interviews and on his own Sunday radio show on top-rating station 3AW, predicting that the Bracks Government's inaction on a crime commission would prove its undoing. 'This will be the end of Bracks,' he told me in an interview in May at his apartment in Regency Towers. 'We will see big changes in this Government. This will taint Bracks so much that I can't see him lasting more than six to twelve months.' The fragmented approach of the Bracks Government indicated a lack of political will to tackle the problem effectively, he said. 'It's common knowledge in the underworld that while this is the strategy of the Government, nothing's going to happen. No one's going to be caught, so they are still pretty free to act as they want – and that's not in the best interests of the people of Victoria. If you don't want them [law enforcement agencies] to get anywhere, you appoint a whole lot of bodies with little jurisdiction to investigate things but no one to oversee it all. If you had a crime commission you would simply refer all these matters to it and have the one body doing it all.'

Faris, a former chief of the National Crime Authority, said the Government had to consider the granting of indemnities against prosecution for villains to testify before a crime commission. 'What we have here is a corrupt system. It is undesirable that anybody is convicted on the evidence of corrupt police. If we are going to fix the system, it's better to let a few people go on indemnities and reward them that way for helping to fix the system rather than have this stand-off where it keeps going forever.' He saw no contradiction in what he was proposing – that his clients go free if they helped clean up the system.

Faris was hammering Bracks almost daily in the media, saying the premier was afraid of what he would find if an independent commission delved into organised crime's links in society: 'The corruption is much wider than the former drug squad, and it's not historic – it's ongoing, and they want to cover it up. And there's corruption that's very close to the Government. It makes it all look more suspicious.'

Finally, in early June, after nine months of my badgering and cajoling, the premier's press secretary decided it was time for Mr Bracks to give me an interview. When I spoke to him on the telephone I could see why she had resisted so stoutly for so long. He was a nice man, but he was clearly out of his depth as a decision-maker. For him, to push forward into the unknown of a judicial inquiry would be like pulling on one thread of a giant tapestry and then seeing the whole thing unravel before his eyes. 'My assessment is that people would expect a government to hold its nerve, to stay the course, to not interfere with the course of justice by the establishment of a body that might throw out existing cases which painstakingly have come before the courts,' he said.

Bracks told me his Government was clean of any links with organised crime: 'There is nothing even remotely of concern to our Government.' I reminded him that nine months earlier, when I had requested an interview on the gangland killings, his press secretary had knocked the idea straight out of court. Now, the revelations of links between corrupt police and the mob had created a media frenzy. I suggested that if his strategy failed, the next gangland corpse might turn up on Spring Street. But the premier wanted to talk tough. 'My message to the villains is: watch out. We are determined to hold the course. We are not going to be diverted. We are going to give more powers to the police commissioner to hunt you down. We are going to give the ombudsman more powers to hunt down corrupt police, so if you think we are going to be diverted you are wrong.'

Then he went overseas for an extended tour of Europe. Winter was closing in, but it was getting too hot for him in Melbourne. Bracks' strategy of doing nothing turned out to be an inspired piece of judgement. He was re-elected in late 2006. Meanwhile, the Opposition leader, Robert Doyle, who had campaigned hard for a royal commission, had been hounded out of office, knifed by his colleagues in a vicious political execution before the election.

20 | A MAN OF VISION

Mick Gatto methodically belted a heavy bag swinging from the ceiling of his exercise yard, pounding out his anger and frustration. He had endured a sleepless night and it was probably my face he was seeing as he jabbed and hooked the bag. After three months in custody, the weight was falling off him and he was barely recognisable from the massive smiling don I had met at La Porcella eight months earlier.

On remand for Benji's murder in Port Phillip Prison, Gatto was locked down twenty-three hours a day. For a time, he was in the same unit as the Rat, who was awaiting trial for the murder of Lewis Caine. On his way past Mick's cell to the exercise yard, the Rat would bang on the door with a little vote of encouragement: 'Keep your chin up, Mick. You'll be good as gold.'

This was great coming from a bloke who was also charged with murder and had also apparently taken a contract to knock Mick. 'What do you think *you're* in here for?' Mick would reply.

He emerged from his cell only for telephone calls to his lawyer, George Defteros, and to belt the bag. That morning he ordered Defteros to get me on the phone as soon as possible. The night before, he had watched *BadFellas*, the documentary I had produced on the war for the Nine Network, in which I had suggested rather airily that this was essentially a drug war and the Carlton Crew were undermanned, particularly as they were the new boys of the drug scene.

I hadn't had a great deal to do with Mick directly since our meeting at La Porcella. I had seen him at Graham Kinniburgh's funeral, surrounded by his boys and greeting his underworld brothers as they arrived. For a man who wanted nothing to do with the press, he had hung around the churchyard for a very long time in full view of the cameras. There was always an element of theatre in these moments, and the newspapers had carried pictures of Mick looking like the monarch of the mob receiving his courtiers.

I had broken ranks with the other journos lined up on the footpath behind the wrought-iron fence of the churchyard and walked straight up to him. He had stiffened when he recognised me, but shook my hand nonetheless. I said, 'I'm sorry for your loss, Mick.'

'I appreciate it. Yeah, I appreciate it, buddy,' he murmured.

A few weeks later I had called him again on his mobile and received a less than warm reception. 'Aah, what is this nonsense? You're bustin' my chops now. I'm going to call you . . . the Sponge. Yeah, you're the Sponge now, buddy,' he said, enjoying his joke.

Mick's were the very last chops I would have sought to bust, but I had a job to do, I told him. 'I know,' he said, his voice softening. 'I understand, but I just don't want to have anything to do with you or the press, okay? It's nothing personal. I let you sit with the boys for five hours and that's plenty. So you take care and have a good day.'

In the six months since then I had studiously avoided venturing down to La Porcella or any of Mick's other haunts. If only Benji had decided to do the same thing, I could have left Mick alone entirely.

In jail he had lots of time for contemplation. He wrote to friends saying that no matter how hard he tried to stay out of trouble, trouble seemed to find him. But there was no remorse for Veniamin, whom he described as 'the little assassin'. He said the people of Victoria should have given him a medal for killing Benji, not a murder charge.

Even from jail Gatto exerted a power and authority that was daunting. I was summoned to Defteros's office in the city the day after Mick had placed his call from jail, and it was arranged that I could be present when he took his regular telephone call from Mick.

First mistake: never ask a bloke on 23-hour lockdown how he's feeling. 'Just terrific, buddy,' Mick said, in a voice heavy with sarcasm.

He had summoned *The Bulletin* to express his displeasure at my recent portrayal of him as the 'Don' of the Carlton Crew. He was 'disappointed' that his name had been associated with a war for control of Victoria's amphetamine industry and he wanted to set the record straight. 'I'm not at war with anyone. I've got no problem with anyone. I want to concentrate on my impending court proceedings. I've got nothing to do with this nonsense. I have been dragged into this.'

The mere suggestion of an involvement with drugs demeaned Mick's integrity: 'I have got nothing to do with drugs, never ever have. And I don't want to inflame the situation. I have nothing to do with this crap or whatever is going on.' Just like he'd said at our very first meeting, Mick wanted out of the whole sordid scene. 'I just want to be left alone. I want to do my own little thing. I want to get through this present headache. And I have got no problem with anyone and I don't think anyone's got a problem with me.'

Mick had joined the chorus of voices calling for a standing crime commission in Victoria to deal with the growing evidence of links between corrupt police and the underworld, but he doubted that the power elites of Victoria would allow a crime commission to uncover corruption at the highest echelons. He claimed police had drawn him into the war for their own ends. 'I'm not at war with anyone . . . I don't know if it's the police that has been feeding you all that nonsense. And it is complete nonsense, just to cause mischief and to create headaches . . . because they are pushing to get new powers and this nonsense that they are going on with today.'

It was loyalty to friends, like the late Lewis Moran and Graham Kinniburgh, that had dragged Gatto into Australia's most bizarre gangland conflict. And now the war he had never wanted had all but destroyed his world. There was talk that the Chief Executive had placed a $400 000 contract on his head, so solitary confinement in jail was about the safest place for him right now. Many of his boys had all but deserted him, having joined the opposing forces of the Chief Executive; his family had fled the state; and, to cap it all off, the Australian Taxation Office was chasing him with a $1 million tax bill.

Mick had made a grave error of judgement that afternoon in a Carlton cafe in late 2002 when he had stood back and let his associates kick the crap out of the Chief Executive. Perhaps from a desire for profit or influence, he had become entangled in too many other people's fights, too many to keep up with. He had believed that senior men had a responsibility to keep the younger guys in line, but had discovered the young guys were well beyond his command. Now his world was a tiny jail cell and the exercise yard. It was said that he was off whether he was in jail or on the streets. If he was found guilty of Veniamin's murder, sooner or later someone would get to him – even in a maximum-security prison. He couldn't serve his entire sentence in solitary.

Still, Mick was more concerned with principle and image than anything else. The indignity of being lumped in with the pseudo-gangsters of the drug scene burned him deeply. Call him a killer and standover man; just don't call him a drug pusher. He had kids and a family – two families, even – and an image to uphold in the community. 'I would very much appreciate if you could set the record straight for me,' he said, summoning all the calm dignity he could under the circumstances.

'Sure, Mick,' I replied.

After the call, George folded his hands and looked at me with a glum expression. 'Do you know what the term "flag" means to people in the underworld?' he asked rhetorically. He waved his hand slowly, theatrically. 'It's when people you thought were friends just blow with the breeze, like flags. A lot of Mick's people have turned into flags these days, Adam. They're going off with whoever comes up with the cash. It's loyalty to the highest bidder. And after all that Mick has done for them.' He paused for effect. 'Most of them have tried to make sure they have exonerated themselves rather than helping Mick.'

Sure, George, I thought. There were more flags in Melbourne at that moment than on Grand Final Day.

I duly wrote what George had said. It was true that many of Mick's boys had switched sides. Some had been seen drinking in clubs with associates of the Chief Executive. Who could blame them? An army marches on its stomach, and with Mick inside there was no one to keep the boys in the style they were accustomed to. And they weren't getting any younger, some of Mick's boys. Some of them had kids to think about. Growing up in this world, they'd had it drummed into them that their own families came second. You owed loyalty to the godfather before everything else. Your life was his. Now, with the boss out of sight, it was impossible to maintain discipline and the boys were thinking for themselves.

That was why I had rung Mario Rocco Condello in early May 2004. He was in the big chair now, but I wondered whether his feet could reach the floor. It would take a real leader of men to keep the boys together, and Condello was facing the sternest test of his criminal career.

With Mick in jail, authority for the Carlton Crew rested with Mario. It was an honour that he believed sat lightly on his shoulders. He was an educated man and a former lawyer, even if he had been disbarred for his crimes. At fifty-two he believed he had the vision to lead his people out of the present circumstances and restore the normal order of things, with the Calabrians at the top of the tree. Once in a generation comes a man with the wit and integrity to unify the rabble of the underworld, and Mario had no doubt that he was that man.

Condello was renowned as one of the most prominent and

effective money launderers in Melbourne. He had deep, serious links with the Honoured Society, and convictions for trafficking in marijuana and insurance fraud. He understood the history of the Mafia, the customs and culture. If he decided to broker a peace with the Chief Executives and Williamses of the world, it would be on his terms. He might even have someone approach a member of parliament to be a mediator, he said. He liked the sound of that. It was appropriate, too, that *The Bulletin* was approaching the Carlton Crew for its opinion on the establishment of a crime commission. But I was hearing other, less flattering stories about Condello – that he was a coward who would faint at the sight of blood. He usually employed others for the physical stuff, parading around as they went to work on the victim. I had heard ludicrous stories, too, like the time Condello had turned up to the beating of a rival dressed like a sadomasochistic freak in a leather face mask and gloves. I hadn't believed it till I read it elsewhere, and I still find it hard that anyone could take him seriously dressed like that. But when you have a pack of goons enforcing your will, I suppose you can wear whatever you like.

On the phone to Mario, I tried my usual routine, saying how I had heard that with Mick in Port Phillip Prison awaiting trial on Benji's murder, he was now the patriarch of the Carlton Crew. Like I had told Mick all those months ago in La Porcella, I wanted Condello to know what I was doing; it was a mark of his authority that nothing I did should come as a surprise.

Mario instantly jerried to my tactics. 'Whaddya beatin' round the bush for, Mr Shand? What are you ringing me for? You think I am going fall for your flattery, eh? Well, you're dealing with Mario

Rocco Condello now, you know.' Condello turned out to be the most insecure of all the gangsters I met. Vain and utterly susceptible to flattery, he was in constant need of approval.

We talked for an hour and a half, the conversation flitting from the history of the underworld through to literary masterpieces of the ancient classical era. He quoted from Virgil's epic poem *The Aeneid* and questioned the philosophy of Socrates, then extolled his personal theories on the great figures of criminal history. 'The greatest gangsters in the world lived without firing one bullet . . . and they died a natural fuckin' death. You take Meyer Lansky, you take Lucky Luciano in America, and even that oddball that ruled Chicago for a while, Capone . . . Well, he died a natural death. He died of a disease, but he died a natural death. They did what they did, yes, but they were different times,' he said wistfully.

In his view, the underworld was divided into those with the wit to lead and those with the muscle to follow: 'Now in any group, whether it's a government, whether it's a local council, whatever it is, a ministry or a group of people, you've got to have people in there who are switched on with the brain. You know what I mean? They can lead them. And then you've got to have other people who can – if something has to be done along a certain area, you know – street things . . . You've got to have people who have been out there and know exactly what's going on.'

It sounded so orderly and honourable, like a parallel government. Everything relied upon the personal integrity and honour of the leader, the boss of bosses. And Mario believed he had the right stuff.

His reputation hadn't been helped by the talk that he and Mick had recently been outwitted by four Nigerian conmen who had relieved them of $200 000. The Nigerians, who told Mick and Mario they were connected with the CIA, had confided that they had US$2 million in black money. It wasn't *all* black, mind you: each note had just a single black mark on one corner, which could be removed only by a special chemical. This chemical, the Nigerians said, could be obtained from a corrupt official within the US embassy in St Kilda Road for the sum of $200 000 in cash. It was a new kind of money-laundering for Mario and Mick, but they were up for the rort, so they sat and waited outside the embassy while two of the Nigerians went in to obtain the chemical. One of them ostentatiously saluted the officials on the door, and Mick and Mario were hugely impressed when the officials saluted back. The Nigerians never came out, and when Mario approached the entrance, the officials saluted him, too. They had been had.

It wasn't the first time that Mario had fallen foul of a funny-money scam. A few years earlier, he had been conducting some business with an associate when he was tipped off that the money he was to be paid was forged. Furious, he battered the hapless associate, forcing him to eat some of the cash right there in front of him. Mario then burned the rest of the money. Later he found out it had been legitimate all along.

Condello had been sleeping only a few hours at a time for the past couple of months and was changing locations almost daily, never giving the assassins on his trail a chance to lock on to his routine. In the underworld it's called sleeping in the trees, the target keeping an eye on the ground below. The idea is to catch the would-be killers in the act of stalking you, to creep up on them as they sneak up on you.

When Mario picked up a copy of *The Bulletin* from his local 7-Eleven at 4 a.m. on 9 June, he saw splashed across the cover a picture of his closest associate, Mick Gatto. As he read my article, Mario felt the anger rising in him. For the next three hours he raged around cursing in fury at what he had read. It was as if I had said the Carlton Crew were finished. In trying to make it up to Mick, I had unwittingly picked a fight with Mario. I had suggested that Mick's mates had switched sides and left him in the lurch, that the guns of Carlton would remain silent. I might as well have called them all fairy godfathers.

At eight o'clock that morning I was preparing to board a luxury cruiser for a leisurely jaunt around Sydney Harbour. It was about as far from the mayhem of Melbourne as I could get, and that suited me just fine. On that glistering morning, I was free, writing an innocent story about a pair of stockbrokers starting their own business. They were young, fresh-faced boys talking big about taking on the opposition and how to avoid getting nailed by their rivals. *Ah, such bliss*, I thought, *to be back in the land of the bloodless euphemism*.

Then my mobile phone rang. It was a producer from a Melbourne radio station wanting me to talk about the latest arrests, which had taken place an hour before. 'What arrests?' I asked, my heart sinking. They told me that at 7.20 a.m., a huge team of police had swooped on two men, Sean Jason Sonnett and Gregg Hilderbrandt, about 150 metres from Mario Condello's fortress-like home in North Road, Brighton. Sonnett and Hilderbrandt were allegedly carrying pistols and two-way radios. Around the corner police had found a stolen Mazda 626, allegedly containing a large can of a flammable liquid. Witnesses told the media they had seen both the arrested men crying as they lay handcuffed on the footpath. One of the men was in such terror he had apparently soiled his trousers. Ten minutes later, another posse of officers had descended on Carl Williams' mother's place in Primrose Street, Essendon. Carl had been out for a big night and was sleeping off his hangover at his mum's when they hauled him away. In Wantirna, another man was arrested. They were all to be charged with conspiracy to murder Mario Rocco Condello.

I asked the captain to take me straight to shore, where I jumped off the boat, not waiting for it to dock, mobile phone in hand. My first call went to Condello. He was still steaming about what he had read in *The Bulletin*. 'What the fuck are you doing writing stuff like that?' he shouted down the phone. 'No one is fuckin' leaving Mick in the fuckin' lurch! You want me to come down there and have a quiet fuckin' chat over a fuckin' shotgun, mate? The Carlton Crew's not finished, and no one's running away. Who told you all that shit, mate?' I had a disturbing flash of Condello dressed up in his S&M wrestling mask, looking like the gimp from *Pulp Fiction*, as his boys began to work on me.

I reluctantly told him it had been Mick's own lawyer, but that didn't quell his anger. He was working himself into a complete lather. It dawned on me that perhaps he wasn't fully aware of the goings-on outside his house just an hour earlier. 'Mr Condello, I appreciate that you are a little upset with me right now, and I will do my best to set the record straight very soon, but do you know what's happened outside your place this morning?' I asked.

There was a pause, then he said, 'Well, I heard there were lots of police officers up and down the street and the helicopter going overhead and so on, but that's all. There was some sort of arrest in the street, I heard.'

'Well, yes, there was an arrest,' I said, trying to find the right words to break the news. 'And it seems the blokes they arrested might have been on the way to see you.'

Whether he already knew this, I still don't know, but he seemed to forget all about *The Bulletin* article and asked me to tell him all I knew about the arrests. He listened carefully, still breathing heavily, recovering from the tirade he had unleashed. I was off the hook, even if it had taken a full-scale police operation to save my arse from a kicking by the Carlton Crew.

'I was waiting for them,' he said, though it later transpired that he had been staying at an apartment in the city. (Of course, he could well have had his own men on the ground at his residence. Sleeping in the trees means always keeping an eye on the ground below, he had said.) 'If they had set one foot on my fuckin' land, at least I would have had a fuckin' defence to say, "Mate, he tried to come into my fuckin' house with a fuckin' gun". Is this self-defence or not? What does it take to fuckin' cause self-defence? Coming into a fuckin' property with a gun and confronting me and next thing you know I pull out a fuckin' shotgun or something and fuckin' kill the fuckin' dog.'

All the expletives and threats in the world could not hide the fact that Condello was scared out of his wits. He knew that Carl was not afraid of him, and could not be bought off. For years, he had covered his faint heart with a big mouth and a ruthless coterie of thugs to do his dirty work. Now he stood alone.

My next call went to Roberta. She had been at home sleeping, amid the rubble of home renovations, oblivious to the arrests. She raced downtown to St Kilda Road police headquarters and got into a minor scuffle with Purana officers. Later that day she called me back, telling me her greatest regret was that Carl's daughter might now have to grow up without a father. The previous weekend Carl had taken his little girl and they had spent time together for the first time. Now it was back to normal: her dad was behind bars again.

The next day, back in Melbourne, I attended Carl's court hearing. There was intensive security as the media filled virtually every row of the public gallery. Roberta was there, looking like she had spent a sleepless night. I remarked upon the security and she fired back in a voice laden with sarcasm: 'Don't you know he's a mass murderer?'

When Carl and his co-accused filed into the court in their bright red tracksuits, they looked more like fugitives from the Wiggles than murder suspects. Sonnett was in a feisty mood, alternating between entertaining everyone with his humour and threatening to kill any journo who took notes on proceedings. Through it all, Carl sat in the dock smiling impassively and chuckling at Sonnett's antics. I tried to catch his eye, but he seemed to be avoiding me. Once I caught him sneaking a glimpse to see where I was and then pulling away. Only a week before he had told me he wanted to distance himself from all these characters. He didn't know who his friends were any more. This was not the life he wanted. This was not how he wanted his daughter to remember him. He was tired of looking over his shoulder all the time and wondering when the bullet was coming for him.

I had said that in thirty years' time we might, he and I, look back on this period and realise we had lived through an extraordinary time in the city's history. He paused for a moment, and then agreed. It had never occurred to him that he might live that long. Yes, I had said, dying was the easy part. Living through the aftermath would be more complicated. And here he was in the dock again, a prisoner of the underworld as much as the state.

All that week flashes of past conversations with Carl came back to me. He had asked me what I knew about Condello, where he went and with whom, the places I had met him and when I would meet him again. He had asked my personal opinion of Condello: did he have dash, or was he afraid? Even at the time, I had been concerned that these were not casual inquiries.

Two days later, Mario Condello was sitting enjoying the autumn sun at an outdoor cafe near the Queen Victoria Market. There were no bodyguards with him and he sat with his back to the street, a tall, distinguished figure wrapped in a long black coat. From behind dark sunglasses, he smiled and sardonically cocked an index finger at me as I approached.

On this fine morning, Condello spoke of peace in a war no one in Carlton wanted, a war that 'didn't have to be'. Magnanimous in victory, he was breaking his customary silence to call for an end to hostilities. He was from 'the old Calabrian school', a culture where you didn't reveal your secrets to outsiders even if you were 'hanging by your fingernails suspended by violin strings'. As an educated man, he believed he should speak out on behalf of his community.

I pulled out a tape recorder, carefully showing him there was no tape in the breach, that I hadn't been secretly recording him. He raised an eyebrow as if to say he appreciated the gesture. Words were just as dangerous as bullets in the city these days.

In particular, Condello said, he wanted to dispel the idea that the Carlton Crew were battling a western suburbs-based syndicate for control of the amphetamine market. 'We really don't have a problem with them, because we are not in the line of business they are in. We don't have anything to do with their line of business and, quite frankly, we despise anyone who has anything to do with that line of business,' he said. It seemed churlish to remind Condello that he had done time for drugs, namely cannabis, and that he had at one time tried to sell kilos of heroin around Melbourne.

'No one wants any further destruction of life. No one wants any further traumas, stress or anything of the like – least of all . . . taking a life. It's absolutely absurd. Put it this way. I have my finger on the pulse and I was pretty focused about matters that were going on . . . Once they reached the other side of the road where my place was, they would not have been able to walk back to the car. I can assure you they would not have been able to return. Now, you make your own assessment of what I'm saying and thank God it turned out the way it did. Thank God for them and thank God for me.'

It was alleged by the Crown that the would-be assassins had planned to hit Condello while he was out walking his two Jack Russell terriers. Had the dogs been injured, Condello's anger and vengeance would have known no bounds, he said. But now, in the glow of survival, he could afford to be forgiving of his enemies.

'I didn't like what happened,' he said. 'I hope it just doesn't continue to happen to others or to myself for that matter, because . . . I am prepared to forgive once and that's as far as it goes. No more.'

Condello said Carl Williams and his father, George, had come to see him three weeks before to talk peace. Carl had told Mario that he didn't want any trouble and that his team would take on anyone in Melbourne except the Calabrians. 'They came and offered peace and goodwill,' he said. 'At first it seemed a little vague, but like any situation, you've got to give it a chance . . . Now how candid and how genuine are people if they're going to come and say we love you and we offer you this and then they come and try to kill you? It doesn't make any sense to me. Does it make sense to you?'

Silly question. None of this made the slightest sense to me at all.

On another occasion, he said, Carl had encountered him in the city. 'I thought he was going to come over and have a cup of coffee with me, but as soon as he spotted myself, he ran like Ben Johnson in the Olympic Games.' (Later, in a letter to me, Carl denied that this flight had ever taken place. I had to concede that it was hard to imagine Carl running.)

Condello had the floor for the moment and he was going to enjoy it. He said he had followed the war through media reports and had heard the story that an earlier victim of the war, Lewis Caine, had been contracted to kill him but had himself been killed by the Rat and the Pug. I asked him whether his conscience was clear. He said it was. 'I slept well last night . . . So the papers say Lewis Caine was contracted to do something, then others were contracted to do something, then these people were contracted to do something. My message is, stay away from me. I'm bad luck for you people. Stay away. Don't come near me, please.'

He asked if he could continue the interview in Latin. He had been classically educated, he reminded me. I replied that my Latin was rusty and I could remember only my old school motto, *Esse quam videre*. 'What's the translation?' he asked. 'To be, rather than to seem,' I replied. He looked at me hard for a moment before continuing on with his policy statement. He was on a roll now, like he was summing up an epic story of tragedy. At the darkest hour victory had been achieved and peace would reign over the kingdom – Mario's kingdom.

'For the first time I have heard some birds singing in the trees, so let's hope these birds continue to sing and everything becomes more peaceful than it has been over the past however-many years, because after all we are not going to be here forever.' (For my story that Sunday on TV, I set his comments to sweeping night vistas of Melbourne. In the background, Dean Martin sang *Return to me . . . if I hurt you I'm sorry, forgive me and please say you are mine*. I called Mario after the show and he seemed well pleased with his national media debut and promised there would be a follow-up.)

As I left him that day on Victoria Street outside the cafe, I shook his hand and he moved closer, clapping a hand on my shoulder. We were standing shoulder to shoulder and looking eye to eye. I could smell his expensive aftershave. I said, 'Mr Condello, I had heard that you were a lot bigger than what you appear in person. Hey, look – I'm standing over you!'

Condello laughed, but he looked a little put out. 'But I'm standing in a hole,' he protested, looking down at his feet. Indeed, he *was* standing in a hole – but it was just about to get much deeper.

A few days later Mario Condello and George Defteros were arrested and charged with conspiracy to murder Carl Williams, George Williams and an unnamed third party. Defteros was later cleared. The police alleged they arranged to pay a shooter $450 000 for the triple hit, which was apparently going to take place in the bar or the foyer of the Marriott Hotel. This was where I had sat with Carl and Roberta and the team at the precise time the assassin was scoping out Carl. It seemed ridiculous to think that as I had been eating and drinking, desperately trying to talk my way deeper into the action, the story had been unfolding all around me. And the man I had just had coffee with could have killed me in his efforts to get at Carl.

21 | NO END IN SIGHT

After a year of working on the gangland wars, I was heartily sick of the whole thing. I was tired of the knot of anticipation that tightened in my stomach every time the mobile rang, tired of judging every single word I said for its unintended meaning, sick of trying to decode what people were telling me. Like Alice, I had fallen through the looking glass. I was too far in and couldn't extricate myself. It would take another six years before I could say I was free of this story.

I had lost perspective on what my role really was. I was part journalist, part counsellor and even part police informer. No other stories interested me now; the ebb and flow of squarehead life with its trivial politics and endless debate bored me senseless. I felt as if the stories I had written before this no longer had any relevance. A fugitive from the world of metaphor, I was now living in the literal. The only thing that mattered was this life-and-death struggle. I had stopped seeing my old friends; dinner-party conversations about economics and middle-class morality left me cold.

Unfolding events still had the capacity to surprise and unsettle, though. A single telephone call could restore that sense of panic and alienation, reminding me that I was still totally ignorant. One night in September 2004, I had been woken by the mobile but it went to message bank before I could get the call. The anonymous message was unambiguous and sent a chill through me: 'You fucking big dog rat. I hope you fucking die, you dog. That's my message.' I hadn't slept again that night. At such moments I sought out new contacts, taking stupid risks to get close to the people I thought could finally lift the veil on all of this. Or perhaps I was seeking their protection. I was never quite sure. (As an anonymous threatening caller, this bloke had left something to be desired. He had called from the mobile phone of someone I knew, and the number was displayed on my missed calls. I called the owner of the phone and suggested he think more creatively next time he wished me dead.)

By now I had made so many contacts that I could drop names to get new ones. About once a week I would get letters from jail from players on both sides of the conflict, offering more insights and clues. Information was coming at me from all sides. People trusted me with their secrets and their opinions of others. The cycle of revenge and pre-emption had taken on a life of its own. It had become life for Carl. You could lay down your weapon, but what of your enemy? Could you trust your friend? Was he positioning you for the kill, as so many others had? As Carl's new shadow, Terrence Chimirri, told National Nine News: 'I use paranoia as an awareness. I'm aware of things, and if they are going to come [they must] be prepared to put me off. No second chances.'

Guys like Chimirri had nothing to lose now. They had seen the hoopla that had accompanied Benji's demise, and it sounded better than dying anonymous in the suburbs. 'We don't come from silver-spoon people, mate. Our parents don't have millions of dollars.

We're from the fuckin' wetlands, if you really want to know. It's all paddocks. If we end up sleeping on the concrete, we sleep on the concrete.'

Chimirri's loyalty to Carl and Roberta was absolute and unquestioning: 'I'll die for them. On the regards as I know they would do it for me.' It seemed only a matter of time before the shooting started again, whether on the streets or in jail.

In mid-August, Roberta's world was threatening to fall apart. She was now living in the Essendon home she part-owned with the Williamses. The renovations were costing more than she had planned and she was running out of money. There was talk in the underworld that Carl had stashed away twenty barrels of pseudoephedrine – enough 'Susie' to make literally billions of dollars of speed. The real amount was probably a fraction of that, and it was more than likely the Chief Executive's, but such stories get around. Anyway, Roberta couldn't get her hands on any of it. Carl had separated his finances from hers and was preparing, not for the first time, to divorce her.

With Carl now in jail and the court process grinding slowly forward, the whole caper was losing its glamour for Roberta. She was forced to call in every favour she could. Every crim who could wield a trowel was pressed into service, and she was looking for backers to help restart her maternity sleepwear business. She had her own legal troubles coming up, with trials for drug trafficking, credit-card deception and home-loan fraud. She would eventually get slapped with an order to pay $142 000 to the Assets Confiscation

Office and a fifteen-month suspended sentence. She was desperate to finish the house before she went to jail on the drugs charges and to enjoy her suburban dream while she could. She knew she had to finish the house before those trials. Who was going to help her finish the place if she went inside for a long stretch? Her girlfriends had deserted her and most of her male friends were either dead, in jail or making themselves scarce. Only her sister Michelle and the kids had stood by her.

Roberta's mobile phone had become a sort of criminal switchboard. Whenever Carl or the Raptor wanted to get through to somebody on the outside they would call her second mobile phone and she would divert the call to wherever it had to go. It was illegal, but everyone did it.

One night my telephone rang. It was Roberta. 'Hi, Adam. Remember you said you could get us tickets to the filming of them shows like *The Footy Show* and *The Price is Right*?'

'Yes,' I said, wincing.

'Well, I wanna go on *The Price is Right*.'

'Okay . . .'

'Hey, and you know what else?'

'What?' *How could this get any more weird*, I thought.

'If they don't call me down, I'm going to run down there and punch on with Larry – on telly.' She was screaming now, howling with laughter. I promised I would get her tickets on the proviso that the small, defenceless and perfectly amiable Larry Emdur was spared a flogging.

On the appointed day, which happened to be my birthday, we lined up with the rest of the hopeful studio audience outside

Channel Nine's Richmond headquarters. All eyes fell on Roberta's noisy little group, which included Michelle, Benji's sister Helen and an aunt of Carl's. For the other punters, any lingering doubts as to the identity of this party were dispelled when the meet-and-greeters stuck big pink name-cards on Roberta and Michelle. I stood alongside in my suit, looking like Roberta's new bodyguard. I was spending my birthday at the taping of a game show with some of Melbourne's most notorious brides of crime – and I was really enjoying it. Roberta gave me a gift of a bottle of aftershave. It was Eternity by Calvin Klein, which she said was Carl's favourite. There was something spooky in getting a gift of Eternity from the wife of an accused murderer.

I looked at Roberta's face as I thanked her. There was a hardness in her eyes: she had seen too much, done too much ever to get away from the life she had chosen. It was all catching up with her. In the heady days of summer her friends had flocked around, everyone wanting to be caught in the reflected glare of fame. Now, in the depths of winter, they had all disappeared. Even the Chief Executive had stopped calling. She was on her own.

She dismissed my thanks. 'You're my friend . . . At least, I think you are,' she said, looking quickly away.

At that instant I understood something that Carl had said to me months before: 'Remember – [in the underworld] a good friend is everyone's enemy.' It had seemed illogical till now. In the squarehead world you could afford to have lots of associates and acquaintances and call them friends. You could be many things to many people without any conflict of interest. In this world, though, if you called someone a friend, it was as strong as declaring someone a dog. Friendship came with obligation. Your new friend's enemies became yours, too, and you could be pulled into a war that was none of your business. Squareheads would say a friend wouldn't do that to you. In the underworld they say, 'What is a friend if he won't go to war with you?'

I weighed up the cost of being a friend of Roberta's. I had seen what happened to Roberta and Carl's friends – Nik Radev, Dino Dibra, Lewis Caine, Benji and others. It had even been rumoured that she'd had a short, torrid affair with Mark Moran. She was mad, bad and dangerous to know, that was for certain. The most terrible things could fall from her lips without a second thought, but there was something deeply attractive in the pure mischief of the woman.

The studio announcer, Shawn Cosgrove, began to warm up the *Price is Right* crowd. 'If there's anybody here who is on the run from the cops, or if anyone's violating their bail conditions by being here, then please let us know now . . .' The audience all laughed except for Roberta and Michelle, who were indeed on bail at that moment. 'That's not funny,' said Roberta. Fortunately for all concerned, the girls didn't get the call to come on down with Larry, and the taping passed without incident.

I watched Roberta's face as Larry whipped the contestants into a frenzy of excitement during the show. Here was a chance to win the showcase of prizes and the perfect lifestyle that went with it. Perhaps crime for Roberta was that showcase win, the short cut to all the things to which she felt entitled. It was the call from the studio announcer to come on down, to put the misery of her childhood and her own bad choices behind her. A father burned to death in a truck accident before she knew him, an uninterested mother who had let her de factos beat up her brood of kids. Growing up on the street, all Roberta had ever wanted was for the world to recognise that she existed. Now, as the wife of an accused murderer, she had at least achieved infamy. She understood the difference.

As far as I knew, no one had ever done a day's jail over Roberta: she was staunch. But as the months of this extraordinary year ground on and the bodies piled higher, she seemed to be increasingly alone. Most of her girlfriends deserted her (some she drove away, others found the heat too much to be near her); her children were getting a hard time at school; shopkeepers would whisper as she went about her daily routines in Moonee Ponds.

During a break in filming we got to talking about Zarah and her legal campaign to be allowed to have Lewie's baby through artificial insemination. 'I wish I had known you could do that when Andrew died,' Roberta said. 'I would have gladly been impregnated with his sperm. I would have been honoured to carry his child for him. 'Cause that's what friends do for each other.'

As winter deepened, I began to lap the block before I pulled into the back lane that led to the rear of my house. I watched the roller door on the garage open ever so slowly and began to appreciate the terror that simple things held for people right now. I thought of the men who had died in this very position. Killing was like scratching an itch, and there was flesh under many fingernails.

When I began my research on the Melbourne underworld war, I planned to grab a juicy piece of low-hanging fruit, taste it and move on. It was a war where the killers operated in broad daylight, seemingly unafraid of being caught. Or perhaps, I thought, they were just too dumb and brutish to care.

To my surprise, once I met the main characters of the story – Andrew Veniamin, Carl and Roberta Williams, Mick Gatto and all the other cast members – a much different picture emerged. I found that within these flawed pitiless characters there was a capacity for goodness and kindness, and perhaps even compassion. There were instances when such finer feelings prompted the commission of evil. If you showed someone mercy, you would pay for it later. But generally their emotions lacked proportion. There was an infinite love for those close to them, but a total absence of it for anyone else.

When I started, the dead were ghosts in my mind's eye as I visited the cafes and restaurants they had frequented and the places where they died. But soon the victims ceased to be just photo identikits. From behind the mug shots emerged complex human beings, and eventually I could hear their voices as I wrote. When this happened, I dropped everything (including some fragile things that I couldn't really afford to drop, like relationships and obligations) in order to follow their stories.

When I began the research I had a nice, easy existence. I was sharing a house with my sister in the leafy suburb of Hawthorn, going to my favourite hotel with mates on a Wednesday night, and picking up the kids from school. As a business journalist, the greatest danger I faced was getting a paper cut or suffering a heart attack from too many free lunches. A year later my sister had moved on and I was living on my own in a dingy Richmond flat wedged between the eastern and southern rail lines. The 5.30 a.m. freight train rattled me out of bed every morning, and in wet weather I put up with the persistent *drip, drip, drip* of rain coming through the leaky skylight, and the smell of damp carpet in my nostrils.

I hadn't realised the place was in the armpit of a rail junction: two major train lines parted company nearby. On the other side of one was the former home of the late Dennis Allen, the house of horrors where he had murdered friends and foes. After three weeks of train noise day and night, I understood why Dennis had become a psycho killer. I am sure that, like me, Dennis eventually got used to the trains, but I wasn't sure the same thing would happen for me with the teenage chromers who wandered the street outside like blue-lipped zombies.

The experience of working on this story challenged my beliefs and my ethics as a journalist and as a person. It challenged my concepts of friendship and personal commitment. I was accused by other reporters and some police of taking the villains' side. In my view, if I were to understand the story, I had to invest something of myself in the telling. To the charge that I had become too close, I would reply that everyone else was too far away.

I was forming relationships of trust and affection with friends and relatives of the dead, relationships that would be shattered with the publication of this book. I had to have a reason for it all, but there was none beyond my enthusiasm for the story and an inability to do anything else.

I decided that Roberta Williams' sentencing in October 2004 on ecstasy-trafficking charges would be my last story on this mess. There had to be a physical separation from the characters, if I was to regain a sense of objectivity. But when I got to court that day, I didn't sit with the other press; instead, I took a seat a few metres from the accused. I watched Roberta as she sat in the dock waiting for judgement. Her arms were folded and entwined. She gripped herself, tightly coiled, as if she might spring up and run out of the courtroom at any moment. Roberta always had something to do, some place to go, two mobile phones ringing constantly in her ear. Now she was a study in perpetual motion denied.

It was cool and dim in the court, but the perspiration was spreading under Roberta's armpits. The muscles in her square jaw were clenched and the sinews in her arms rippled as she looked around the courtroom, challenging anyone to stare her down. Rows of journalists sat in the jury benches, trying to avoid eye contact with her. Across the bar table, a female Crown solicitor, neatly coiffed and suited, stared blankly at the prisoner in the dock as she prepared for her day's work, the task today to put this mother of four away for as long as possible.

Roberta's mouth curled into a half-smile, half-sneer. 'You are so ugly, so ugly,' she said, softly at first. 'You're the ugliest *thing* I have ever seen.' For a brief, shining moment Roberta's team had been on top of the heap. She wasn't going to let some jumped-up lawyer bitch stare at her like a picture at an exhibition. 'Come on,' she said, her voice rising. 'Let's go outside and sort this out right now. Let's go and fuckin' punch on. I've got nothing to lose now – it's the end of the line.'

At thirty-five, Roberta was about the same age as the solicitor. They might have gone to the same hairdresser and shopped in the same boutiques, such was the style of Mrs Carl Williams. That morning, in her late-model Pajero, Roberta had driven two of her daughters to their private school in Essendon. She had then driven to town, leaving behind her newly renovated home in Moonee Ponds. So what if she had to live behind bulletproof screens? Her visitors would still respect the little sign asking them kindly to remove their shoes, even if they had come to kill her. And she had survived, even if the cost had been high. Around her neck she was wearing the silver heart-shaped locket containing Benji's picture; his dark angry eyes blazed out incongruously from the photograph.

Roberta had been forced to call in every favour she could. Fearing a nervous breakdown, she had checked herself into a psychiatric hospital for a couple of weeks, but had lasted only a few days. 'I can't participate in the group therapy sessions,' she told me. 'I can't share what it's like to be me, because everyone knows who I am.'

She would receive only an eighteen-month sentence for her part in the trafficking of $100 000 worth of ecstasy. With time off for good behaviour, she served only six months in jail for her crime, but with her sentencing there was a sense that an era was ending.

One day Roberta and I had met for lunch in a cafe and she had poured her heart out to me, trying to describe what her life was like. She was moving in a circle where treachery was the daily currency, a world where her friends and enemies were interchangeable in short order. In December 2003, she had thrown a huge christening party for her and Carl's daughter and every prominent criminal in Melbourne had been there, drinking and eating with gusto as they swore loyalty to their host and hostess. *Where have they all gone?* I wondered as we sat in that cafe. Some, like the late Andrew Veniamin, had legitimate excuses; others had simply moved on to the next big thing in town.

She turned to me and with surprising vulnerability asked if I was her friend. Yes, I could be her friend, I told her. She knew that I respected the fact that she'd kept her household together through a gang war, just as she knew that I could laugh with her at the absurdity of her situation but I could never live in her world. She said she longed for ordinary things: life inside the square with a conventional man 'who went to work and came home and sat down to the tea that I had made for him'. I wished her luck in finding that in her next marriage.

For the time being she was going to have put up with Carl, at least until he filed the divorce papers. Of course, he was in 23-hour lockdown in Barwon Prison, facing years of trials and appeals. His only pleasure was the chance to hassle Mick Gatto as Mick went by Carl's cell en route to his own court appearances. 'You might have been the Don of Carlton, Mick, but in here, mate, you're the Dog of Barwon!' Carl would call out, much to the amusement of the unseen gallery of inmates behind their cell doors. Sooner or later the combatants would find a way to get to each other. If found guilty of their crimes, they would have a lifetime inside to plot and scheme. As Billy Longley had said, some things only blood can settle.

For now, an uneasy calm had fallen over the ganglands. By Christmas 2004, with all the main players on remand awaiting trial, the killings had stopped. La Porcella, which was Mick Gatto's headquarters and the scene of Benji's death, had re-opened as an upmarket Chinese restaurant. Mick's table was gone. The public was afforded a brief glimpse into the ganglands, but the portal to this netherworld had closed over once more.

22 | KITES FROM BARWON

Now in the maximum security Acacia Unit at Barwon Prison, Carl's world had shrunk dramatically. Unable to communicate as he had on the outside, he turned to letter-writing to express himself. Prisoners call them 'kites', and a number landed on my desk in 2004 and 2005.

Sunday 11th July

Hello Adam,

Well it was good to hear from you as it always is. As for me, I'm back here at HOTEL ACACIA [Acacia is the maximum-security isolation wing of Barwon Prison], just taking a break for a while, everything's good no problems.

Time goes quickly here, if you don't keep track of it, it seems to get away from you. A good way to look at it is things always get better and I will be back to have a drink with you. Just not sure when, but it won't be too long.

I was going to run for PM. Didn't think that would have been an idea though, because I'm too honest, and to be in that department

you have to be an out and out LIAR, that's not me as you for
one know.

Sunday 8th August

Hey, buddy, lucky you never got shot with me at the MARRIOT.
I would have jumped in front of you anyway. But we live another
day. Every day above ground is a good day. And that bloke's
[Mario Condello] trying for bail. He has a headache. Why don't
he just see a doctor? I've never seen on Panadol packets if pain
persists go for bail. It says if pain persists see a doctor. Some of
the new Australians (WOGS) aren't too bright. Might be good at
standing over hardworking family people, that's not something
I'd like to be known, or remembered for, but that's ME.

Wednesday 1st September

You were saying about people not likeing what Chopper said about
plastic godfathers.

I always thought people were brought up to tell the truth, sometimes the truth hurts, and some people shy away from that, and
prefer to believe they belong in the movies, they could be right, but
just have the wrong scene.

You are my friend, well I consider you as a friend anyway.
You've always paid me respect and I will always pay you the same
right back.

We will be having a few drinks again before we know it, don't
you worry about that.

Tough men last, tough times don't. As much as the POLICE want to keep me here they are wasteing there time, doing their heads in over me, because I will be back out there when I finish these court cases, no rush at the moment, but I have no doubt that everything will work out, time tells everything.

Well only a short letter today to say thanks for writing to me, as its always good to hear from you.

Until I hear from you again, 'be good or be good at it'.

Take care, your friend always.

Carl

He who searches for friends with faults will never have a friend.

A good friend is hard to find, hard to lose, and IMPOSSIBLE TO FORGET.

A Purana's Tale
(as edited and augmented by Carl Anthony Williams and the Raptor)

Acacia HMP Barwon

Dear Mum and Dad,

Gee it's grouse in the Victoria Police Force, sorry Service, Purana Taskforce. My very first day at the station at the St Kilda Road Complex, Sergeant Stuart Bateson says: 'Don't just sit there counting money son, come on the beat with me.' So I buckled up my pistol and truncheon and radio and capsicum squirter and handcuffs and electric pod and thermos and brown paper bags and chased after him. We went down Lygon Street, which is in Carlton, to see what information we could gather from the Carlton Crew, the likes of Mick (the Don) Gatto, Mario (the Bull) Condello just like the opening credits of *The Bill*. Big Boots, moving slow, plus the use of the hips as they taught us in the academy, like a Friesian cow smuggling parrots in condoms through customs, and we took an apple off a fruit store for free, just like in the NYPD, because fruiterers know we are looking after them. And then we got a coffee for free and a donut for free and a side of lamb each for free, and a um, massage for free and heaps of money in brown paper bags and we're just coming up to the trattoria at lunchtime and the Sarge says, 'This is real community policing.' Then the Sarge says, 'Strewth, what day is this, Lightning?' (They call me Lightning, I'm not sure why – give me time and I'll work it out.) And I says, 'Tuesday' and he says, 'Cross the road now. We need some brioche, urgently.' So we just settle down to some free brioche and the front of the trattoria over the road explodes in a hail of gunfire and there's blood everywhere and screaming and there's these blokes laid out on the pavement in a pool of veal parmigiana and blood and I say to the Sarge, 'Those blokes look dead!' And the Sarge says, 'A good copper never jumps to conclusions. Wait for forensics.' And I say, 'Sarge what about those blokes in balaclavas? Are they the killers here?' And the Sarge says, 'Don't jump to conclusions about balaclavas, son. It's nearly the start of the ski season. Or perhaps they tan easily. Have some more of this uncommonly good brioche.' Then he got on the radio and placed a couple of bets. So, to reassure the civilians, I crossed the road and stepped over the alleged bodies and booked a bicycle courier for angle parking.

Dear Mum and Dad,

Me and the Sarge went undercover to the alleged crim's funeral. It wasn't very undercover. We parked across the road with the lights flashing and the cones out and we had some donuts and some chips and brioche and pizza and KFC, but the Sarge has certainly got the drop on the crims. He showed me how to spot them. They were all in their uniforms, black suits with wraparound sunglasses, guns drugs and photographers. And also they all waved, and the Sarge waved them over. The Sarge placed a couple of bets on the car radio, and a couple of the crims came up and asked him to put a couple of monkeys on for them. I said, 'Sarge you've got them where you want them. They can hide but they can't run.' The Sarge said, 'Lightning your two pizzas short of a patrol car.' Then some blokes in balaclavas ran out of the mourners and shot the Sarge's mates. Sorry allegedly shot them. Blood everywhere, sorry alleged blood everywhere. In the carwash, the Sarge said, 'The first rule of good policing is this. Avoid domestic disputes.' OK I've got stuff to learn.

Dear Mum and Dad,

Back at the station, in a quiet moment when people weren't placing bets, I asked the Sarge about Organised Crime. Everyone knows who the crims are and what they do, and is this Organised Crime?

'Organised Crime,' he said, 'is when thugs stand over people and demand their money, with no return in goods or services.' Then he showed me some Sydney newspapers about the Carr and Egan mini-budget, and all I could do was whistle, just like the people in

NSW have to do. He said that this was the work of the mob, the mates of Bob, going through people's pockets, and also, strictly speaking, this was disorganised crime. The NSW ALP is not so much *The Sopranos* as *The Falsettos*, or possibly *The Castratos*. So I said, 'What about the multi-million dollar trade in amphetamines and stuff that has led to so many shootings there?' And the Sarge said, 'Alleged shootings of alleged dead people, in alleged pools of blood, in alleged public places. Given the usual lawyers, these may never have happened. Lightning, who makes and takes and sells these drugs? Heavily armed bikie gangs? Heavily armed crims? Huge wired truckies? Sparking party goers?' I thought this was likely. And Sarge said, 'What do these people have in common?' And he helped by answering 'lawyers' and 'Bracks' Judges'. Then he took some more bets over the phone and I went out for Maccas and brioche. Oh, and he also said, 'If these people trouble you, you try to bring them in.'

Dear Mum and Dad,

I'm learning. And apparently, the Sarge's book is on who gets shot next. I got the trifecta! Also when there's the next gangland slaying, I get to stand out the front of the police station with a sign saying, 'HE WENT THAT WAY'.

P.S. I hope you had a laugh.
Your friend always,
Carl

Some of Carl's letters were not so funny. By December 2004, he was desperately trying to discredit Purana's star witness, Goggles, who would soon give evidence in the Michael Marshall murder trial (the Raptor was yet to roll). The only problem was that Goggles' name had been suppressed by the courts and couldn't be mentioned by the media; at this point he was being referred to as '161'. Yet Carl believed it was time to call in the debts of friendship.

Wednesday 15th December

Adam,

Hope you are well, as for me im fine. Received your letter today dated 6-12-04 and it was good to hear from you. The media don't really care about the truth as long as they can make up a good story what sells.

They don't care whos life they put at risk, whos trials they make hard to win by poisoning the protential jury's mind. they are the lowest of Low.

The media people no about witness known as 161 prior conviction of dishonesty, different stories to POLICE and proven lies but yet wont report on any of those stories, as they don't suit the police, the media is an outlet for the police and most reporter are worse than the lying Police.

I was once told the public needs a true portrayl of the FACT but no one wants to report the facts [in fact, it was me who told him this], when someone with any balls [does] that they'll get and earn my RESPECT.

Hopefully you can do something as I thought you were my friend, if I could ever HELP you I would and I believe you no that.

A few reporter should watch a good movie I seen the other week VERONICA GUERIN.

All the best regards <u>Carl</u>

The movie Carl referred to starred Cate Blanchett as Irish reporter Veronica Guerin, who was murdered in 1995 after investigating a drug lord with links to the IRA. Despite this hint of menace, I stayed on Carl's Christmas card list that year.

Adam,

I could think of better holes to be stuck in over the x-mas period.

Merry Christmas and Best Wishes for the New Year

Your friend Always <u>Carl</u>

23 | SLEEPING IN THE TREES

When Mario Condello was shot dead on the night of 6 February 2006, I recalled his words to me: 'For the first time I have heard some birds singing in the trees, so let's hope these birds continue to sing and everything becomes more peaceful.'

Perhaps if Condello had not been busy birdwatching he might have seen the danger approaching. He believed the war was over with Carl in jail. He told me that he was confident of beating the incitement-to-murder charge he faced at his forthcoming trial.

The charges against his lawyer George Defteros had already been withdrawn. Condello had been granted bail, much to the surprise of many, and he was even working legitimately at a friend's concrete business. (I thought he'd been joking at first when he told me about the job. Every time I saw their trucks, I wondered whether Mario was in the back making the shoes.) Under his bail conditions, Mario had to be home by 10 p.m. and could no longer use a range of other addresses to help avoid danger. He had given up his bed in the trees, and could no longer scope out the grounds below, I thought.

The killer waited for Condello to drive his car into the garage.

The remote-controlled garage door was closing as the killer stepped inside and shot Condello; he was out again before it shut. The killer was rumoured to be the Savage, still taking care of business for Carl like his criminal father figure.

Less than eight hours later I was standing in front of Condello's home doing a live interview for the *Today* show. I made the point that Chief Commisioner of Police Christine Nixon had only hours earlier, in press comments, congratulated Purana for bringing the gang war to a close. It was far from over, I said: there was talk that the Chief Executive was bragging he would pay someone a million dollars to hit Gatto. Gatto was on the phone just minutes later with a less than subtle warning: 'You're trying to get me killed!' he fumed. 'You're throwing oil on the flames again with all this nonsense. If I see you, you had better keep out of my way.' The pressure was clearly telling on Mick.

Camera crews gathered outside his home, waiting for him to emerge. He didn't disappoint. Storming out of his house in a striped dressing-gown, he pelted the media with eggs. By now Mick had been acquitted of the murder of Andrew Veniamin and he seemed to think that everyone was supposed to leave him alone. He had taken the decision to go straight. Most of the rorts that he and the Carlton Crew had enjoyed for years were gone now, in a blaze of publicity. But if he thought eggs and threats would deter the media, he was mistaken.

In the autumn of 2006, the Gunsmith, now resident in the Acacia Unit of Barwon Prison, kept a series of appointments with detectives from the Purana Taskforce. After nearly two years in 23-hour lockdown, the Gunsmith was at breaking point. Inside his tiny cell, he was shrinking literally. He had lost lots of weight, he had lost his wife and he was fast losing his mind. He knew that the jacks had acquired evidence linking him to at least three murders. He hadn't pulled the trigger in any of them but he'd still get the full whack for murder. As he saw it, he wasn't going down for life for giving Carl two sawn-offs.

'The reason why I got youse here, right . . . I plead to something I haven't done but I want youse to put it all as a package deal. Whatever I know, I tell yas. What I want is if the cops can look after me,' he said. 'I've had enough. I can't fight any more. I got no more fight in me. Look, I should have listened to you from the start and a lot of crap wouldn't have come out. I should have said something, and Moran wouldn't have been shot, no one would have been shot.'

But the Gunsmith's actions had nothing to do with conscience. He knew that the Raptor had already had his own appointment with Purana in March 2006. He had fingered Carl over all the murders and a good deal besides. The Raptor had also fingered the Gunsmith for his involvement in several of the murders, so his meeting with Purana was entirely motivated by self-preservation. 'I'm telling you now, I know for a fact [the Raptor] is lying. I can't fight it.'

The Gunsmith made sixteen statements in all. He talked enough to make a stack of paper that represented one of the most comprehensive insights ever into the workings of the Melbourne underworld. His statements detailed the rise of big players in the speed trade in the 1990s, and the methods they had used to import cocaine and ecstasy. He told how he had helped the Williamses in the pill-making business, setting up a press, one of several George and Carl operated in the garage of the Williams family home in Broadmeadows. He implicated George in a plot to kill Lewis Moran. He dobbed in dozens of co-conspirators in the speed trade and showed the cops where to find their assets. He sketched the background plotting of murders, how he had supplied two sawn-off shotguns to Carl for the murders of the Moran brothers, how he had helped lure Nik Radev to his death.

More than 53 000 hours of electronic bugging and 20 000 hours of physical surveillance hadn't been able to extract what was spilling out from the Gunsmith. Purana was finally getting their evidence, and all they had to do was sit and listen. As the officers told their witness, they had scuttlebutt coming out of their ears; what they didn't have was evidence.

The Gunsmith turned his confession into a community service announcement. 'No one else wants to do the right thing and put their hand in and tell 'em the truth, so what else am I gunna do?' he asked.

When I interviewed the Raptor in Barwon Prison a year earlier, it was clear the Acacia experience was wearing thin. He had stayed staunch to Carl for longer than he'd thought he could. For Carl, the Raptor had even agreed to his lawyer's suggestion to put on thirty kilos to throw the jury's ID of him in the Moran–Barbaro murders.

Maybe it was partly out of guilt. If only he had listened to Goggles' warning about the tracking device he'd found in the car they had used in the Marshall killing. If the jacks hadn't recorded the whole thing, they wouldn't be here now. They would still be having fun and killing people. He and Carl had become mates in jail, but this was no ordinary boob. When the Raptor met Carl, they set up a supply line of drugs, mobiles, food, alcohol – basically anything you wanted – through a dodgy contact in the outside catering company that served the Port Phillip prison. Jail with Carl had actually been better than life on the outside. The Raptor did time easy as it was. He'd been in custody for most of his life. In his last year of freedom, life had consisted of nothing more than contract killing, punting and visiting his mother. Jail held no terrors but Acacia was much worse. Standing right next to Carl, the Raptor predicted that he would break under the 'protracted torture' he was undergoing.

'The will of the individual becomes overborne by the torturous conditions in here,' he said in a quiet voice. The screws hadn't let any mail in or out for weeks now. I had fortuitously been at Carl's mum's place when the boys called. As soon as prison authorities knew that a journalist was speaking to their prize remand prisoners, they cut the call. The Raptor called back and talked of his daily routines inside Acacia Unit and the phone was cut again. He called back. 'See how petty they [the prison officers] can be? Surely I have the right to discuss my daily routines!' he fumed.

Six calls were terminated in the space of ten minutes. Each time the phone cut, the Raptor and Williams had used up another of their fourteen calls each per week. The screws took away their telephone privileges entirely for speaking to me. Now there was nothing to do but watch TV, read piles of legal briefs for their upcoming trials or walk in tiny circles in their cells, waiting for the next shakedown by the screws.

It would take another year for the Raptor to betray Carl. He only did it after he learned that Carl was trying to have his own charges on the Moran–Barbaro murder heard separately from the Raptor's. And this after Carl had short-changed him on the fee for killing the pair.

Even Carl had been feeling the walls of his four- by three-metre cell closing in on him. There were no more amusing letters. His writing now reflected a man coming to terms with the reality that he would never see freedom again.

'The moment you become a prisoner, you lose all sorts of legal rights and social respect. Even the value of your life is downgraded in one big thud,' he wrote. 'Prisoners are not considered as people. Your death or mutilation does not particularly concern the judges, prosecutors, police, prison officers or other state officials, providing it does not cause too much embarrassment . . . Very few people in society even want to hear about the dozens of people that commit suicide or are killed in jail. Death in jail is such a common occurrence that it is rarely reported in newspapers and even other prisoners find it too painful to dwell on.'

Needless to say, the public showed little sympathy for Carl's new sensitive attitude to death. So did the prison authorities. Carl and the Raptor lost their telephone rights as a punishment for speaking with me and my letters went unanswered, probably blocked by the screws. The dialogue had ended. Now it was a test of endurance:

two killers versus their steel-and-concrete cage. Acacia was steadily chopping them up into bits.

On 3 February the Raptor wrote to the Office of Public Prosecutions with a proposition. 'Before anything can be discussed my mother would first have to be relocated and I would also have to be moved from my current placement . . . I would then provide you with some explosive allegations in relation to numerous matters involving and not exceeding 10 individuals.'

It was February 2007 and Roberta Williams was sitting on her bed in a Melbourne psychiatric clinic, where she was being treated for stress and anxiety. She was speaking of the family's bloody ascension to gangland power in a strangely disconnected way. She seemed a bewildered observer with the rest of us, not 'a player up to her back teeth', as one policeman had described her.

'Someone should make a movie about all this shit,' she said, shaking her head in mock disbelief. 'You would never believe that all this could have happened.'

A few days later Carl Williams would put his hand up for three murders: Jason and Lewis Moran and Mark Mallia. Police would say that he had killed ten men, but with the 2005 conviction for the Marshall murder and the guilty pleas on Mallia and the Morans, it seemed the law's thirst for revenge had been quenched. He'd already got twenty-six years with a 21-year minimum on the Marshall murder.

A week earlier over lunch, Carl's father, George, had told me the authorities had offered something of plea bargain to his son:

plead guilty to three murders and the rest of the clan would be spared murder and conspiracy charges. Carl would also receive a minimum jail sentence, which meant that one day, even as an old man, he would be free.

For the four years I had known the Williams family, we had acted out a pantomime where we danced around the truth: Carl was innocent and framed, they said, just a drug dealer fighting corrupt police and their henchmen in the city's Italian mafia. Now it was over. Carl's plea of guilty would keep his father out of jail. There was no talk of beating the murder raps, just damage control. If George, who suffered a heart problem, went to jail, he would die for sure, he said. It was more likely an inmate would knock him for a shot of heroin on behalf of the Williams' many enemies, but either way it was a deal that proved irresistible.

Someone had already made that movie, I told Roberta. Geoffrey Wright's 2006 film *Macbeth* retold Shakespeare's play with Melbourne's gangland as the backdrop. She hadn't heard of the film or the play, so I told her Shakespeare's story: the minor Scottish lord driven by his ambitious, manipulative wife to murder his king and a string of associates; the pretender's short, unhappy reign as King of Scotland; the final denouement with Macbeth's betrayal and beheading.

If Roberta got the connection she didn't let on, but when she spoke of her stress and anxiety, Lady Macbeth's famous sleepwalking scene sprang to mind. Consumed with guilt about the crimes she and her husband have committed, Lady Macbeth frantically tries to wash imaginary bloodstains off her hands. She can't do it – no more than Roberta Williams could distance herself from the blood and gore of the past eight years. No more than her great rival, Judith Moran, can distance herself from the criminal activities of her late sons, Mark and Jason, and her husband Lewis.

Roberta was the only one of the group that the informers had not dobbed in for something. Now she was moving on, talking of converting to Islam because in that faith 'you can wipe the slate clean and start again'. She spoke of donning the hijab and learning the Koran, but she seemed an unlikely convert sitting there in her pink tracksuit with her laptop, flicking through an online catalogue of Peter Alexander sleepwear.

She showed me a photograph of her 'new friend', Mohammed. She said he was a legitimate businessman with taxi cabs and nightclubs. Okay, yes, Mohammed had been to jail, but he was a good man, a pious man, and he was standing by her. 'Not like the rest of those dogs and rats we once called friends.' She spat the words in disgust. 'Where are they now?'

Where were the people who had attended the lavish parties, Carl and Roberta's wedding in 2001, their daughter Dhakota's christening two years later, she asked. It seemed churlish to point out that Carl had killed some of those partygoers. Or that some were fast friends indeed. The Chief Executive had disappeared a year earlier, days before he was to be charged with a murder. Though the cops would turn up a couple of stook holes stuffed with cash and jewellery, it was thought that he had spirited millions away.

However, it seemed only a matter of time before someone gave up the Chief Executive for the money. As Keith Moor of the *Herald Sun* newspaper said, the Chief Executive had to be lucky every day to evade capture, while police only needed to get lucky once.

And besides, the Chief Executive was a Melbourne boy through and through. Sooner or later, this homesick hoodlum would slip up. In the meantime, he could fool himself that he had left the wreckage behind.

Zarah Garde-Wilson, the glamorous solicitor, had moved on too. When Roberta was in jail Zarah had stayed in her house and driven her Pajero; now she didn't want to know her client any more, 'cos the money's run out,' said Roberta. Zarah had her own battles, having had her practising certificate suspended after allegations she had lied to the Australian Crime Commission. She was supposed to have passed Lewie's gun to a police informer and then tried to bullshit her way out of it. But she was in too deep. She faced contempt of court charges for giving evidence to the ACC and was also charged with possessing an unregistered gun. When she was called to give evidence before the ACC she swore on oath that she had communicated with spirits who told her where Lewie was murdered. (Of course, she had also been convinced that Lewie was murdered by a contact of mine who had head-butted him in a Brunswick hotel two weeks before his death. So maybe even the spirits couldn't be trusted now.) She also beat a Legal Services Board ruling that she was not a fit and proper person to practise law. The police had publicly shamed her by revealing she had an off-and-on sexual relationship with the Chief Executive and was a sometime resident in one of his homes. She would also be accused of tipping off the Chief Executive that he was about to be charged with a murder, which prompted his flight. If all this were true, I found it hard to understand why she had done it. What was the benefit to her? She had all but trashed a promising career for the love of drug dealers, thugs and murderers. But she'd had her fifteen minutes of fame, later scooping up $90 000 for a television interview.

Roberta was writing a book now – a salutary tale for other young women who believed that hanging off the arm of a gangster was a dream come true. 'It's all glamorous at the beginning – the parties, the money, the power. You walk into a nightclub and every-one steps back. You could flog the bouncer and he can't do nothing to you. But it don't last, it don't last,' she said. 'All I want now is to be with a man that goes to work and comes home of an evening. I would have his dinner on the table for him and talk about his day, kids runnin' round, you know what I mean?'

The Islam conversion and talk of burqas made sense now: it was just another mask for Roberta. But it couldn't cover the empti-ness. No man could replace her dad who had died after the blazing truck accident when she was just eight weeks old. Nothing could heal the scars from being rejected by her mother, the floggings she'd got from her first husband, Dean, who had been aligned with the Moran clan.

Roberta's mother died in 2006 unreconciled with her wayward daughter, and then her eldest sister Sharon died from cancer. Not-withstanding the fact that Roberta once chased her sister with a shovel in a murderous rage, she felt her circle getting ever smaller. It was little consolation that she has the celebrity she always craved. She knows that when the tabloids have moved on and the blood money's been spent, the hollowness will return.

Even as a pretty blonde girl named Renata Laureano took Rob-erta's place at Carl's court appearances, she couldn't dismiss her husband. She was going to flog Renata (who turned out to be the sister of the goddaughter of the ex-wife of a man who betrayed Carl), but she could forgive her as a silly girl caught up in the illusion of glamour – just as Carl had forgiven Roberta for sleeping with his one-time best friend, Andrew Veniamin. Benji, it turned out, had also had a contract to kill Carl. So Islam and Mohammed would have to wait. Here in the last act, all Carl and Roberta had was each other.

I went to the Williams family home in Broadmeadows in early March 2007, after Carl had pleaded. George was all by himself, sitting in a recliner, with the races on the television and the form in front of him. The house was so quiet now, he said. It used to be so busy, with a dozen boys around any time of the day or night, playing snooker in the garage, splashing about in the above-ground pool. Now, with Kathleen away in Bali, it was just George.

There was a plaque on the wall for his first born, the late Shane, and a letter on the table from Carl in jail. George and Barb had bought this house for $11 000 back in the 1970s, with the money that George had saved from a decade with the Board of Works. He had been the youngest inspector ever, and tipped for better things, but still he didn't mind digging ditches alongside the men down in the sewers of Richmond.

'You've seen the real underworld, George,' I told him. He couldn't help but smile. He'd started off in the shit and that's where he would end up – with nothing, and trying (unsuccessfully) to stay out of jail.

But he'd been a big shot for a while, hadn't he? They had owned properties and fancy cars, loads of gold jewellery; they had sent Roberta's kids to private schools. He and Carl had even built Barb her dream home, in Primrose Street, Essendon. They had been up by about $15 million until the whole thing crashed. Now there was just this old Housing Commission home that had been his and Barb's escape from the slums of Richmond. Now it was mortgaged to pay legal fees – when this was all over, George would be lucky to still be holding the property. It didn't matter too much: the Turks had taken over the street long ago and it wasn't the same any more.

As I went to leave, we talked about his security – the roller shutter on every window, the thick hedge of mature cypresses that shielded the property. Carl had wanted George to cut them down when things got dangerous: 'He said too many blokes could hide in them.'

George would lie in bed all that night watching the flickering security monitor at his feet. With four different camera views of the garden, he could watch the approach of his own executioner.

'The police told me to leave the cameras on so they could find the body,' he said, closing the mesh grille. 'Imagine that.'

24 | PARTING SHOTS

There was no remorse – not a flicker – even as Carl contemplated a life sentence in jail.

Two weeks before sentence he told his mother he wished he could turn back the clock, that the last ten years of his life had been a waste. But that was it. There would be no giving up other crooks, no expectation of forgiveness in this life or the next. He was an atheist, Barbara Williams said.

In the Victorian Supreme Court (sitting in the County Court for security reasons) on Monday, 7 May 2007, Carl maintained a studied defiance as Justice Betty King sentenced him to life imprisonment with a minimum of thirty-five years, commencing immediately. With nearly three years already served, it was an effective 38-year sentence. He would be eligible for release in 2042, when he would be aged seventy-one.

Most of the supporting cast were on hand. Judy Moran, severe in black with matching cowboy hat, came dressed for a hanging. Carl's girl of the moment, Renata Laureano, enjoying a brief infamy, walked into court like Paris Hilton on a red carpet. She could enjoy her minor celebrity safe from Roberta, who had been barred entry after putting on a huge show inside and outside the court a week earlier. Roberta had been wearing a beanie, having had her thick locks razor cut – possibly as part of her short-lived conversion to Islam. She had threatened to deny Carl any contact with his daughter if Renata continued to visit him in prison. Despite pleas from Carl in a letter to Roberta not to speak to anyone, the estranged Mrs Williams had threatened to cave Renata's head in, taunted Judy Moran with jibes that she would never see her loved ones again, and complained bitterly that Barbara Williams had never accepted her as a daughter-in-law. Roberta's ferocity and loopy aggression at the court had so intimidated Barbara that her knees shook.

But all this was just a sideshow. The only woman who really mattered that day was sitting on the bench in wig and gown, peering at Carl over her glasses.

And with her sentence came withering condemnation. Justice King gave Carl an old-fashioned dressing-down. It was the most humiliating part of the entire exercise, like your grandmother telling you off in front of company. He tried to ignore it but the hot flush on his cheeks belied his cool. Some reporters said he appeared to smirk when the sentence was handed down, but I couldn't see it. But earlier he agreed to be photographed in the dock (one shot could be published) and offered a goofy smile.

The judge was concerned that Carl had become a hero to people in the community. 'You are not,' she said. 'You are a killer, and a cowardly one, who employed others to do the actual killing whilst you hid behind carefully constructed alibis. You should not be the subject of admiration by any member of our community.'

She found it repugnant that Williams had enjoyed his notoriety, giving interviews and making statements to the media.

As the court adjourned, Williams, now on his feet, wanted to fire a parting shot: 'I have something to say.'

Opening a clipboard, he began to read from a prepared text. 'I expected nothing better of you. You are not a judge. You are only a puppet of the police. You are a puppet for Purana—'

Justice King cut him short and ordered that the prisoner be removed. His speech interrupted, Carl still managed the last word. 'Aah, get fucked!' he cried as they led him away.

And with a wave of his hand, Carl Williams was gone.

In a dingy bluestone lane by the old Waterside Hotel on Flinders Street in Melbourne's CBD, crime-scene tape swayed on a summer evening breeze. The lights of a police car flashed red white and blue in the gathering darkness, illuminating a chalk outline of a body marked on the ground.

Two enormous stretch Hummers pulled up, disgorging their well-dressed passengers. They were young, good-looking and arrogant; or old, belligerent and bejewelled. It was a vision of Italian suits, sunglasses and silicone. They walked nonchalantly over the chalk lines as photographers and TV crews jostled for position.

This is just how Carl Williams wanted it to end. Somehow all the blood would wash away and he and his crew would be feted as celebrities, the new generation who had vanquished the old. He would play himself in his own movie, he once told me.

But the gangsters were lookalikes, the cast of *Underbelly*, arriving for the launch of what would become the most successful drama series in Australian television history. A function room of the old wharfie pub was decorated with bullet-riddled logos and billboards, just like the first story I had written for *The Bulletin*. The Melbourne gangland war had long ceased to be a factual event – it was now a made-for-media spectacle. The actors were remarkably well-cast, at least physically, and the more you watched the more they seemed to become the characters. With the real people dead or in jail, the cast of *Underbelly* became their stand-ins.

Earlier, for the *Sunday* program, I had interviewed Gyton Grantley (Carl Williams), Kat Stewart (Roberta Williams) and Les Hill (Jason Moran). I felt a little disappointed that Damian Walshe-Howling, who played Benji, wasn't available. He was such a dead ringer for the fallen hit man, I could have picked up my last conversation with him – but the real Benji was in Keilor Cemetery. And Carl was in Barwon Jail in a red tracksuit, frozen in time

It was a most odd experience. The actors were the idealised media images of Melbourne's underworld that I had helped to create. Now they were interpreting the lives of the characters they had played for me. 'His essential quality was likeability,' said Grantley of Carl Williams.

'That's why Carl was so successful in his pursuits He treated all of his people well. He paid them well, he was fun to be around, he was quite a loveable guy, always joking and smiling. He never seemed too threatening. He dressed normally. He was an average kind of guy,' Grantley said.

'[Williams] almost gives Australia a bit of pride in their own gangster. The new Australian gangster has been born – not the stereotypical gangster mafia man from Italy, but the tracksuit-wearing bogan from Sunshine that drives a Monaro.'

And that image would go around the world, as *Underbelly* was sold to the United Kingdom, Italy, the Balkans, Portugal, Russia, South Africa, Turkey and Asian markets such as Korea.

The actors brought well-thumbed copies of early editions of this book for me to sign. It was so unexpected I signed the wrong date on a couple. As I fielded their questions, I realised I had become a relic of the story myself, an extra in a drama.

I relayed the critiques of how the real players had been portrayed. Carl wouldn't appreciate being portrayed as a brain-dead goose, I told a nervous Grantley. Later Roberta told me she was outraged that in the series Kat Stewart had given 'husband Carl' a blow job in a car outside court. Never mind the murder and drug dealing, she was no cheap dick-sucking slut, she screeched. Never had she performed such a disgusting act, she said. She wanted to challenge Stewart to a boxing match to sort it out, with the proceeds going to charity.

Carl also took umbrage at being portrayed as a driver for the Morans – he never was. He was a player in his own right. But far from hating the show, I think he enjoyed the renewed notoriety it gave him. How many inmates from Barwon Prison had television shows made about them?

'Whatever people might say, I'm the king of the castle and they're the dirty rascals. Or dead rascals, in fact,' Carl said through Roberta.

His mother had to visit him in jail, but Judy Moran had to visit her sons and ex-husband in the cemetery. It was some small comfort to him. All was in ruin. In November 2007, his father George, health failing, got four and a half years' jail, with a minimum term of twenty months. But Carl could still claim victory because Barb could come visit.

Requests I made to interview Carl in jail or to be placed on his visitors list were ignored by Corrections Victoria. They were determined to deny Carl the power and influence he had once enjoyed through the media. It was probably just as well – who knows what trouble he could have sparked. There was already talk he had ordered the stabbing of a rival in another unit at Barwon.

Meanwhile Roberta, with my full encouragement, sought to launch a full-scale media blitz off the profile she received from *Underbelly* and this book. Publishers and broadcasters had made a good living off her stories, so why shouldn't she (if she could satisfy proceeds of crime legislation)? The opportunity would be short-lived, I told Roberta. She had kids to feed and legal bills to pay – she should go for everything she could. Besides, writing books and doing TV interviews and making documentaries would leave less time for crime and mischief. It did concern me that despite surviving on a Centrelink pension with four kids she often had a roll of banknotes on her, but perhaps she was just thrifty.

In July 2008, the summit of tackiness was finally reached when Roberta posed in skimpy swimwear for a lad's magazine, *Zoo Weekly*. Finally, she was enjoying the fame and recognition she had always craved. To the innocent family members who lost loved ones to Carl's murderous revenge, the world had become a bizarre place indeed.

Mick Gatto, in the throes of writing his own book, had re-established his profile after beating the murder charge over Benji. He threw a gala $1000-a-head dinner for one of Victor Peirce's accused killers (who cannot be named for legal reasons). A cross-section of union leaders, building industry figures and minor celebrities turned up to help fund the man's defence. Gatto's mate still went down, convicted of acting as Benji's driver in the Peirce hit. Later he was charged with involvement in Paul Kallipolitis' murder in 2002.

Undeterred, Gatto's business was booming, and despite his dislike of the media he couldn't stay out of it. He showed he had a big heart. He raised $1 million to help the Country Fire Authority after the devastating Black Saturday fires in 2009. Not to be outdone, Roberta also held a fundraiser in a nightclub. In February 2010, Gatto announced he would stage a telethon with the legendary US comedian Jerry Lewis to raise money for sufferers of muscular dystrophy. The rebirthing of Mick Gatto from accused gangland killer to public benefactor was breathtaking to watch, rather like Roberta's outing as bikini model. It strained credulity but was within the bounds of this ridiculous story. Two media images endured: Gatto playing straight man to Jerry Lewis and a photographer nonchalantly primping and fluffing Roberta's cleavage.

But behind the charity and the glamour, Roberta and Gatto were what they had always been; they were hostage to their former lives. Gatto remained a suspect for the Purana Taskforce over the murders of Victor Peirce and Frank Benvenuto. Roberta had the Tax Office on her tail – she hadn't put in a return for eight years. She wanted a second chance in life, for the public to know the real

Roberta, not the *Underbelly* version. Perhaps naively, she wanted to be a squarehead because in that world friends stuck by you. But she was still surrounded by her old life. In December 2009 her son Tye, twenty-two, was locked up for two years after a crime spree that netted him more than $60 000. He had been storing the loot in a caravan at Roberta's place.

After Carl was sentenced, Barbara Williams lost her will to go on. She had promised to keep fighting to free her son. For a long time she just blocked out what Carl had done. 'Whatever he done had been to protect his family,' she would say. To her, Carl would always be Mummy's boy, a cheeky loving kid who had built the house Barb had always wanted. Now the authorities were threatening to sell the property under her to pay off about a $1 million dollars in taxes and fines.

She had lost her son Shane to drugs, then Carl to the drug business, and her marriage to George had broken up. She had only been living for the delight of seeing Dhakota grow, but one night it seems the last flicker of light went out. In despair, it was to Dhakota she turned one last time. She rang to say she couldn't sleep without speaking to her. She asked Dhakota to sing her a favourite song.

Then she took the pills, washed them down with a glass of champagne, lay down and drifted away.

On the morning of 22 November 2008, Barb was found dead from an overdose of sleeping pills in her bedroom. For once the press and the police seemed to have a little sympathy for the Williams family.

'Here's a mother whose brought up her children the best that she can and unfortunately Carl's in jail and her husband's in jail, and that's obviously had a massive effect on her,' Detective Senior Sergeant Ron Iddles told the *Herald Sun*.

Roberta asked me to write the eulogy for her to read at Barb's funeral and I readily agreed. Barb had once told me that I was her man in the press, that I would help them get Carl freed. Of course I could do no such thing, any more than she could change the past, but she had stayed staunch to desperate dreams until the reality of her family's demise descended upon her.

As I wrote in the eulogy: 'There is no greater champion in this world than a mother who wants the best for her kids through thick and thin. That is the legacy of love she leaves behind.'

She cared more for them than for herself. She stuck by them even when she knew they were wrong. She stood up to their enemies, the police and even Supreme Court judges because she believed loyalty was a lifetime thing, not just a luxury for when things were going well. She knew loyalty was a sacrifice and she was prepared to pay the cost.

And what had loyalty earned Carl Williams? A short, thrilling ride to the top of the underworld, a fleeting public infamy and finally a four-by-three-metre cell where he would spend the best years of his life in a red prison tracksuit. Now his best friends were dead and gone, or bearing witness against him. Even his mother had deserted him.

And still the blood flowed. On June 15 2009, Desmond 'Tuppence' Moran, brother to Lewis and uncle to Mark and Jason, was shot dead in a delicatessen on Union Road in Ascot Vale. One of the first on the scene had been his former sister-in-law Judy Moran, wailing for the loss of another family member. The next day she was charged with his murder, along with Geoffrey 'Nuts' Armour and Suzanne Kane, the daughter of slain 1970s underworld figure Les Kane. Another man, Michael Farrugia, was arrested in Bacchus Marsh, north of Melbourne, and also charged with Moran's murder. Police alleged that Moran was killed because he had not shared his late brother Lewis' hidden fortune with his widow.

It was the first Moran that Carl had felt any sympathy for. He had no quarrel with Des, he didn't deserve to die like that, he told me. But the manner of his death had confirmed his low opinion of the Morans.

In our last conversation a year later, Carl Williams had been full of regret at how his life had turned out. He didn't feel tough or defiant, just lost and alone.

'People reckon my life has been glamorous, well if this is glamour, then they're just off their heads,' he said.

He had been the king of Melbourne's underworld for a brief moment; now his realm was nothing more small cell in Barwon Prison. He spent his days staring at television, tapping away at his computer, reading the occasional book and enjoying a brief few hours of exercise with a couple of hand-picked inmates.

He always believed he was a target, even inside. In his short murderous spree, he had learnt that if someone wanted to get him badly enough there was nothing he could do. He wouldn't make it easy for his killer – when they came for him he would fight it to the death. But he was fatalistic.

'What can you do?' he said. 'Que sera, sera.'

There was a still a string of women prepared to visit him in jail to bask in the underworld legend. He couldn't understand why they still came but he didn't discourage them. It was a link with the world that he once enjoyed. Almost all of the old crew had dropped off him now. The only other visitors he received were his father George – released in June 2009 after serving twenty months – and a couple of his old school mates from Broadmeadows, he said. It was a slow daily torture for a man who had once been so social and gregarious.

Now he relied heavily on his ex-wife Roberta. Without her, he said, he would have gone mad long ago inside Barwon. She kept him in touch, ran errands for him and talked him through the prison blues that descended on him from time to time. They were divorced and there were frequent nasty verbal battles with her, usually over other women.

'But I will always be connected with her, whether we are married or not,' he said. 'We probably should never have got married, but just stayed best friends. We will always stay that way.

'Bert's the one who stuck by me when everybody else just disappeared.'

Every day he would ring her and Roberta would put the call on speaker phone and update him on the domestic goings on in the family. Life was moving on and Carl was was just a voice in the corner of the room. That he wasn't even allowed to attend his mother's funeral had cut him deeply. He had been up $15 million at his peak, now drugs had completely destroyed his family. He had seen his former allies turn and give evidence against him.

What kept him going was the hope that one day he might live to see his daughter Dhakota again, as a free man. He wanted to secure her future, but there was no hidden loot, no cache of drugs that his family could fall back on. All they had to sell was their story, and everyone else, it seemed, had made money from it. Carl wanted Roberta to negotiate more media deals, a documentary or even a reality series. He wanted to write his own book too. He would serve up the truth on a string of unsolved murders, but only for a huge price.

Initially he had refused to cooperate with Purana in solving the other murders or fingering corrupt cops, so he had received no discount on his sentence. But something in him changed when Barb had killed herself. I hope that he thought of the suffering he had caused and felt some pang, but I doubt it. Carl had one last cheque he could cash; he could exert the only leverage that remained to him. He knew his testimony could put a policeman in jail for murder, he could expose the dark nexus between the underworld and Victoria Police. From inside a maximum, the Premier could still run affairs.

At the end of December 2008, it was reported that Carl and George Williams had spent nearly a week over Christmas with police in a secluded location, thought to be a military brig inside a special forces training base on Swan Island, near Geelong. Purana chief Simon Overland became the Chief Commissioner of Victoria Police in March 2009. Yet he knew he hadn't won any war on drugs. This was but a minor skirmish in an unwinnable conflict.

'We're never going to eradicate it, and I think to pretend otherwise is just silly,' Overland told the *Herald Sun*.

It was another day in Barwon. On Monday, April 19 2010, Carl was sitting with the *Herald Sun* at a table outside his cell in an enclosed exercise yard he shared with two other inmates. On the front page, the headlines screamed: YOU PAY CARL'S SCHOOL FEES.

Carl had been waiting for this day for some time. He had been made aware the previous weekend that the *Herald Sun* planned to run the story. There had been tension in George's voice when he called me that Saturday asking exactly what the newspaper would publish. I couldn't tell him. It would be just one more story, I said, no more or less remarkable than the thousands that had been written already, but I was left with a sense of foreboding.

Just before 1 p.m., Carl was reading the newspaper. His staunchest ally Tommy Ivanovic was on the telephone; another inmate, who can't be named, was close by. For the past year and a half Carl had been allowed out of his cell for four to six hours a day with Tommy and the other man. It was a mind-numbing routine, but at least he could feel secure. This was Acacia Unit – the safest space in any jail in Victoria. The screws supposedly watched their every move on the closed circuit television monitors. With many still wishing him dead, he was fortunate to be in Acacia.

He never saw the blow coming.

At the *Underbelly* launch in February 2008, I recognised one of the Purana investigators. He had doubtless listened to the hours of phone taps as I had spoken to Carl through the summer and autumn of 2003–04. He had heard me joking and jollying Carl along, getting enough of his confidence to do the job I was assigned. And he hated me for it. That anyone would go beyond the police line to speak with the accused was cheeky; to question their methods inexcusable.

'You chose a side,' he said, contemptuously.

'Are you saying I joined the wrong team?' I asked.

'Yes,' he said.

'I wasn't aware it was a game.'

'You're not a journalist at all', he said. 'You are, are . . .' He struggled for the right put-down. 'A storyteller!' he exclaimed.

Seeing I was quite pleased with that description, he dug deeper.

'You're an . . . *entertainer!*' he snorted.

I wonder if he saw the irony. He, a public servant, was at a TV function, toasting (with the network's beer) a drama series for which Purana members had played technical adviser. Sorry Sarge, we were *all* in the entertainment business. Ganglands is a drama you can catch on an endless loop, courtesy of our drug laws.

I thought of that exchange as I sat in the back row at Carl's funeral at St Therese's Church in Essendon, 30 April 2010.

With Williams' death, any chance of convicting the Savage for his role in the Hodsons' murder evaporated, but it mattered not. Convicted of a 1987 double murder, he wouldn't see the light of day till he was ninety-one. There was no way left to punish him. The other informers were held in other local and interstate jails and continued to sing, but it was all for nothing with Carl dead. If there was any lasting social significance from a decade of this plotting, scheming and bloodletting, I couldn't think of it at that moment. And I still struggle to. As one tragicomedy ends, another begins. Only the names and faces change.

I sat in the back row of the church as Roberta and her children gave eulogies to Carl as a loving father and husband. There was no mention of murder, drugs and corruption. Apart from a few wannabes, the mourners were the old crew from Broadmeadows he had grown up with. The loyalty and the friendships he had made in the underworld had all been superficial.

Beside me Deana Falcone was sobbing uncontrollably. She had buried her boyfriend Shane, Carl's brother, thirteen years earlier. Now it was Carl's turn, but through Deana's tears I could sense something like relief. His death might end this tragic cycle now. The killing might finally be over. I felt the same way, even though the murders had been my business for nearly seven years. Enough was enough. Perhaps now I could finally extricate myself from this, move on to a story where my role was clear-cut once more. I didn't know whether I was there as reporter or as a friend that day. All I knew was that Carl and I had shared this ride for too long and it was time to get off.

I watched the $50 000 gold-plated coffin, held aloft by the pall-bearers, make its stately way from the church to the hearse and the waiting media. A hundred cameras flashed, a news helicopter hovered over the scene. One last curtain call, I thought, and then into the cold earth for Carl. He had granted the media's fervent wish: a final headline; the villain was gone. But there was no joy, no feeling of justice done, just a pervading sense of futility and waste. I was out of the churchyard before the tailgate of the hearse had closed. If I had lingered, I might have asked myself too many awkward questions.

16 January 1998 – **Alphonse Gangitano,** 40, shot in his Templestowe home. Coroner Iain West finds Gangitano's associates Jason Moran and Graham Kinniburgh are 'implicated in the death'.
3 August 1998 – **John Furlan,** 48, bombed in his car in North Coburg.
23 November 1998 – Notorious criminal **Charles 'Mad Charlie' Hegyalji,** 42, shot in the front yard of his home in Caulfield South.

9 January 1999 – **Vince Mannella,** shot outside his North Fitzroy home.
28 May 1999 – Bankrupt fruiterer **Joseph Quadara,** 57, gunned down in a Toorak supermarket car park.
9 September 1999 – Brighton businessman **Dimitrios Belias,** 38, shot in an underground car park in St Kilda.
20 October 1999 – **Gerardo Mannella,** 31, shot in a North Fitzroy street after talking to and trying to escape from two men.

8 May 2000 – Melbourne Fruit & Vegetable Market wholesaler **Francesco Benvenuto,** 52, shot dead at the wheel of his car in Beaumaris.

16 May 2000 – Career criminal **Richard Mladenich**, 37, shot in a St Kilda motel room in front of three other people.

15 June 2000 – **Mark Moran**, 36, known to have criminal underworld links and facing drugs and firearms charges, shot after getting out of his car outside his Aberfeldie home.

14 October 2000 – **Dino Dibra**, 25, shot outside a Sunshine West home.

1 May 2002 – **Victor Peirce**, 42, a career criminal acquitted of the murders of police officers Steven Tynan and Damian Eyre in South Yarra in 1988, shot in his car in Bay Street, Port Melbourne.

15 October 2002 – **Paul Kallipolitis**, 33, found shot dead in his Sunshine West home.

15 April 2003 – Bulgarian migrant **Nikolai Radev**, 47, formerly jailed for assault, burglary, attempted arson and drug-related offences, shot in the head and chest in Queen Street, Coburg.

21 June 2003 – **Jason Moran**, 36, and **Pasquale Barbaro**, 40, gunned down in the front seat of a van in the car park of the Cross Keys Hotel, Essendon North, while five children watch from the back seat.

21 July 2003 – **Willy Thompson**, 39, shot in his car in Waverley Road, Chadstone.

18 August 2003 – The charred remains of **Mark Mallia**, 30, an associate of Radev, found in a drain in West Sunshine.

11 September 2003 – **Housam Zayat**, 32, a violent criminal, forced from his car and shot in a paddock near Werribee, south-west of Melbourne. Nicholas Ibrahim charged with the murder.

25 October 2003 – **Michael Marshall**, 38, kickboxer and hotdog dealer, shot in front of his five-year-old son outside his South Yarra home.

13 December 2003 – Semi-retired crook **Graham Kinniburgh**, 62, ambushed and shot outside his home in Kew.

23 March 2004 – 'Person of interest' to police, **Andrew 'Benji' Veniamin**, 28, gunned down in a Carlton restaurant.

31 March 2004 – Crime patriarch **Lewis Moran**, 58, shot at the Brunswick Club in Sydney Road, Brunswick.

8 May 2004 – Williams associate **Lewis Caine**, 39, shot and dumped in a Brunswick lane.

16 May 2004 – Police informer **Terry Hodson**, 56, and his wife, **Christine**, 55, executed in their East Kew home.

6 February 2006 – Carlton Crew elder **Mario Rocco Condello**, 53, shot in the garage of his Brighton home.

15 June 2009 – The last of the Moran clan, **Desmond 'Tuppence' Moran**, 60, shot while sitting in his favourite cafe on Union Road, Ascot Vale.

19 April 2010 – **Carl Anthony Williams**, 39. Bashed to death in Acacia Unit, Barwon Prison.

ACKNOWLEDGEMENTS

This book would not have been possible without the cooperation and patience of many, many people on both sides of the law.

I owe a debt of gratitude to Penguin Books, especially the Publishing Director, Bob Sessions, for championing a different kind of true crime book. And also my eternally optimistic editor, Katie Purvis – together, we got it done and learned a new language on the way. Penguin's Michael Nolan picked up the baton for the revised edition and brought us home superbly.

Thanks also to my bosses at the late and lamented *Sunday* program, John Lyons and Paul Steindl. The editors of the now defunct *Bulletin* magazine, Garry Linnell and John Lehmann were unwavering in their support and encouragement.

I am very grateful to Brian 'Skull' Murphy and Billy 'The Texan' Longley for their friendship and the Melbourne stories they shared that you won't find in history books. They never put any 'side' on the truth. And thanks also to their comrade, who took me places they couldn't.

I would like to acknowledge the assistance and friendship of Johnny Auciello. With courage to face his past, he shared his journey out of the underworld. Johnny, I hope you make it for the sake of your kids and your mother's memory – not to mention all those mates who died for money and power.

Thanks to Sue and Sam Chisholm, who provided me with the sanctuary and hospitality of Bundarbo Station near Jugiong, New South Wales, for the writing of the manuscript when Melbourne was a dangerous place.

And thanks to all who shared the private, human stories behind the news. These include the Peirce/Pettingill, Williams, Ivanovic and Veniamin clans, Deana Falcone, Roberta Williams and a host of others who I have missed or simply can't name. The truth was often unpleasant, but I hope I have done justice to the character of the men you knew, loved and lost.

Thanks also to my parents, Dr John and Robin Shand, who taught me that unpopular opinions are not always wrong and should still be heard.

GANG WARS OF THE NORTH

The inside story of the deadly battle between
Viv Graham and Lee Duffy

Stephen Richards

Viv Graham and Lee Duffy led parallel lives as pub and club enforcers, raging their gangland turf wars with a fierce frenzy of brutality and unremitting cruelty. This is a riveting double portrait of two of the North East's most feared men, whose bloody rivalry was only cut short when they each met horrifically violent ends.

With unprecedented access to friends, family members and associates, Stephen Richards dispels many of the myths surrounding these legendary figures to create the ultimate biography of Britain's deadliest rivals.

ISBN: 978-1-84358-380-6

RRP £7.99

Available now in paperback from all good bookshops,
online or direct from the publisher.

To order call +44 (0) 207 381 0666

Free P&P and UK delivery
(Abroad £3/copy)

Or visit our website: johnblakepublishing.co.uk

THE CROSSBOW CANNIBAL

The definitive story of Steven Griffiths –
the self-made serial killer

Cyril Dixon

There was a gut-wrenching feeling of déjà vu… three decades after the industrial city of Bradford found the Yorkshire Ripper living and killing in its midst, someone was targeting vulnerable women once again. During Midsummer 2009, three women disappeared; it was as if the cobbled backstreets had opened up and swallowed them. All of them had paced the windswept kerbs and corners of Bradford's red light district to fund their drug habits. Who could know many how more there were?

Stephen Griffiths was a shy, eccentric student of criminology who always had a word of cautious advice for the working girls. He wandered the same bleak landscape, dressed in black, hair slicked back with baby oil, happy to chat and share a cigarette. Here, surely, was someone they could trust…

Top journalist Cyril Dixon – who attended the hearing – tells the chilling story of how an attention-seeking oddball fashioned himself into a serial killer for the sole purpose of becoming famous. *The Crossbow Cannibal* exposes the dark, nether world of vice which exists in the shadows of a proud and bustling city, and reveals how, inspired by books on homicide, Griffiths turned it into his own murderous fantasy land.

ISBN: 978-1-84358-359-2

RRP £7.99

Available now in paperback from all good bookshops,
online or direct from the publisher.

To order call +44 (0) 207 381 0666

Free P&P and UK delivery
(Abroad £3/copy)

Or visit our website: johnblakepublishing.co.uk

DANGEROUS PEOPLE, DANGEROUS PLACES

Norman Parker

'My assignments took me from London to Colombia, from Haiti to Israel. I visited the darkest corners of the world and lived to tell the tale...'

While serving 24 straight years in jail for murder and manslaughter, Norman Parker gained a degree in criminology. He emerged from prison a changed man and, in his bestselling *Parkhurst Tales* series, graphically detailed the cruel realities of live on the inside.

In *Dangerous People, Dangerous Places*, he turns his attention to the world's most terrifying organisations – from notorious drug dealers and violent gangs, to coldblooded professional killers and terrorists who will stop at nothing to achieve their goals. To seek them out he travelled from London to Colombia, and Haiti to Israel. He uncovered stories of violence and corruption – both at home and abroad – and he relates them with the insight that comes from spending decades alongside Britain's most dangerous criminals.

Written with compelling frankness, this is a must-read for anyone intrigued by the darkest corners and most dangerous characters on the planet.

ISBN: 978-1-84358-312-7

RRP £7.99

Available now in paperback from all good bookshops, online or direct from the publisher.

To order call +44 (0) 207 381 0666

Free P&P and UK delivery
(Abroad £3/copy)

Or visit our website: johnblakepublishing.co.uk